Concrete Bridge Designer's Manual

Concrete Bridge Designer's Manual

E. Pennells

A Viewpoint Publication

Frontispiece: Tarr Steps, Devon

186067
624.2
~~13.60~~

Viewpoint Publications

Books published in the Viewpoint Publications series deal with all
practical aspects of concrete, concrete technology and allied subjects in
relation to civil and structural engineering, building and architecture.

Contributors to Viewpoint Publications include authors from within the
Cement and Concrete Association itself and from the construction
industry in general. While the views and opinions expressed in these
publications may be in agreement with those of the Association they
should be regarded as being independent of Association policy.

12.072 First published 1978

Reprinted with amendments 1981

ISBN 0 7210 1083 0

Viewpoint Publications are designed and published by the
Cement and Concrete Association,
52 Grosvenor Gardens, London SW1W 0AQ

Printed by The Whitefriars Press Ltd. London and Tonbridge

© Cement and Concrete Association 1978

Preface

This book has grown from the need for a series of design guides for use in a bridge design office. Its purpose is to help an engineer coping with the day to day tasks of design, and to bring together in one volume some of the information he needs to have close to hand.

Ideas have been collected from a wide range of sources and the author acknowledges the contribution of numerous colleagues, particularly those at E. W. H. Gifford and Partners.

A number of commercial organizations have generously made illustrations and data available for inclusion in this manual.

Ernest Pennells first became involved in bridge design during the reconstruction of numerous small railway overbridges to accommodate overhead electrification of the London—Liverpool railway line.

His initial training with Contractors, and subsequent experience with Local Authorities as well as Consulting Engineers, covered a diversity of types of work: highways, buildings, heavy industrial construction and water-retaining structures. But bridges became the dominant factor in the development of his career.

In 1967 Mr. Pennells joined E. W. H. Gifford and Partners. He was their Resident Engineer for the Braidley Road and Bourne Avenue bridges at Bournemouth, which gained a Civic Trust Award, and commendation in Concrete Society Awards. This was followed by a short tour in Chile representing the interests of the practice. He was subsequently made an Associate of the practice and became responsible for several of their bridgeworks contracts through all stages of design and construction.

In 1976 Mr. Pennells went to Oxford University for a period of further study, and was later ordained as a Minister in the Baptist Church.

A Fellow of the Institution of Structural Engineers, Mr. Pennells is also a holder of their Murray Buxton Award Diploma.

Contents

Data sheets and illustrations

The following list of data sheets and illustrations also acknowledges
the sources of the material, where appropriate

Figures

CHAPTER 1

The bridge deck

The simplest form of bridge deck is a reinforced concrete slab. It is, of course, only economic for short spans, and where such a slab is employed it is often connected monolithically with the abutment walls, forming part of a box or portal section. This arrangement leads to the more efficient utilization of the structure where the proportions of height to span are favourable.

Slabs play a part in many other forms of construction, and where a slab is spanning between open spaced beams or adjoining webs in a box deck which are spaced at intervals approximating to the width of a traffic lane, the slab thickness will usually be 200mm (8in.), or thereabouts. Assuming that the thickness has been kept to a modest dimension to suit the span, continuous support is usually provided for solid slabs because they have a limited capacity to span transversely between isolated bearings, and a simple rubber strip bearing is adequate to cater for the small movements involved.

The thinnest possible slab is not necessarily the most economic. It is worth investigating the relative costs of concrete and reinforcement with various thicknesses of slab. Fluctuations in the costs of concrete and reinforcement make it impossible to state a universal rule for this, and the question is discussed further in the chapter on economics.

Once the depth of a cast-in-situ concrete deck slab exceeds about 700mm or 28in., it becomes practical to introduce voids, thereby reducing the self weight and material content of the deck. Various types of void former have been used. Spirally wound sheet metal was an early type. It has been known for voids to become full of water during construction, and the possibility of this taking place in a permanent structure cannot be overruled entirely even if drainage holes are provided. This could result in significant overstressing of the deck. With spirally-wound metal sheet it is only possible to produce a cylindrical void so that, where it is necessary to change shapes, it becomes essential to utilize an alternative material to form the special shape required.

The use of expanded polystyrene overcomes the potential objection of water filling the void, since the material consists of a series of small closed cells, resulting in very low porosity compared to the total volume involved. The material has the further advantage of being readily cut, either by using a hot wire in the factory or, on site, simply a hand saw. The latter may not give the smoothest result but is effective enough.

Other methods of void forming have been tried, with varying degrees of success. Formers have been built with timber frames overlain by tough cardboard, but the ability of this type of former to maintain its shape after prolonged exposure on a construction site is arguable.

Any void former requires very secure fixing to prevent flotation during concreting. The flotation force can be substantial – even more so when combined with the vibration used to compact the concrete. Fixing the void to the reinforcement cage is not a wise procedure – some engineers have suffered the embarrassment of having their reinforcement float with the void formers!

Although there is no compulsion to use a cylindrical void, and other shapes could be exploited to advantage in some circumstances, the circle does allow the concrete to flow easily underneath the void. Any attempt to employ a wide flat void could be disastrous for the concrete finish on the soffit. The choice of dimensions for the spacing and depth of voids must make due allowance for the practicalities of concreting, particularly when bearing in mind the space occupied by prestressing tendons, where they form part of the deck construction. Due allowance for practical tolerances in construction should also be taken into account. For reinforced concrete construction the recommended minimum dimension for the concrete thickness above and below a circular void is 150mm (6in.), but for prestressed concrete construction this might be reduced to 125mm (5in.). Voids of other shapes require increased thicknesses. The spaces between voids should be not less than 200mm (8in.).

The saving achieved by introducing voids stems from the reduction in self-weight. Forming the void is likely to cost a similar amount to the actual concrete replaced, so the resulting saving in materials consists of a saving of reinforcement, which is reduced because the load due to self weight is lower. In prestressed concrete the prestress required is further reduced as a result of the diminished area requiring precompression.

Other benefits arise from voided slab construction. It becomes possible to introduce strong transverse diaphragms within the depth of the deck, simply by stopping-off voids. Costs are also less sensitive to increases in depth than is the case with solid construction, so that it becomes more attractive to vary the shape of the overall cross-section of a deck, introducing transverse cantilevers at the edges. This not only gives economic benefits but also improves the appearance of a structure by lightening the

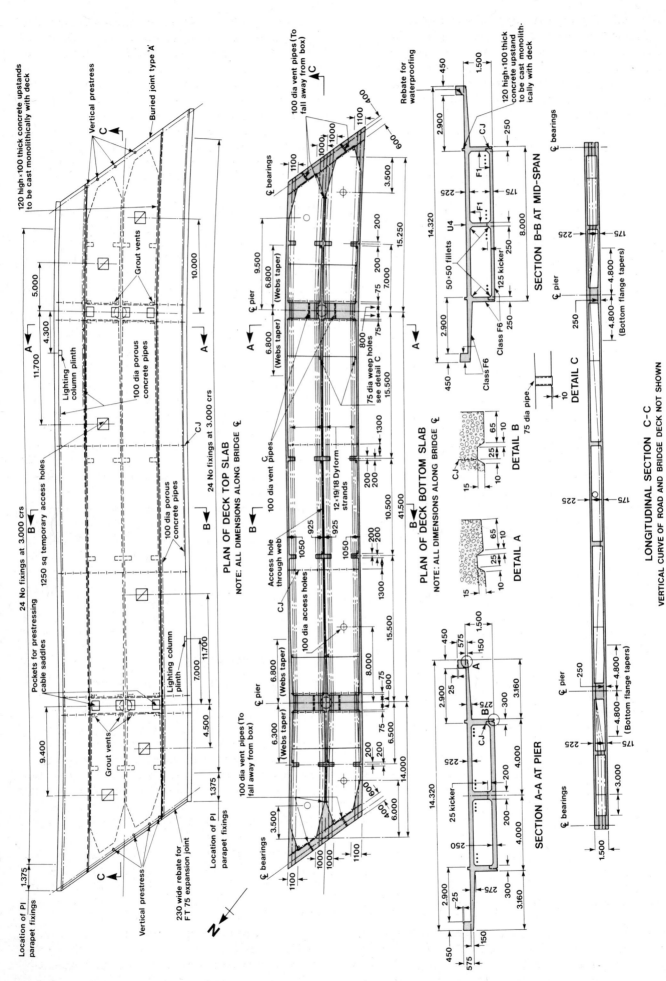

Figure 1. Deck layout drawing.

2

edge and giving an interesting profile to the soffit.

In a wide bridge it is also worth while breaking up the deck into a series of broad "spine" beams of voided slab construction, introducing linking slabs spanning transversely to provide a connection between them and to form a continuous deck surface. In addition to its affect on the appearance this arrangement introduces benefits in construction. There are difficulties in building wide decks, particularly where prestressing is involved. The relative movements between one part and another due to the elastic deformation on stressing, and the subsequent shrinkage and creep, can result in awkward problems. Trying to cater for relative movement during construction and yet to achieve fully continuous behaviour in the completed deck can be particularly difficult with load-carrying diaphragms. By breaking up the width of the deck into distinct sections, each can be treated as a separate constructional problem, and the linking slabs can then be concreted following the completion of all the main structural elements.

Where this approach to construction is adopted, the transverse diaphragms should be kept within the width of each spine element, and not taken across the linking slab. Supports are provided separately for each spine.

The fact that a voided slab deck can be provided with transverse diaphragms within its own depth allows a simple form of bridge pier to be utilized. A cantilevered diaphragm member can span up to 3 to 4m (or 10 to 14ft) depending on the proportions of the span and the width. With a plate pier 3 or 4m wide, plus cantilevered edge slabs spanning 3 or 4m, the effective width of each "spine" element could be up to 16m or 50ft, which is sufficient to accommodate a three-lane all-purpose road.

The plate type of bridge pier is not only pleasing in appearance because of its simplicity of line, but is also straightforward to construct. It blends well with the lines of a deck of this type.

The economic change-over point between reinforced and prestressed concrete construction in a voided slab depends on the prevailing relative costs of concrete and steel. The economic choice therefore changes in differing circumstances, but is probably within the range of 20 to 25m or 65 to 80ft. That is to say for spans of up to 20m reinforced concrete is cheaper, between 20 and 25m further investigation is necessary, and above 25m prestressed concrete should be the economic answer.

One important factor in the economy of a prestressed concrete deck is the layout of prestressing cables adopted. It is fundamental to the efficiency of a cable that its profile should move through as great a height as possible, to give maximum eccentricities at both midspan and support. Where twin cables are used between adjacent voids, the maximum range of eccentricity is exploited by bringing the cables from a parallel, side-by-side position at midspan to a similar side-by-side position over the pier. The path followed by each cable, when viewed in cross section through the deck, therefore describes an "X" through the length of the span, as shown in Figure 3.

Where a voided-slab deck is a continuous prestressed structure of more than three spans it becomes necessary to use serial construction (see Data Sheet 57). This involves building one or two spans at a time, coupling the prestressing cables for subsequent spans on to the end of those spans that are already built and stressed. The details necessary to accommodate suitable anchorages can impose restrictions on the eccentricity that can be achieved at pier positions. If the construction joints for the span-to-span connections are provided adjacent to the pier, the prestressing anchorages force the cables down into the deck to a lower level than that required by the cables themselves, in order to achieve the necessary edge clearances. To avoid this restriction it may become necessary to move the span-to-span construction joint away from the piers.

With the construction joint within the span, the point of connection becomes subject to deflection during the course of construction and prestressing. This can be difficult to deal with in a manner consistent with obtaining a good finish.

One disadvantage of serial construction is the constraint imposed on the constructional sequence. The work effort required from the differing trades in contributing towards the progress of construction tends to come in short, concentrated efforts that do not provide the continuity of work which is so desirable to achieve optimum productivity.

There are also limits to the rate of construction which can be achieved, and since serial construction demands that erection proceeds sequentially, span by span, from the starting point, long construction periods become inescapable in the case of viaducts. To speed construction it is sometimes necessary to produce a design requiring the construction of two spans at a time. The disadvantage of this arrangement is that frictional losses will be high at the end remote from the stressing point, which can only be the leading edge of construction. It is inevitable that the effective prestress will differ at adjoining piers (due to the different frictional losses). The range of stresses that must be catered for during design becomes a further constraint on achieving the maximum economy in terms of the balance of forces on a cross-section.

Beam-and-slab construction

Cast-in-situ construction using beams and slabs — as commonly adopted in building construction — is rarely used in bridges in the UK, other than locally within the context of other forms of construction to provide trimming around openings. Where beam-and-slab construction is used, it invariably occurs in conjunction with precast beam units. Early forms of such construction were based on the use of I-beams with slabs spanning transverely, as is common in steel construction. Composite action between the precast unit and the deck slab then forms a T-section. A number of variants have been employed for the shape of the precast unit in an attempt to achieve the optimum economy in the design condition for the precast unit while it is acting independently (i.e. during construction) as well as in the completed structure.

To streamline construction, it can also be beneficial to precast part of the slab itself. This usually means precasting a sufficient thickness of slab to support the dead weight of the full slab, and completing the thickness

Figure 2. Bourne Avenue Bridge, Bournemouth. Prestressed voided slab with reinforced concrete side cantilevers, built using serial construction with couplers.

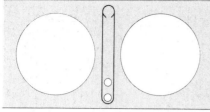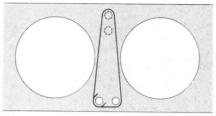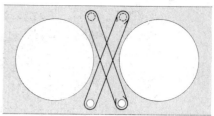

Figure 3. Layout of prestressing cables.

with cast-in-situ concrete (see Figure 5).

When railway modernization was in progress in the UK, with the accompanying change from steam to electric and diesel motive power, the inverted-T bridge deck became very popular. It provided a means of constructing a bridge deck without recourse to falsework which could otherwise impinge unacceptably on railway clearances. Also, while steam traction was still common, it had been desirable to have a bridge with a flat soffit, in order to avoid smoke traps which had the effect of worsening the deterioration of a structure by trapping hostile elements in the exhaust from the locomotives and thus promoting corrosive attack. A wide range of T-beams came on to the market, and steps were taken towards standardization, as it was felt that this would produce economies. This development gave rise to the marketing of rapidly-designed bridge decks. By the simple expedient of selecting the appropriate standard units, and stacking them side by side on a drawing: "BINGO!"; the design was virtually complete. This procedure held considerable attractions for design offices with limited experience in bridge design.

The use of bridge decks based on the use of contiguously placed precast units still has a place in particular circumstances where there are severe restrictions on temporary headroom during construction, where speed of erection is a prime consideration for the deck, or where safety requirements favour this approach. The current standard unit in the UK for this form of construction is the M-beam, a particular version of an inverted-T. There are also box sections and other types of inverted-T on the market. Details of some types of precast deck beams currently available are given on Data Sheet 1.

Where precast beam units are used in a bridge deck and the span is such that prestressing is the economic answer, the choice remains between pretensioning and post-tensioning. Where a small number of units are being utilized, post-tensioning is likely to be more economic because pretensioning requires a fairly elaborate set-up for fabrication. Such expense can only be justified where the number of units to be produced is sufficient to gain advantage from the fact that with pretensioning the anchorages are re-usable through the fabrication of a number of components.

It has often been argued that precasting should represent the economic solution to most bridge problems. This impression arises from the relative simplicity of the constructional procedures on the site. Against this must be set the fact that most forms of precast construction involve more total work, and additional handling operations are needed above those required to complete cast-in-situ forms of construction. It is also necessary to finance the overheads at a precasting factory in addition to those on the construction site, which must increase the already substantial margins added to the direct cost.

In many instances the cost of a cast-in-situ form of construction, as represented by the prices tendered by contractors, is cheaper than the precast alternative. Comparisons of this kind are difficult and can only be valid where alternative designs of equal merit are used as yardsticks. Even in a structure where the spans cover a range favourable for precasting, most practical bridge decks have geometrical complications which demand dimensional variations in the length of the units or their spacing, thus robbing the work of fabrication and assembly of that repetitiveness which gives the prime potential saving in precast construction.

There are obvious limitations in the length and weight of precast units which can be transported, so that only spans of less than 30m or 100ft can be dealt with by using single precast beams.

It is sometimes possible to construct a precast deck in a manner which results in continuity as regards imposed loading only. The adjustments which would be necessary during erection to counteract the deflection due to self weight make it impracticable to achieve full continuity for the dead loading when precast beams are used. The effects of continuity are sometimes simulated by providing articulated joints within the span acting in conjunction with cantilevers from the support. The drawback with this solution is that the joints in a bridge deck invariably leak and, whereas the consequences of this can usually be concealed at the abutments, the siting of a joint within the span usually leads to disfiguring staining on the elevation. Unless the joint is successfully masked, it can also detract from the lines of the structure.

Where a bridge of precast beam construction consists of several spans, the intermediate supports invariably require a portal frame, the cross member of this portal usually being located below the deck. Although attempts have been made to conceal the cross-head within the depth of the beam-and-slab construction, the resulting details are complex, and are therefore unattractive.

Box-section decks

Precast construction has been applied to post-tensioned prestressed concrete box decks, but the circumstances where this is justified and provides an economic solution are the exception rather than the rule. The arrangement involves heavy handling on the site and a good deal of labour in forming joints.

The precast solutions which have been adopted are generally based on the use of segments which represent the whole of the deck cross-section. These are precast in short lengths which are then jointed by cast-in-situ

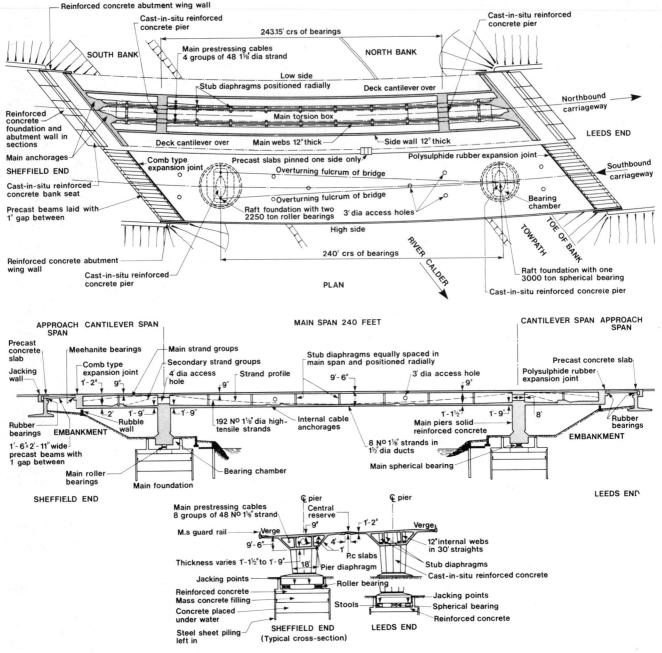

Figure 4. Box construction applied to Calder Bridge.

concrete, usually in joints about 100mm (4in.) in thickness. An alternative solution, in which precast segments represent only part of the cross-section of the deck, has been adopted where there were stringent limitations on the size of unit which could be handled on site (see Figure 6). Such a precast solution requires extensive falsework to support the components until jointing is complete and prestressing has been carried out. The need for this falsework detracts from the potential advantages of precasting and makes box construction generally better suited to cast-in-situ concrete work.

The natural flexibility of cast-in-situ concrete construction can be well exploited in a cellular type of deck. The external profile of the cross-section can be maintained, while variations in the relative positions of webs, as well as their thickness, can be made to suit the geometry imposed on a structure by the highway layout.

There are a number of variations on the basic theme of a box section. Not only is there a choice as to the number of cells which can be included but the soffit profile can be varied, providing a haunch at the pier locations where the bending moments tend to be higher. Nor is there any necessity for the web members to be kept vertical. A number of boxes have been constructed with sloping outer webs, which gives an interesting profile to the bridge soffit. Whether or not this adds to the cost of a structure is arguable in the light of the proportions of an individual deck but, where such a solution is appropriate, the additional labour involved in forming the unusual shape should be offset by reductions in material content necessary. Of course, where such shaping is introduced purely as a gimmick without having functional relevance it must be expected to add to the cost.

The argument supporting the provision of sloping outer

Figure 5. Interior of box deck under construction. External prestressing cables located ready for stressing.

webs is that the width of the upper slab of a box deck is enforced by the width of the pavement to be carried. Although a box could be built with its outer webs on the extremities of the section, it may be advantageous to limit the width of the box itself, thereby reducing the material content. Providing transverse cantilevers at the edges of the deck is one significant step towards this, and sloping the outer webs can further reduce the width of the bottom slab, if the box is sufficiently deep to make this worthwhile. Whether or not such a shape is appropriate depends on the width of the highway and the depth of the box.

The bottom slab of a box has only to maintain equilibrium with the prestressing cables at midspan. Adjacent to the supports it has the primary function in resisting the reverse bending moments over the continuous supports, and it is then a relatively simple matter to thicken the slab in this region without incurring the penalty of significantly increasing the bending moments due to self-weight.

Where box construction is adopted another fundamental alternative presents itself: whether to provide internal or external prestressing cables. Internal cables are buried within ducts contained in the concrete forming the deck cross-section. External cables are suspended freely within the voids of the box, stressed in that condition, and subsequently protected by a casing of concrete, grout, or some other means.

If internal prestressing cables are used and the structure has several spans, the same limitations arise that apply to voided slab construction. That is to say, serial

construction must be adopted because it is only possible to prestress one, or possibly two, spans at a time from one end because of the rapidly accumulated friction within the length of the ducted cables. It is also likely that the dimensions of the box, in terms of web thicknesses, will be dictated by the concrete required to accommodate the prestressing ducts and to cover them.

The use of external prestressing cables removes these restrictions. The frictional losses accumulated along the length of an external cable are very low, so that it becomes possible to stress a number of spans at one time with quite modest losses. This can make a marked impact on the design of a multi-span structure. Not only does it become possible to dispense with intermediate anchorage positions for prestressing, which would be required with serial construction, but the sequence of construction for the bridge can be freed from the strait-jacket of serial construction, demanding its span-by-span approach.

It is unlikely that accumulated friction will limit the number of spans which can be constructed and prestressed in a single operation. It is more likely that restrictions will arise from the prestressing equipment, in that it is necessary to stress a cable by a series of bites, i.e. strokes of the jack, and it is desirable to limit the load at which a further bite is commenced. This limitation arises from the fact that in commencing a fresh bite the prestressing jack must first overcome the resistance to withdrawal of the wedges, which have locked-off temporarily at the end of the preceding bite. If a cable is to be stressed to 70% of its characteristic strength, it is desirable that the last bite should commence at a figure not higher than 65%, to allow for the overload due to withdrawal of the wedges, so that the length of cable must be no more than that which will allow a single stroke of the jack to raise the cable through 5% of its characteristic strength. If the working stroke of the jack is 150mm (6in.), this implies a limiting length of 200m or 650ft where stressing is to be carried from one end only.

Where a box section is cast-in-situ it is obviously necessary for the section to be built up in a series of operations. For deep boxes it may be necessary to cast the bottom slab, webs and top slab separately. For shallower sections the webs and top slab may be cast together. In a single-celled box there may be advantages in casting the bottom slab and webs together, and subsequently adding the top slab. Difficulties in securing the web forms make this arrangement unattractive for multi-celled boxes.

To simplify the casting sequence in a long length of deck, a considerable advantage can be gained from allowing the construction of the box itself to precede the concreting of such diaphragms and stiffeners as may be necessary along its length. This arrangement enables the formwork for the box to proceed without complications due to the transverse reinforcement and formwork. Special attention must be paid to detailing the reinforcement for the stiffeners and diaphragms if free movement of the box formwork is to be attained.

The main limitation on the size of boxes at the lower end of the span range becomes the practicability of casting a shallow box. It is necessary to work inside to strike and remove the formwork and, where external cables are used, to thread and protect the prestressing cables. Where a box is to be built with re-usable timber forms the clear height inside the deck should not be less than 900mm (3ft), which implies a minimum overall depth of 1.2m (4ft). If external cables are used and they are to be protected by a casing of cast-in-situ concrete, the headroom inside the box should not be less than 1.5m (5ft). Lesser headrooms are acceptable where alternative forms of protection are provided.

Optimum deck proportions

In spite of the fact that a substantial proportion of on-site constructional costs in the UK are due to labour,

experience has shown that the forms of construction which require minimum material content are those which tend to prove the economic solution, even though alternatives may exist which are simpler to assemble and which call for fewer man-hours to be worked on site.

Economic designs make the best structural use of the material contained within the deck, and the non-working parts of the structures are kept to a minimum. The penalties to avoid are the provision of heavy webs at midspan, where shearing stresses are only nominal, and unnecessary areas of flange at points having nominal bending moments. For example, in many forms of precast construction it is necessary to provide a flange on the precast element in order to maintain stability prior to its incorporation in the finished deck. In many beam sections this temporary top flange is stressed at low levels in the permanent structure but adds significantly to the self weight. In voided-slab construction the shape of the web is structurally inefficient and where significant depths are involved the amount of structurally-unnecessary material carried by such a section becomes substantial. In wide box construction the top flange is necessary throughout to support the pavement, but the bottom of the box, which acts as a flange, is only nominally stressed at points away from support or midspan locations. A source of self-weight common to many forms of construction is the concrete added to a section solely to protect the prestressing tendons.

To achieve an economic solution it is necessary to assess critically any concrete which is included for non-structural reasons. It is also essential to make the maximum use of those elements of the structure which are indispensable. The prime example of this is the slab surface provided over the full width of the deck to support the road pavement. For optimum structural efficiency this slab member must be well utilized. It forms a natural flange to resist longitudinal bending, and the minimum thickness which it can practically be given provides sufficient capacity to span transversely between longitudinal members that are spaced at about a width of one traffic lane apart.

To make the best structural use of longitudinal members a prime consideration is that their number should be kept to the minimum compatible with the capacity of the deck slab. Since it is impossible to design a

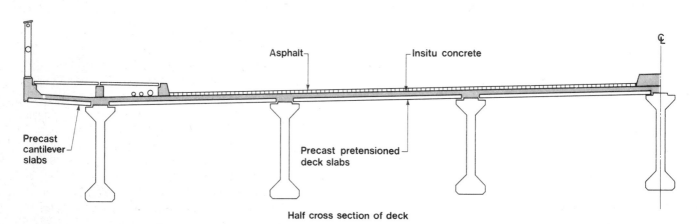

Figure 6. Precast beam-and-slab construction.

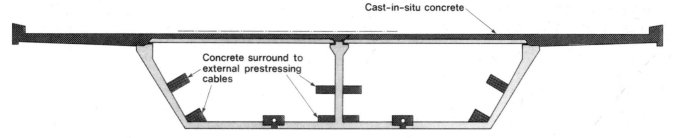

Cast-in-situ concrete

Concrete surround to external prestressing cables

Typical cross-section of deck structure

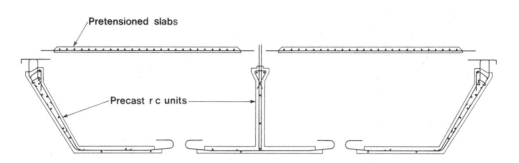

Pretensioned slabs

Precast r c units

Exploded typical cross-section showing precast units

Figure 7. Precast construction applied to box-section deck.

beam of any type which is 100% structurally efficient, the idea of using a minimum number of longitudinal members ensures the provision of the minimum of structurally-surplus material in the deck.

The best use is made of the upper surface of a deck slab spanning transversely by allowing it to make the maximum possible contribution to carrying the load across the width of a deck. For example it can cantilever a significant distance beyond the outer members to support parapets, verges and part of the carriageway itself. The presence of a verge lowers the intensity of loading, and transverse cantilevers of 3 to 4m or 10 to 14ft are quite practical. Longitudinal members spaced at a width of one traffic lane apart are well within the capacity of a reinforced concrete slab about 200mm (8in.) in thickness. This provides an economical layout whether the longitudinal members are the webs of a box-section, or precast beams.

A structure of the minimum depth is not necessarily the most economic. To achieve maximum economy the balance of cost between the concrete and steel for reinforcing (or prestressing) needs examining. This matter is discussed further in the section on economics. For economic design the costs of approach roads also need to be taken into account, which may give rise to substantial extra costs that are proportional to the deck thickness.

Of course economy is not the sole consideration and a slender structure is often preferred for the sake of appearance.

Selection of deck

Physical constraints arising from the nature of the site may eliminate some solutions. Restrictions on the depth available for construction may demand a deck having the minimum depth or may eliminate the use of falsework where the restrictions apply during construction. Access to the site, or the height of a deck above the ground can also be factors limiting the choice in extreme circumstances.

In most cases several options remain. Appearances are important and, assuming the deck to be well proportioned, the complimentary consideration is the form chosen for the intermediate supports. Portal frames have little to commend them in this respect – they add to the apparent overall depth of construction and interrupt the lines of the deck. The plurality of numerous supporting columns can add confusion to the general appearance beneath the bridge, which may already be busy with traffic routes. If skew is present this confusion is compounded. To simplify the form of the supporting piers a deck structure must be of a type which has some capacity to span transversely as well as longitudinally, thus replacing the cross-beam of a portal. This means using a voided-slab or box-type structure.

For a long length of bridge or viaduct, there may be circumstances where the ground features admit a range of options in terms of the number and dimensions of the individual spans. Obviously in such circumstances full advantage must be taken of the benefits of repetition by adopting an even spacing for the piers, although the end spans should, if possible, be shorter than the intermediate spans to achieve optimum structural economy. Where the length of a structure is such that a large number of spans becomes necessary, the rate at which it is practicable to construct the bridge must be taken into consideration. If serial construction is adopted it is unlikely that the rate of construction can exceed one span per month even after working has settled into a productive rhythm. Although the cheapest structure might be a voided slab with a span of less than 30m or 100ft there could be a case for building longer spans by using box construction so as to enable the adoption of external prestressing to achieve a faster rate of construction. Substructure costs often influence the economic layout.

For multi-span structures the preferred articulation is to adopt full continuity. Serial construction introduces varying moments in adjoining spans as construction proceeds. These moments are subsequently modified by shrinkage and creep, eventually converging on the values which would occur in a structure built in the fully-continuous state. Because time is taken to achieve this situation a range of figures must be taken into account in the calculations, adding to the margins of residual stress to be provided and thereby adding to the material content in the deck.

Where the choice of deck construction remains open, cast-in-situ concrete box construction will prove to be the most-economic solution for spans in excess of 35m. For spans of 30 to 35m or 100 to 115ft the box will be economic where a depth of not less than 1.2m (4ft) is acceptable. For spans of 25 to 30m a prestressed concrete voided slab is the appropriate choice, changing to a reinforced concrete voided slab at some point between 25 and 20m or 80 and 65ft span. Where the depth of the deck is less than 700mm (about 28in.) a solid reinforced concrete slab is appropriate.

Data Sheet 2 summarizes the limiting dimensions and spans for various types of deck construction.

Precast construction should be used where restrictions on the temporary headroom preclude the use of falsework under the deck, where safety considerations demand the provision of a continuous soffit during construction by using contiguous precast beams, or where the speed of erection is a prime consideration.

Standard bridges

During recent years the Department of Transport has undertaken an extensive study of bridge standardization, as a result of which it hopes to publish a range of detailed designs that are applicable to commonly recurring bridging problems associated with highway construction.

Although the forms of construction adopted for this standardization are well known and proven bridge deck types, the task has nonetheless proved to be complex because of the bewildering number of combinations of factors controlling the basic geometry of a bridge. In view of the fact that standard solutions can only be applied to a small proportion of total bridging problems, the effort required to resolve this difficulty, combined with the consequent cost of the exercise, raises questions as to whether this approach to design standardization is economically productive.

Standard precast beams are prominent in the standard designs, which is likely to have the effect of strengthening their dominance of the scene where precast construction is concerned. The incidence of precasting other than for standard beam sections has become rare in bridge building. Either this argues for economic advantages having arisen from the use of standard sections, or it argues for conservatism in the design approach where precasting is concerned.

Cast-in-situ reinforced concrete slab decks and composite steel-and-concrete construction also figure in the range of standard designs prepared by the DTp, so that a choice of types of construction can be offered to the contractor at tendering stage, enabling him to select the type of construction best suited to his resources and methods of working.

Section No.	Depth mm	Area mm²	Ht.N.A. mm	I_{NA} mm⁴ ×10⁻⁶	Self weight kN/m
B1	510	337 550	251	9 765	7.95
B2	585	356 300	287	14 095	8.39
B3	660	375 050	323	19 430	8.84
B4	735	396 925	361	26 175	9.36
B5	810	418 800	400	33 995	9.87
B6	885	437 550	435	42 450	10.31
B7	960	456 300	471	52 200	10.75
B8	1035	478 175	510	63 970	11.26
B9	1110	500 050	548	76 930	11.79
B10	1220	527 550	600	97 240	12.43
B11	1220	604 625	580	105 800	14.25
B12	1260	616 625	598	114 810	14.53
B13	1310	633 501	623	127 660	14.93
B14	1360	651 001	649	141 660	15.34
B15	1410	667 877	674	149 830	15.74
B16	1460	682 876	697	170 330	16.09
B17	1510	697 876	720	185 415	16.44

Section No.	Depth mm	Area mm²	Ht.N.A. mm	I_{NA} mm⁴ ×10⁻⁶	Self weight kN/m
WB1	510	419 032	251	12 556	9.88
WB2	585	447 245	290	18 300	10.54
WB3	660	465 995	326	25 172	10.98
WB4	735	487 870	364	33 716	11.50
WB5	810	500 282	398	42 923	11.79
WB6	885	528 495	439	54 419	12.46
WB7	960	547 245	475	66 718	12.90
WB8	1035	569 120	513	81 310	13.42
WB9	1100	581 532	545	95 794	13.71
WB10	1220	622 495	607	123 490	14.67
WB11	1220	707 270	579	133 235	16.67
WB12	1260	719 270	598	144 475	16.95
WB13	1310	736 770	623	160 455	17.37
WB14	1360	753 645	648	177 062	17.76
WB15	1410	770 520	673	194 566	18.16
WB16	1460	785 520	696	212 027	18.52
WB17	1510	800 520	719	230 464	18.87

Section No.	Depth mm	Area mm²	Ht.N.A. mm	I_{NA} mm⁴ ×10⁻⁶	Self weight kN/m
U1	800	469 390	354	30 010	11.08
U2	850	485 895	377	35 640	11.44
U3	900	502 400	400	41 880	11.85
U4	950	518 905	424	48 760	12.24
U5	1000	535 325	447	56 270	12.61
U6	1050	551 830	471	64 450	13.00
U7	1100	568 335	495	73 320	13.40
U8	1200	601 345	543	93 220	14.19
U9	1300	634 270	590	116 100	14.96
U10	1400	667 280	638	142 200	15.72
U11	1500	700 205	687	171 500	16.52
U12	1600	733 215	735	204 400	17.29

C&CA BOX BEAM

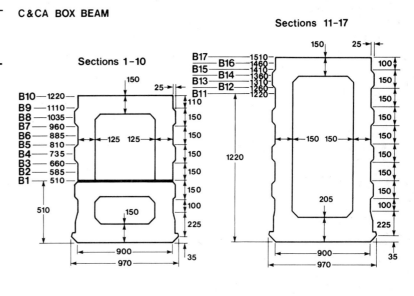

DOW MAC WIDE BOX BEAM

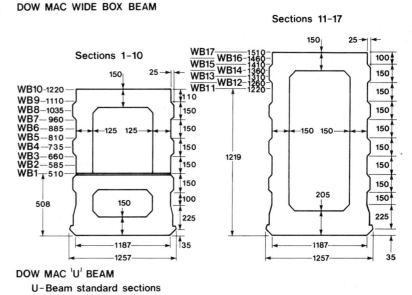

DOW MAC 'U' BEAM

U–Beam standard sections

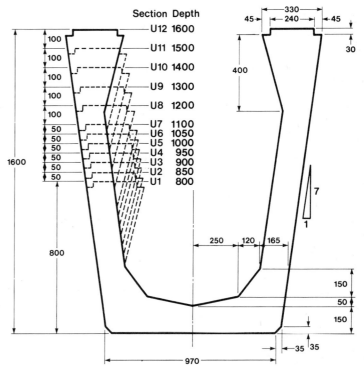

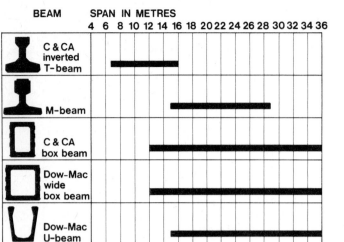

Section No.	Depth mm	Area mm^2	Ht.N.A. mm	I_{NA} mm^4 $\times 10^{-6}$	Self weight kN/m
T1	380	98 000	140	12 45	2.31
T2	420	106 200	160	17 55	2.50
T3	535	114 275	196	32 45	2.69
T4	575	122 475	220	42 30	2.89
T5	615	130 675	244	53 20	3.08
T6	655	138 875	267	65 00	3.27
T7	695	147 075	289	77 80	3.47
T8	735	155 160	312	91 90	3.66
T9	775	163 360	334	107 20	3.85
T10	815	171 560	356	141 60	4.05

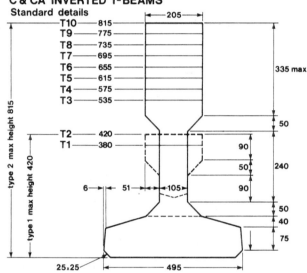

C & CA INVERTED T-BEAMS
Standard details

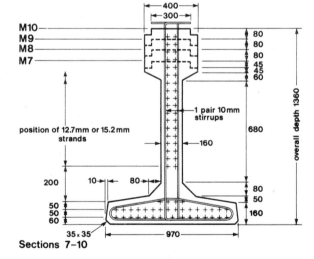

M-BEAM

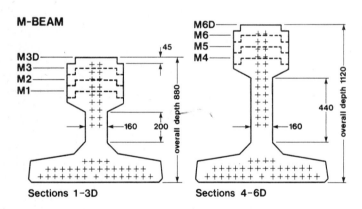

Sections 1-3D

Sections 4-6D

Sections 7-10

Section No.	Depth mm	Area mm^2	Ht.N.A. mm	I_{NA} mm^4 $\times 10^{-6}$	Self weight kN/m
M1	640	284 650	220	10 380	6.71
M2	720	316 650	265	16 200	7.46
M3	800	348 650	310	23 020	8.21
M4	880	323 050	302	25 080	7.61
M5	960	355 050	357	35 810	8.37
M6	1040	387 050	409	47 560	9.12
M7	1120	361 450	393	48 350	8.52
M8	1200	393 450	454	65 190	9.27
M9	1280	425 450	512	82 980	10.02
M10	1360	457 450	568	101 880	10.78

Reinforced concrete slab

Suggested applicability: spans up to 8 m.
Max depth: 800 mm without voids.

Reinforced concrete spine beam

Suggested applicability: spans from 6 to 12 m.
Max. depth: 750 mm without voids.

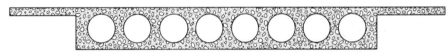

Reinforced concrete voided slab

Suggested applicability: spans from 10 to 20 m.
Max. depth: 1.000 m.
Span/depth ratio: 1:17 for simply-supported spans;
1:20 for continuous spans.

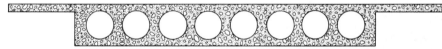

Prestressed concrete voided slab

Suggested applicability: spans from 20 to 30 m.
Max. depth: 1.000 m, extended to 1.200 m in some circumstances.
Span/depth ratio: 1:22 for simply-supported spans;
1:27 for continuous spans.

Prestressed concrete box deck

Suggested applicability: spans in
excess of 30 m.
Minimum depth: 1.200 m.
Span/depth ratio:
1:24 for simply-supported spans;
1:30 for continuous spans.

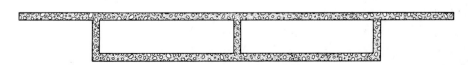

SWANN, R. A. *A feature survey of concrete spine-beam bridges.* London, Cement and Concrete Association, 1972. pp. 76. Technical Report 42.469.

WOOLLEY, M. V. and PENNELLS, E. Multiple span bridge decks in concrete. *Journal of the Institute of Highway Engineers.* Vol. 22, No. 4. April 1975. pp. 20–25.

WOOLLEY, M. V. Economic road bridge design in concrete for the medium span range 15–45 m. *Journal of the Institution of Structural Engineers.* Vol. 52, No. 4. April 1974. pp. 119–128.

CHAPTER 2

The sub-structure

Because of the close interaction between a bridge deck and its supporting structure it is essential that the two be considered together in formulating outline proposals, to ensure that they are compatible. Ground conditions may be such as to make some settlement of the foundations inevitable, and where the magnitude of settlement involved is substantial, this may rule out the use of structural forms involving continuous spans or a torsionally stiff deck, because these would be unable to accommodate large displacements at the points of support.

The techniques of ground investigation by means of boreholes are well known and widely practised. However, it is important to realize that an investigation carried out without proper supervision and understanding may be of little value, and can even be positively misleading in ways that may give rise to major problems during construction, or to the unsatisfactory performance of the completed bridge.

The supervision of ground investigations needs to be in the hands of personnel who know the techniques of investigation well enough to differentiate between real difficulties and a lack of care on the part of the operatives, and who are also able to identify the strata encountered during the investigation. In many instances the latter requirement calls for little more than common sense, but some subsoil formations present variations which may only be identifiable by trained geologists. Even so, the consequences of these differences may be very significant in terms of the design, construction and serviceability of the foundations.

Information regarding the allowable bearing capacities of granular and cohesive soils is summarized on Data Sheet 4, Data Sheet 5 deals with the field identification and classification of various types of soil, as required by CP2001, while Data Sheet 6 tabulates approximate foundation pressures according to CP2004 : 1972.

Abutments

Mass concrete construction is economic for retaining walls of small height, but is not normally competitive with alternatives in reinforced concrete at the height required for a bridge abutment giving highway clearance. The simplicity of construction suggested by mass concrete is offset by the need to taper the section in order to limit the quantities of materials involved. An interesting solution to this requirement occurs where the cross-section is given a triangular shape with the front face battered, resulting in a sloping front to the abutment.

Cantilevered reinforced concrete walls are probably the most widely used form of construction for typical highway bridges. They require simple formwork, but as the height increases, the reinforcement can become very heavy and the section thickness substantial.

With increasing height it becomes economic to shape the section of the wall stem in plan, creating a T, which allows the use of wall panels of the minimum practical thickness in combination with cantilevered T-beams. This arrangement results in a reduction in the quantities of concrete and reinforcement required but adds complexity to the formwork arrangements needed.

The traditional counterfort wall employs T-ribs that extend right to the back of the footing, but at intermediate heights this is not necessary – the T-ribs need only be sufficiently deep to enable them to resist the shearing forces involved, and to keep the amount of tension reinforcement required within reasonable limits. The resulting stub-counterfort wall provides an intermediate solution between the cantilever and the full counterfort, and can be economic at heights which are appropriate to providing the necessary highway clearance.

Where types of wall involving more-complex formwork requirements are to be utilized it is important to keep the spacing between counterforts regular, so that the formwork panels can be given the maximum amount of re-use without modification.

For the bases of retaining walls it is often the shearing stresses that control the thickness of footing needed. This is particularly true as regards the recent requirements of the Department of the Environment (DoE) in its Technical Memorandum BE1/73 which limits the shearing stress in relation to the amount of main tension steel provided.

For large abutments where the ground is rising away from the bridge spans there can be advantages in using a hollow abutment. This consists of four walls forming a box in plan and supporting a deck of simple cast-in-situ reinforced concrete beam-and-slab construction. The front and side walls simply act as supports to the deck, while the rear wall retains the earth fill to the approach embankments. The potential advantage of this arrangement is that the height of the retaining wall at the rear of the hollow abutment is much less than would be required if the retaining wall were the front wall of the abutment.

The various types of abutments are illustrated on Data Sheet 7, and their design is dealt with on Data Sheet 10. The various modes of failure that may occur are discussed on Data Sheet 9.

Piers

The choice of construction of a bridge deck will dictate how much freedom exists in choosing the pier construction. If support is required at intervals across the full width of the bridge deck, some form of supporting wall or portal frame is called for. However, where a deck has within itself some capacity to span transversely at intermediate-support positions by means of a diaphragm within the depth of the deck, then a wider choice is possible.

Simplicity in the form of the pier not only has the merit of providing easier, and therefore more-economical, construction but is also more likely to produce an attractive result. Complex shapes have been used with success, but for every good example there are several poor imitations and it is evident that piers of a complex shape should only be adopted after a careful investigation of their potential appearance. It is probably better to limit their use to situations where good modelling facilities enable a realistic representation to be made of the final result. Although perspective sketches can be prepared, they are frequently misleading because they can at best only represent the appearance from a single viewpoint.

One choice to be made in relation to the overall articulation of a structure is whether the bearings should be placed at the heads or the feet of piers. A monolithic connection between the head of a pier and the bridge deck is undoubtedly a clean and tidy solution visually, but bearings at the foot of a pier require a chamber and introduce associated drainage problems which usually combine to create additional expense. There are also problems in providing stability for the pier during construction, and for these reasons bearings at the heads of piers are usually preferred.

Banks seats

Where no abutment is provided and the end of the bridge deck is supported at the head of a slope formed by a cutting or embankment, the foundation may be a strip footing, a buried skeletal abutment or a piled bank seat, depending on the level of suitable founding strata.

The choice of a bank-seat support usually follows from a designer's wish to minimize the interruption to the flow of lines of the deck. It is possible to detail such a foundation in a way that enables the deck profile to continue into the earthworks without the supporting foundations being visible. To achieve this it is usually necessary to construct part of the bank seat with an edge profile to match that applied to the deck itself. With this arrangement the movement joint in the deck is likely to pass through the parapet clear of the earthworks. Attention to draining this joint is therefore important in order to avoid weathering defects.

Several types of bank seat are illustrated on Data Sheet 8.

Transition slabs

Opinions differ as to the merits of providing transition slabs on the approaches to a bridge. Maintenance problems have been known to arise with transition slabs, but those who favour their use attribute this to poor original design or detailing. Where ground conditions are such that the embankment supporting a road will settle significantly, depressions are liable to develop immediately adjoining the ends of the bridge deck, giving a very poor riding characteristic to the carriageway. This in turn increases the settlement as a result of pounding from traffic on the poorly-aligned section of road. This problem is aggravated by providing rigid supports at the ends of the deck such as would occur if this element were piled. It is also apparent that embankments of a substantial height will be subject to settlement within themselves, quite apart from that of the supporting sub-grade, thus further adding to the problem.

A well-designed transition slab distributes the relative settlement between a bridge deck and the approach embankments, thereby very much improving the riding characteristics of the pavement and eliminating the recurring maintenance problems associated with the formation of depressions immediately behind rigid end supports to the deck.

Piling

It often becomes necessary to employ piled foundations for bridgeworks where the ground near to the surface is too soft to sustain spread footings or would be susceptible to substantial settlement. In addition to providing a means of supporting the foundation loads, the use of piling can make it possible for the other ground works (such as the construction of pile caps in the place of spread footings) to be carried out at higher levels than might otherwise be possible. This can be beneficial where the foundation is to be built adjacent to a waterway or in waterlogged ground.

The various types of pile that are available are listed on Data Sheet 11. Data Sheets 12 and 13 give charts for the design of precast concrete and steel bearing piles respectively according to the well-known Hiley pile-driving formula.

The choice of the type of pile to be used is influenced by ground conditions. Where rock or some other hard bearing stratum occurs at an accessible depth, preformed piles driven to provide end bearing can be an attractive proposition. Steel H-piles are more easily driven, cut and extended than their reinforced concrete alternatives. However, it is self-evident that reinforced concrete is a more suitable material where corrosive conditions exist. Preformed piles can be driven at a rake of up to 1:4, thereby absorbing horizontal forces without inducing substantial bending moments in the pile section. Loadings in pile groups which include rakers can be assessed by the elastic centre method described in the Civil Engineering Code of Practice No. 2: "Earth Retaining Structures". To minimize the risk of high bending moments developing in piles, any arrangement adopted should be such as to avoid the intersection of all the pile centre-lines at a single common point, because with such an arrangement the rotation of the pile cap about that point is possible. This risk is avoided by ensuring that the layout adopted produces intersections of centre-lines at no less than two well-separated points.

Large-diameter piles are normally installed vertically, but it is still possible to absorb horizontal loads although these do give rise to bending in the pile. Methods of assessing the horizontal-load capacity of large-diameter piles have been developed which utilize the subgrade resistance in combination with the stiffness of the pile.

The techniques of constructing large-diameter bored piles are best suited to cohesive soils. Granular layers near to the surface can be successfully dealt with, but at greater depths the risks of the shaft sides collapsing become too great.

Piling adds to the cost of a bridge, so that the practicability of providing traditional footings always merits careful investigation. Even where the soil will only permit low bearing pressures it is usually cheaper to provide extensive spread footings than to employ piles.

Groundworks

For work within the ground, simplicity of construction can have considerable merits. A mass concrete foundation may be bulky, but is worth consideration as a means of speeding construction in difficult ground conditions and it provides a firm base for continuing the work in reinforced concrete with the added complexities involved. In waterlogged ground the use of circular cofferdams filled with mass concrete minimizes the temporary works and leads to the rapid completion of the work in the ground.

Diaphragm walls

For vertically-sided cuttings, such as those required for lengths of sunken road, the work of excavation can often be minimized by using such constructional techniques as contiguous bored piling or diaphragm-wall construction, in place of conventional retaining walls. Since these techniques are usually associated with particularly-difficult ground conditions, such as those arising with over-consolidated clays, the design approach involves consultation with authoritative experts.

The construction of a diaphragm wall requires the excavation of a deep trench in short lengths, using a bentonite slurry to support the faces of the excavation where necessary. A prefabricated cage of reinforcement is lowered into the excavation and concrete is placed by tremie. Each short length forms a panel, and the joints between panels introduce some measure of structural discontinuity into the wall. Precast wall panels have been used in some instances, and involve the use of a bentonite drilling mud which develops a strength appropriate to the surrounding ground.

Reinforced earth

A rapidly-constructed and lighter form of retaining wall construction has been developed in recent years which is based on the use of facing panels that are stacked without any attempt to provide fixity or bond with adjacent units, but where each panel is tied back to the earth fill by straps that are buried in the retained embankment during construction. The facing to a reinforced earth wall can consist of concrete panels, metal troughs or — more recently — lightweight panels of fibre-reinforced concrete. The technique has been widely demonstrated on the Continent, and several examples have now been built in the UK. In addition to giving a lighter wall than could be achieved in traditional reinforced concrete construction, this technique has the merit of allowing construction to proceed on ground which may not be suitable to form the foundation for a conventional wall.

Joints between the facing panels are usually made to accept movements which may arise due to settlement, and the flexibility of the finished construction makes it highly tolerant to differential settlement without affecting its structural integrity. The technique has been used for bridge abutments as well as free-standing walls. Some settlement is likely to occur, although this can be nominal where ground conditions are firm. In circumstances where the use of conventional abutments would involve extensive groundworks associated with foundations, it may be found that the use of reinforced earth could provide a solution which makes substantial savings by eliminating much of the groundworks.

Granular soils

The bearing capacity of a granular soil is closely related to its density. The more tightly compact the soil is, the greater its capacity.

The standard penetration test is the technique adopted for assessing in situ the compactness of granular soils.

The bearing capacity can therefore be related to standard penetration test values N.

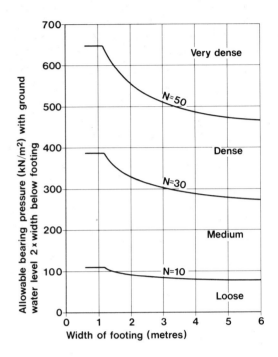

Bearing capacity of sand

Cohesive soils

The ultimate bearing capacity q_d per unit of area of a continuous footing is

$$q_d = 5.70c = 2.85q_u$$

and of a circular or square footing is

$$q_{dr} = q_{ds} = 7.4c = 3.7q_u.$$

The ultimate bearing capacity of a rectangular or oblong footing of width B and length L is approximately equal to

$$q_{do} = 2.85q_u\,(1+0.3B/L)$$

Suggested allowable bearing values for clay

N: number of blows per 300 mm in standard penetration test.

q_u: unconfined compressive strength.

q_d: ultimate bearing capacity of continuous footing.

q_{ds}: ultimate bearing capacity of square footing.

q_a: proposed allowable bearing value (where $G_s = 3$).

G_s: factor of safety with respect to base failure.

Description of clay	N	q_u	q_d	q_{ds}	q_a	
					Square $1.2q_u$	Continuous $0.9q_u$
Very soft*	<2	<25	<75	<100	<30	<20
Soft*	2 to 4	25 to 50	75 to 150	100 to 200	30 to 60	20 to 45
Medium	4 to 8	50 to 100	150 to 300	200 to 400	60 to 120	45 to 90
Stiff	8 to 15	100 to 200	300 to 600	400 to 800	120 to 240	90 to 180
Very stiff	15 to 30	200 to 400	600 to 1200	800 to 1600	240 to 480	180 to 360
Hard		>400	>1200	>1600	>480	>360

All values in kN/m².

Field identification and classification of soils

Types	Size and nature of particles — Principal soil types — Field identification	Composite types	Strength — Term	Strength — Field test	Structure — Term	Structure — Field identification
Coarse-grained, non-cohesive						
Boulders	Larger than 8 in. in diameter					
Cobbles	Mostly between 8 in. and 3 in.					
Gravels	Mostly between 3 in. and No. 7 BS sieve	Boulder gravels, Hoggin, Sandy gravels	Loose	Can be excavated with spade. 2 in. wooden peg can be easily driven.	Homogeneous	Deposit consisting essentially of one type.
			Compact	Requires pick for excavation. 2 in. wooden peg hard to drive more than a few inches.		
			Slightly cemented	Visual examination. Pick removes soil in lumps which can be abraded with thumb.	Stratified	Alternating layers of varying types.
Sands — Uniform	Composed of particles mostly between No. 7 and 200 BS sieves, and visible to the naked eye. Very little or no cohesion when dry.	Silty sands, Micaceous sands				
Sands — Graded	Sands may be classified as uniform or well graded according to the distribution of particle size. Uniform sands may be divided into coarse sands between Nos. 7 and 25 BS sieves, medium sands between Nos. 25 and 72 BS sieves and fine sands between Nos. 72 and 200 BS sieves.	Lateritic sands, Clayey sands				
Silts — Low plasticity	Particles mostly passing No. 200 BS sieve. Particles mostly invisible or barely visible to the naked eye. Some plasticity and exhibits marked dilatancy. Dries moderately quickly and can be dusted off the fingers. Dry lumps possess cohesion but can be powdered easily in the fingers.	Loams, Clayey silts, Organic silts, Micaceous silts	Soft	Easily moulded in the fingers.	Homogeneous	Deposit consisting essentially of one type.
			Firm	Can be moulded by strong pressure in the fingers.	Stratified	Alternating layers of varying types.
Fine-grained, cohesive — Clays — Medium plasticity	Dry lumps can be broken but not powdered. They also disintegrate under water. Smooth touch and plastic, no dilatancy. Sticks to the fingers and dries slowly.	Boulder clays, Sandy clays, Silty clays, Marls	Very soft	Exudes between fingers when squeezed in fist.	Fissured	Breaks into polyhedral fragments along fissure planes.
			Soft	Easily moulded in fingers.	Intact	No fissures.
			Firm	Can be moulded by strong pressure in the fingers.	Homogeneous	Deposits consisting essentially of one type.
Clays — High plasticity	Shrinks appreciably on drying, usually showing cracks. Lean and fat clays show those properties to a moderate and high degree respectively.	Organic clays, Lateritic clays	Stiff	Cannot be moulded in fingers.	Stratified	Alternating layers of varying types. If layers are thin the soil may be described as laminated.
			Hard	Brittle or very tough.	Weathered	Usually exhibits crumb or columnar structure.
Organic — Peats	Fibrous organic material, usually brown or black in colour.	Sandy, silty or clayey peats	Spongy	Fibres compressed together.		
			Firm	Very compressible and open structure.		

Presumed bearing values under vertical static loading

NOTE: These values are for preliminary design purposes only, and may need alteration upwards or downwards.

Group	Types of rocks and soils	Presumed bearing value		Remarks
		kN/m²*	kgf/cm² or tonf/ft²*	
Rocks	Hard igneous and gneissic rocks in sound condition	10000	100	These values are based on the assumption that the foundations are carried down to unweathered rock
	Hard limestones and hard sandstones	4000	40	
	Schists and slates	3000	30	
	Hard shales, hard mudstones and soft sandstones	2000	20	
	Soft shales and soft mudstones	600 to 1000	6 to 10	
		600	6	
	Hard sound chalk, soft limestone Thinly bedded limestones, sandstones, shales Heavily shattered rocks	To be assessed after inspection		
Non-cohesive soils	Compact gravel, or compact sand and gravel	>600	>6	Width of foundation B not less than 1 m (3 ft). Groundwater level assumed to be a depth not less than B below the base of the foundation.
	Medium dense gravel, or medium dense sand and gravel	200 to 600	2 to 6	
	Loose gravel, or loose sand and gravel	<200	<2	
	Compact sand	>300	>3	
	Medium dense sand	100 to 300	1 to 3	
	Loose sand	<100	<1	
Cohesive soils	Very stiff boulder clays and hard clays	300 to 600	3 to 6	Susceptible to long-term consolidation settlement.
	Stiff clays	150 to 300	1.5 to 3	
	Firm clays	75 to 150	0.75 to 1.5	
	Soft clays and silts	<75	<0.75	
	Very soft clays and silts	Not applicable		
	Peat and organic soils			
	Made ground or fill			

* 1 tonf/ft² = 1.094 kgf/cm² = 107.25 kN/m².

Undrained (immediate) shear strength of cohesive soils

Consistency			Undrained (immediate) shear strength		
In accordance with CP 2001:1957	Widely used	Field indications	kN/m²	kgf/cm² or tonf/ft²	lbf/ft²
Very stiff	Very stiff or hard	Brittle or very tough	Greater than 150	Greater than 1.5	Greater than 3000
Stiff	Stiff	Cannot be moulded in the fingers	100 to 150	1.0 to 1.5	2000 to 3000
	Firm to stiff		75 to 100	0.75 to 1.0	1500 to 2000
Firm	Firm	Can be moulded in the fingers by strong pressure	50 to 75	0.5 to 0.75	1000 to 1500
	Soft to firm		40 to 50	0.4 to 0.5	750 to 1000
Soft	Soft	Easily moulded in the fingers	20 to 40	0.2 to 0.4	375 to 750
Very soft	Very soft	Exudes between the fingers when squeezed in the fist	Less than 20	Less than 0.2	Less than 375

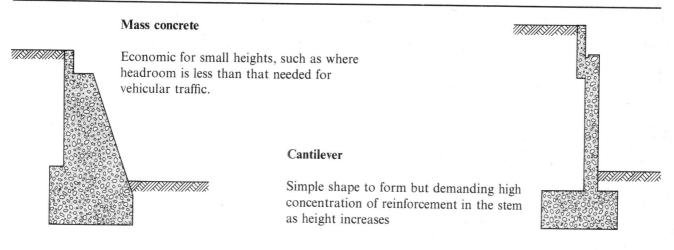

Mass concrete

Economic for small heights, such as where headroom is less than that needed for vehicular traffic.

Cantilever

Simple shape to form but demanding high concentration of reinforcement in the stem as height increases

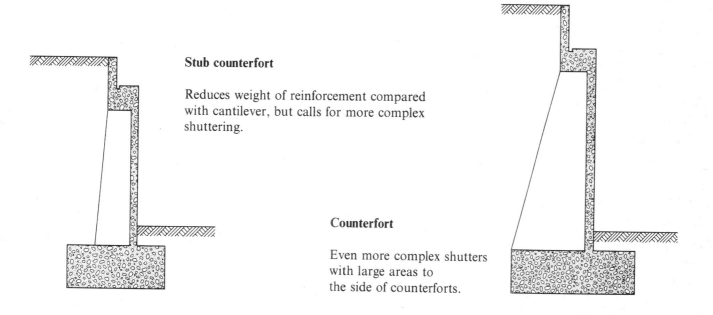

Stub counterfort

Reduces weight of reinforcement compared with cantilever, but calls for more complex shuttering.

Counterfort

Even more complex shutters with large areas to the side of counterforts.

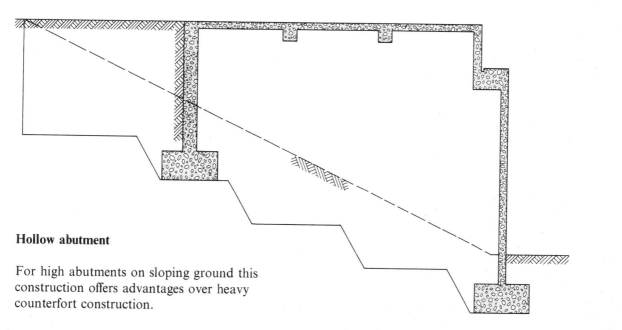

Hollow abutment

For high abutments on sloping ground this construction offers advantages over heavy counterfort construction.

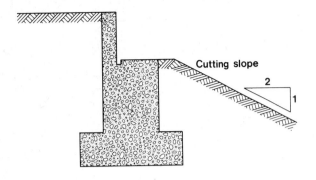

A bridge constructed at existing ground level to span across a road in cutting may need only nominal bank seats if good foundation strata are available at shallow depths. This may give rise to particular problems where negative reactions are likely to develop.

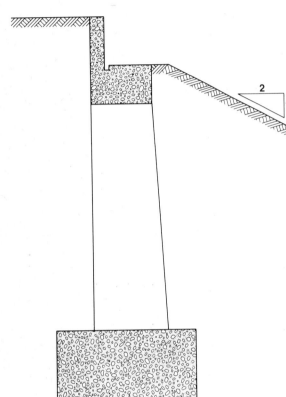

"Spillthrough" or "skeleton" abutments are suitable where spread footings are needed at a level well below a bank seat. It is often advantageous to design a footing to offset the foundation in relation to the bearings, because the permanent horizontal loading shifts the reaction.

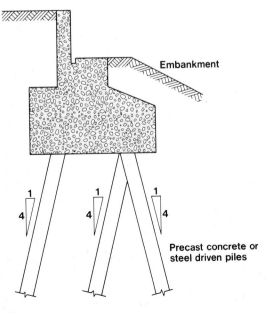

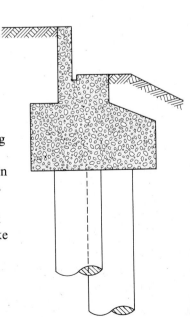

Where the load-bearing strata are at a considerable depth below the bank seat level, piled foundations are called for. Driven piles are usually preferred where the bearing strata are of rock or granular material: bored piles are suitable in cohesive ground. Horizontal loads are accommodated in bored piles by their resistance to bending, but driven piles can be placed at a rake to form a framework.

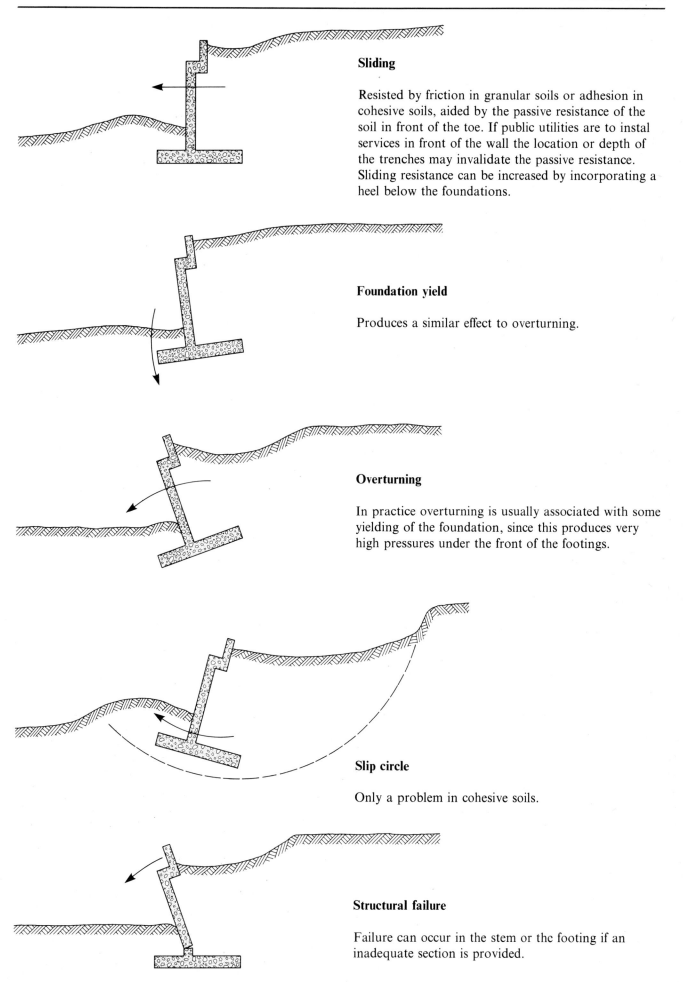

Sliding

Resisted by friction in granular soils or adhesion in cohesive soils, aided by the passive resistance of the soil in front of the toe. If public utilities are to instal services in front of the wall the location or depth of the trenches may invalidate the passive resistance. Sliding resistance can be increased by incorporating a heel below the foundations.

Foundation yield

Produces a similar effect to overturning.

Overturning

In practice overturning is usually associated with some yielding of the foundation, since this produces very high pressures under the front of the footings.

Slip circle

Only a problem in cohesive soils.

Structural failure

Failure can occur in the stem or the footing if an inadequate section is provided.

Loading case — The following loading conditions should be considered when designing the section:

Construction cases:

1 abutment self-weight + wing walls

2 abutment self-weight + wing walls + deck load + temperature rise

3 abutment self-weight + fill behind abutment + HA surcharge

Working-load cases: HA loading

4 abutment self-weight + fill behind abutment + fill on toe + deck dead load + temperature fall + shrinkage + HA surcharge

5 abutment self-weight + fill behind abutment + fill on toe + deck dead load + temperature fall + shrinkage + HA surcharge + HA live load + HA braking away from abutment

Working-load cases: HB loading

6 abutment self-weight + fill behind abutment + fill on toe + deck dead load + temperature fall + shrinkage + HB surcharge

7 abutment self-weight + fill behind abutment + fill on toe + deck dead load + temperature fall + shrinkage + 1/3rd HA surcharge + HB live load + HB braking away from abutment

8 abutment self-weight + fill behind abutment + fill on toe + deck dead load + temperature fall + shrinkage + HB surcharge + 1/3rd HA live load + 1/3rd HA braking away from abutment

25% overstress on steel and concrete stresses and bearing pressures, and reaction allowed to fall outside middle-third for cases 1, 2, 3, 6, 7 and 8

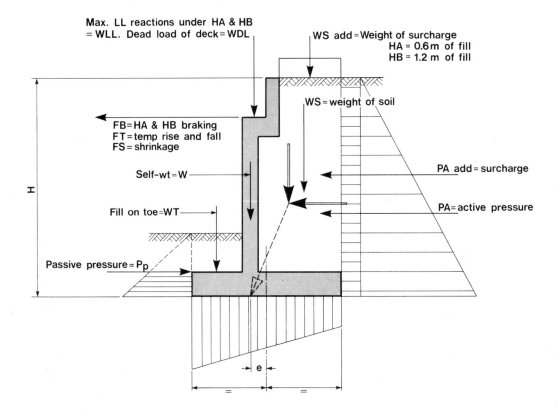

Displacement piles

Pile type			Normal range of sizes available		Normal range of load
			Cross-section	Length	
Preformed	Timber		Up to 400 mm × 400 mm	Up to 20 m	Up to 600 kN
	Concrete	Normal reinforced	Up to 450 mm × 400 mm	Up to 27 m	Up to 1000 kN
		Prestressed	Up to 400 mm square Up to 750 mm dia. hollow	Up to 27 m	Up to 1000 kN
	Steel	Box	Rendhex standard Frodingham octagonal Sheet pile fabrication	Up to 36 m	Up to 1500 kN
		Tubular	Heavy gauge up to 900 mm dia.	Up to 36 m	Up to 1500 kN
		H-section	200 mm × 200 mm to 300 mm × 300 mm	Up to 36 m	Up to 1700 kN
		Screw	600 mm to 2400 mm dia. helices	Up to 24 m	Up to 2500 kN
Partially preformed	Precast and cast-in-situ concrete		450 mm to 600 mm dia.	Up to 50 m	Up to 2000 kN
	Steel and cast-in-situ concrete		250 mm to 500 mm dia.	Up to 18 m	Up to 800 kN
Driven in situ	Concrete		250 mm to 600 mm dia.	Up to 24 m	Up to 1500 kN

Replacement piles

Pile type			Normal range of sizes available		Normal range of load
			Cross-section	Length	
Percussion bored	Small diameter		450 mm to 600 mm dia.	Up to 24 m	Up to 1200 kN
Flush bored	Large diameter		600 mm dia. and over	Up to 45 m	Up to 10 000 kN
Rotary bored	Large diameter	Straight shaft	600 mm to 1800 mm dia.	Up to 45 m	Up to 10 000 kN
		Under-reamed base	As above with bell up to 3 times shaft diameter	Up to 45 m	Very high loads possible
	Small diameter		225 mm to 550 mm dia.	Up to 36 m	Up to 1000 kN

With acknowledgements to Ground Engineering.

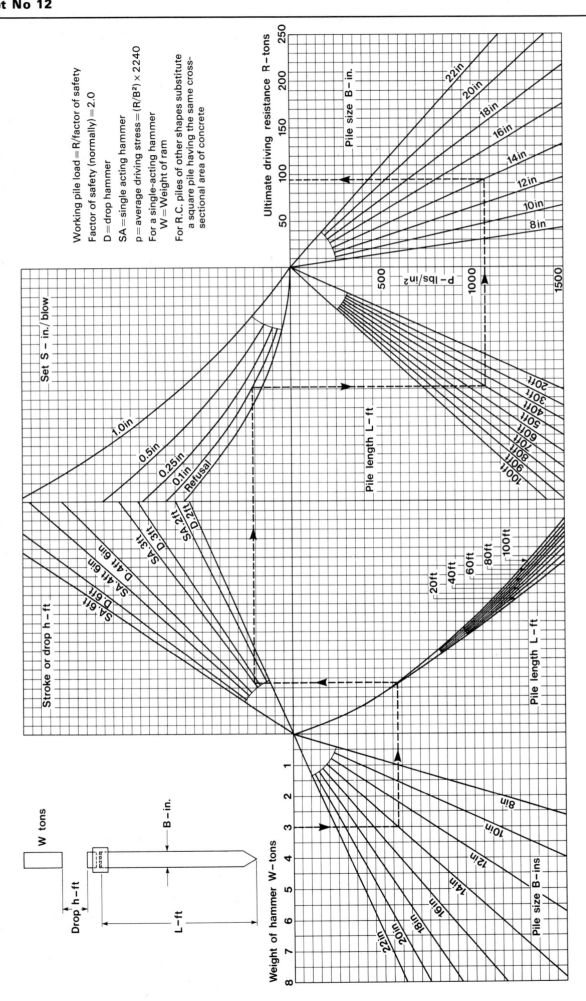

NOMOGRAM FOR THE HILEY PILE-DRIVING FORMULA

Square reinforced concrete piles driven with a single-acting steam hammer or a drop hammer
Pile head fitted with helmet, timber dolly and packing

Working pile load = R/factor of safety
Factor of safety (normally) = 2.0
D = drop hammer
SA = single acting hammer
p = average driving stress = $(R/B^2) \times 2240$
For a single-acting hammer
W = Weight of ram
For R.C. piles of other shapes substitute a square pile having the same cross-sectional area of concrete

Set S – in./blow

Ultimate driving resistance R – tons

Pile size B – in.

p – lbs/in.^{2}

Pile length L – ft

Stroke or drop h – ft

Weight of hammer W – tons

Pile size B – ins

Pile length L – ft

W tons

Drop h – ft

B – in.

L – ft

NOMOGRAM FOR THE HILEY PILE-DRIVING FORMULA

Steel bearing piles driven with a single-acting steam hammer or a drop hammer
Pile head fitted with helmet and plastic or Greenheart dolly

INSTITUTION OF STRUCTURAL ENGINEERS. *Earth retaining structures*. Civil Engineering Code of Practice No. 2. London, 1951. pp. 224.

INSTITUTION OF CIVIL ENGINEERS. *Behaviour of piles*. Proceedings of the conference organized by the Institution of Civil Engineers. London, 1971. pp. 222.

BRITISH STANDARDS INSTITUTION. CP2001:1957. *Site investigations*. London. pp. 124.

BRITISH STANDARDS INSTITUTION. CP2004:1972. *Foundations*. Amendment AMD 1755. London, June 1975. pp. 158.

BROMS, B. B. Lateral resistance of piles in cohesive soils. *Proceedings of the American Society of Civil Engineers*. Vol. 90, No. SM2. Paper 3825. March 1964. pp. 27–63.

BROMS, B. B. Lateral resistance of piles in cohesionless soils. *Proceedings of the American Society of Civil Engineers*. Vol. 90, No. SM3. Paper 3909. May 1964. pp. 123–156.

BURLAND, J. B. and COOK, R. W. *The design of bored piles in stiff clays*. Garston, Building Research Establishment. Paper CP 99/77.

CHELLIS, R. D. *Pile foundations*. Second edition. New York, McGraw Hill, 1961. pp. 704.

POULOS, G. Lateral load-deflection prediction for pile groups. *Proceedings of the American Society of Civil Engineers*. Vol. 100, No. GT1. January 1975. pp. 19–34.

TOMLINSON, M. J. *Foundation design and construction*. Third edition. London, Pitman Publishing, 1975. pp. 816.

INSTITUTION OF CIVIL ENGINEERS. *Diaphragm walls and anchorages*. Proceedings of the conference organized by the Institution of Civil Engineers in London, September 1974. pp. 223.

HAMBLY, E. C. and BURLAND, J. B. *Bridge foundations and substructures*. Building Research Establishment Report. HMSO, London, 1979 pp. 93.

CHAPTER 3

Furnishings

Parapets

The minimum function of a parapet is to prevent pedestrians from accidentally falling from a bridge deck. In recent times it has become expected that they will also provide some measure of similar protection for vehicles.

The requirement for a parapet to provide a safeguard against a vehicle which is out of control plunging over the edge of a bridge cannot be specified in terms of a static loading condition. The ability to absorb or redirect the energy of an errant vehicle is a function of the flexibility and constructional details of a parapet as much as on the nature and speed of the vehicle. Design regulations have therefore been based on the containment requirements in terms of a specified weight of a vehicle and its approach angle, and the assessment of suitable parapet designs has become a matter of tests rather than design calculations.

It would be impracticable to stipulate that a parapet should be capable of containing any vehicle travelling at any speed. Requirements must be rationalized, and very few incidents have arisen in which vehicles have plunged through parapets, although there is inevitably much publicity in instances where this does occur with a consequent loss of life.

The selection of the type of parapet for a bridge is of fundamental importance to its appearance. In fact, for traffic users crossing a bridge the parapet is likely to be the only indication that they are on a bridge structure. The fundamental choice is between a solid concrete parapet, usually surmounted by a single rail, and a more-open metal parapet. Each can have visual merits depending on the general configuration of the bridge structure. In the case of a simple bridge that is required to provide a single span over a single two-lane carriageway and with solid abutments, the short span will inevitably be slender and may be visually weak by comparison with the mass of the abutment wing-walls. A deep concrete parapet can offset this, particularly if the parapet is continued as a distinctive element along the full length of the wing-walls as well as over the span. On the other hand, if a three-span or four-span bridge is required over a motorway to carry a local road, with consequent light loading, it would seem inappropriate to introduce heavy concrete parapets onto a structure which would otherwise be slender.

Because it is very important to the finished appearance of a bridge, the parapet and its supporting upstand merit particular attention during detailing. The main potential hazard is weathering as a result of water staining. Even where the parapet is non-corrosive, such as where it is of aluminium, if water running off the parapet is allowed to run over the front face of the supporting upstand, this will lead to severe staining in time which will have a disfiguring effect. The width of the supporting upstand therefore needs to be ample to accommodate the parapet post fixings and base plate, with a sufficient margin of width to ensure that the water drains into the bridge rather than over the front face.

The choice of fixings can also create hazards as regards appearance. If some form of pocket is detailed it is possible for these pockets to become filled with water during the course of construction, and to give rise to frost damage to the upstand. Even the introduction of anti-freezing agents to prevent this does not always solve the problem.

Where a metal parapet is to be used a choice must be made between steel, which will then require painting (not only in the course of construction but as a regular item of maintenance), and aluminium, which has gained widespread favour. Its colour is complementary to concrete, and the absence of any need for routine maintenance in the form of painting is a significant advantage.

Data relating to the design of parapets are summarized on Data Sheet 15.

Expansion joints

Fundamental requirements for an expansion joint are that it should allow free movement of the structure under the influence of thermal, elastic and creep movements, and that any constraining force that is applied should be easily absorbed by the structure. It should also provide good riding quality for traffic passing over the joint, and it should either be waterproof or be associated with drainage details which prevent any disfiguring weathering of the structure below the deck surface. The joint should be serviceable and it should require the minimum of maintenance. Since it is unlikely to last the life of the structure it should also be replaceable without prejudice to the viability of the structure, and at a moderate cost. Expansion joints not only have to cater for the surface of the main carriageway, but must also make provision for movements in kerbs, verges and parapets.

However good an expansion-joint detail may be, the

Figure 8. Controlled impact test on rectangular hollow-section barrier.

joint presents an interruption in the traffic surface which is likely to give rise to noise in use, and to a problem of some degree as regards maintenance. Where long structures are constructed it is preferable to minimize the number of joints, accepting the need to cater for large movements where they do occur rather than to have joints at frequent intervals. The range of types of construction of bridge decks now in common use makes it feasible to produce long lengths of continuous structure. Even where precast beams are being used which will not themselves be made continuous under added load, it is possible to detail the deck slab as a continuous member but with the provision of simple articulation joints at the deck-support locations.

The mechanical type of expansion joint is used for large ranges of movement. Such a joint may be based on the use of opposing sets of finger plates which interlock to provide a running surface throughout a range of movement up to the length of the projecting fingers. This type of joint has been well proven over the years. Its disadvantage is the need for heavy fixings because of the cantilever action of the finger plates. With smaller ranges of movement, however, the fingers can be shallower in depth and in some instances may be partially supported by a flat plate on the opposing side of the joint, thereby reducing the cantilever and also the weight of the fixings needed.

For lower ranges of movement several types of joint are available that are based on the use of compressible

neoprene or rubber membranes. If a wide strip of rubber or neoprene is exposed on the traffic face it can give rise to difficulties in the riding quality of the joint. At various ranges of compression the upper surface will tend to change profile and therefore alter the riding characteristics. In any event, some traffic noise must inevitably arise from the juxtaposition of two different riding surfaces. In some joints this potential difficulty has been offset by introducing a series of steel members, breaking up the width of the compressible membrane into narrow strips which are set below the traffic surface, so that the running surface is provided by the steel members themselves. These joints obviously become simpler as fewer membranes are needed to cater for reducing ranges of movement, until only a single membrane is provided.

Fillers based on foamed plastics are alternatives to the use of rubber or neoprene as compressible membranes. Such fillers can be effective in joints catering for small movements, provided that the filler material remains in compression at all stages of movement in the joint. Although the filler is normally bonded to the supporting edges of the joint, and certain types of foam plastics are capable of working in a stretched as well as a compressed state, adhesives do not usually show the degree of reliability in service which would warrant relying on tension across such a joint. Although the materials themselves may be capable of performing in this way, a civil engineering site does not permit the close control of workmanship which would be necessary to guarantee results throughout long lengths of joint.

Because it is necessary to install the joint filler in a state of compression, nosings must be established before the installation of the filler. It is important to achieve a strong and true-to-line shoulder on each side of the joint. This may be done by using high-strength concrete or epoxy nosings. The latter have come into widespread use in recent years, but difficulties have been experienced where the shape of the nosing results in high shearing stresses under the impact of vehicle wheels. It is important that the shoulders of the nosing should be square.

Where the range of movement being catered for is very small, flexible sealants may be used. There are a variety of types available on the market in the form of polysulphides. Again, it is important that the shoulders of the joints should be firm and true to line.

For the smallest movements, perhaps associated with points where the deck support permits rotation without translation, carriageway finishes can be continued over a joint in the structure.

Types of expansion joints form the subject of Data Sheet 16, and information relating to deck movements is collated on Data Sheet 18.

Bearings

The advent of PTFE (polytetrafluroethalene), giving low frictional surface-to-surface contact, has meant that mechanical types of bearings such as rollers and rockers have largely been superseded. The working pressures that PTFE can sustain are such that the design of bearings gives contact areas well matched to the capacity of the concrete, and the sliding surfaces permit substantial movement without the need for enlarged bearing dimensions.

The objective of a bearing layout in a bridge deck is to allow those movements which must take place as a result of thermal changes, creep, shrinkage and articulation of the structure to occur, while maintaining the deck in position. Restraints against longitudinal and lateral movement must be provided, and bearing manufacturers have various details in their products to provide restraint in certain directions while allowing specified movements. Some of these devices restrain movement in one direction only while others are bi-directional. In some instances the restraint is sensitive to direction and care must be taken to ensure that a pair of bearings do not act against one another in service conditions, and that they allow lateral as well as longitudinal movements to take place.

Rotations are accommodated by spherical or cylindrical interfaces in a PTFE bearing, acting in combination with a second, plane, sliding surface. Where a cylindrical surface is adopted, it is essential that any set of bearings acting together along a single line of rotation should have a common axis – not only in plan, but also in elevation. Where there is any doubt about the practicability of achieving the accurate setting of the bearings, spherical surfaces must be used in preference to cylinders. Some bearing manufacturers recommend this as a matter of course.

Where small movements and rotations are to be accommodated, it may be appropriate to use rubber bearings which permit movement by shear displacement. The choice is a matter of cost, but the capacity of rubber bearings is limited to lower ranges of load and movement.

The service life of a bearing may not equal that of the rest of the structure. It is important to make adequate provision for inspection during the life of the structure because any tendency for the capacity for movement to be restricted quickly leads to the deterioration of the structure, in the form of cracking and spalling. It is possible that the bearings will need to be replaced during the life of a bridge. This is obviously a fairly major operation, and it is not appropriate to prepare the details with a view to making simple replacement a prime requirement, unless no resultant penalty of cost or serviceability will arise. However, it is obviously appropriate to see that the details are such that replacement is possible without prejudicing the viability of the structure.

Many bearings contain steel components that are susceptible to corrosion. A high standard of protective coating is appropriate on these because, within the context of the concrete structure, the need for painting maintenance does not generally arise, and it is therefore unlikely that the paintwork on small components will be given regular attention. In any event, to obtain access to the bearings in order to repaint them would usually be extremely difficult.

Further information regarding bearings is given on Data Sheet 17.

Waterproofing

Mastic asphalt is a long-established and widely used material for waterproofing bridge decks. It provides a continuous membrane which can follow the shape of the bridge deck without difficulties. One disadvantage that it has, however, is that it requires good weather conditions for successful laying. While a bridge deck is damp, laying is delayed by the fact that the heat leads to the "blowing" of the freshly laid material so that, during adverse weather conditions, there may be lengthy periods during which it is not possible to make progress with waterproofing, which can cause embarrassment regarding the time required to complete the works. Preformed bituminous sheeting is less sensitive to laying conditions but the evaporation of moisture trapped on the deck surface can cause the subsequent lifting or blowing of the sheeting.

Recent developments include the introduction of materials which are applied by spray. These bond directly to the deck surface, thereby preventing any migrant path for water beneath the impermeable layer, such as can occur with unbonded materials with the result that one weak spot allows the water to travel over large areas, finding its way to the lowest corner of the deck where leaks develop.

Sprayed material and bituminous sheeting require protection before the road pavement materials are added. This protection may take the form of sand asphalt or concrete tiles.

Several products are now marketed which are based on preformed sheets and combine a water barrier and a surface that can withstand constructional traffic during completion of the road pavement, without requiring secondary protection. The drawback in using such materials is that they involve special details wherever problems of shaping arise, as inevitably occurs at the edges of the bridge deck or where changes in camber occur across the width of the formation.

Where a bridge deck carries a dual carriageway with a continuous gradient (due to superelevation) from one side of the bridge deck to the other, problems can arise from the migration of water through the central reservation. The heavy finishes in the central reserve may act as a reservoir in which the water collects, discharging slowly on the downhill carriageway so that this pavement surface does not dry out with the rest of the carriageway surface. This can present an icing hazard. Its prevention requires the introduction of a water barrier within the central reservation, together with filter drains in the finishes unless these are formed of materials that are completely impermeable.

P1 Vehicle parapet with plinth 700 mm high or more. For use on motorway under-bridges.

P1 Vehicle parapet with plinth less than 700 mm high. For use on motorway under-bridges.

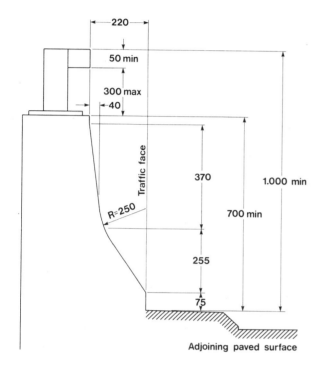

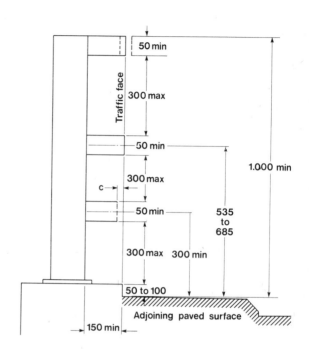

P2 Vehicle pedestrian parapet. For use on all-purpose road bridges, the design speed being stated.

P2 Vehicle pedestrian parapet. For use on road bridges where speed is restricted to 48 km/h.

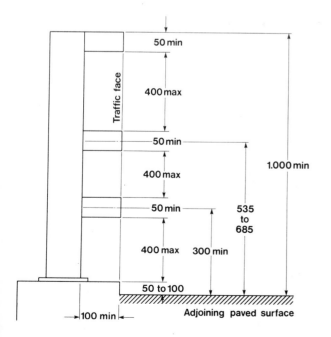

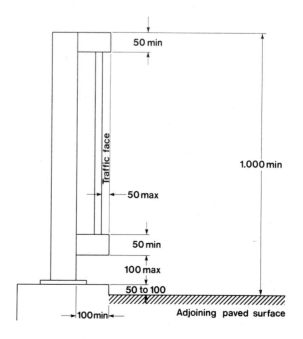

Above left: FT expansion joint panel.

Above right: FT joint installed.

Left: Specimen section of Rheinstahl joint.

Below left: Installation of Rheinstahl joint.

Below right: Transflex joint installation.

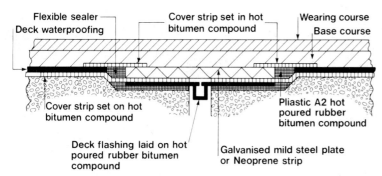

Flexible sealer
Deck waterproofing
Cover strip set in hot bitumen compound
Wearing course
Base course
Cover strip set on hot bitumen compound
Deck flashing laid on hot poured rubber bitumen compound
Galvanised mild steel plate or Neoprene strip
Pliastic A2 hot poured rubber bitumen compound

BURIED JOINT – MOVEMENT UP TO 25mm

Recent years have seen a rapid growth in the number of proprietary expansion joints available on the market.

Some of these offer a waterproof joint while in other cases drainage is needed below the joint. This is a particularly important consideration in the event of a joint being introduced within the total length of the structure at points where it would be difficult to provide positive drainage immediately below the joint.

There are wide differences in the provision that must be made for installation and fixing, which may be very significant in cases where details at the end of the bridge deck are already congested.

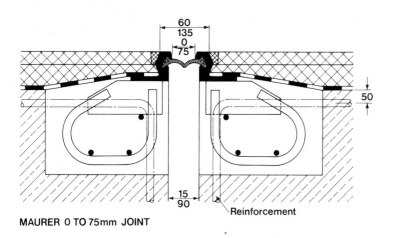

Reinforcement

MAURER 0 TO 75mm JOINT

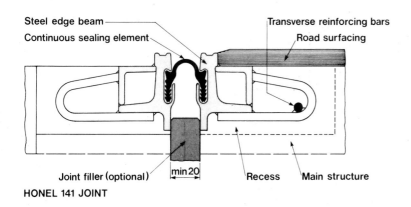

Steel edge beam
Continuous sealing element
Transverse reinforcing bars
Road surfacing
Joint filler (optional)
min 20
Recess
Main structure

HONEL 141 JOINT

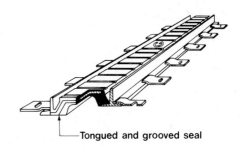

Tongued and grooved seal

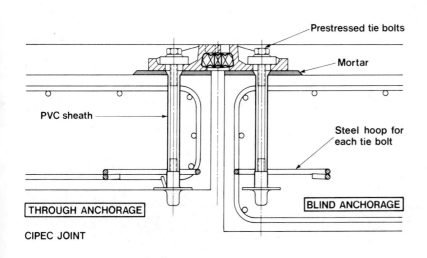

Prestressed tie bolts
Mortar
PVC sheath
Steel hoop for each tie bolt

THROUGH ANCHORAGE **BLIND ANCHORAGE**

CIPEC JOINT

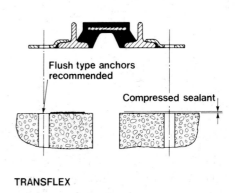

Flush type anchors recommended
Compressed sealant

TRANSFLEX

Spherical PTFE bearing allowing movement in any direction and rotation about any axis by low-friction contact surfaces.

Cylindrical PTFE bearing allowing movement in any direction and rotation about cylinder axis by low-friction contact surfaces.

Combined PTFE and reinforced rubber bearing, allowing rotation by deformation of rubber, and translation by sliding.

Laminated rubber bearing allowing movements and rotations by deformation of rubber.

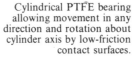

Rocker bearing allowing translational movement in one direction only, and rotation about axis of rollers.

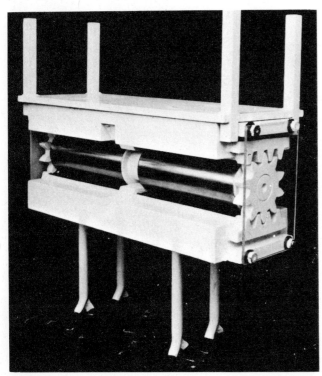

"Pot" bearing allowing movement in any direction within the plane of the bearing by low friction sliding surfaces, and rotation about any axis by deformation of an enclosed rubber membrane.

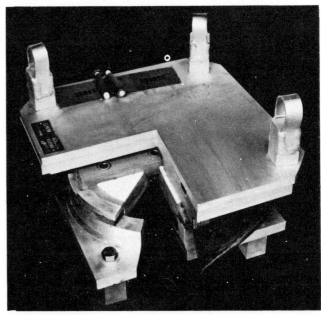

Movements to be catered for at bearings and expansion joints arise from the following causes.

1) Thermal expansion and contraction (see Data Sheet 31).
2) Shrinkage of the concrete (see Data Sheet 58).
3) Creep in the concrete (see Data Sheet 58).
4) Elastic shortening under prestress.
5) Displacements of the structure under load.

Because expansion joints are installed at a late stage in construction some of these movements will already have taken place, and less total movement has to be catered for than in bearings at the same location.

Elastic shortening under prestress is normally assessed on the mean stress induced in the deck section by the prestress.

In most bridges displacements of the structure under load produce very minor movements.

Bearings at fixed points, or those providing restraint in a given direction must be designed to resist the following lateral forces arising from the articulation of the deck.

1) Friction in sliding bearings.
2) Wind.
3) Horizontal loading from traffic:
        e.g. centrifugal force, braking and traction.

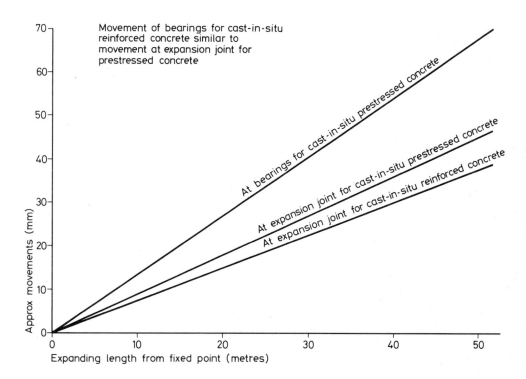

Movement of bearings for cast-in-situ reinforced concrete similar to movement at expansion joint for prestressed concrete

At bearings for cast-in-situ prestressed concrete

At expansion joint for cast-in-situ prestressed concrete

At expansion joint for cast-in-situ reinforced concrete

Approx movements (mm)

Expanding length from fixed point (metres)

Data used for the graph:

Coefficient of expansion	12×10^{-6} per 1°C
Temperature range	38 to -12°C
Coefficient of shrinkage	300×10^{-6}
Creep coefficient (post-tensioning)	36×10^{-6}
Elastic modulus	$32 \cdot 5 \, \text{kN/m}^2$
Average prestress	$7 \, \text{N/mm}^2$

CHAPTER 4

Loading

Normal loads

The basic (Type HA) highway loading which is applied to public highways in the UK is given a simplified form comprising a uniformly distributed load combined with a line load across the width of each traffic lane, thereby allowing easy calculation of the design bending moments for the main span of a bridge deck.

This loading is considered to be adequate to represent the effects of closely-spaced vehicles of 24 tonnes laden weight on loaded lengths up to 30 metres. Where the loaded length exceeds this figure the equivalent vehicles of 24 tonnes laden weight would have to be more widely spaced and interspersed with lighter vehicles of 10 tonnes and 5 tonnes laden weight to give design forces matching the HA loading specified.

Heavy lorries with weights significantly greater than 24 tonnes have now become commonplace, but the regulations governing the design and operation of commercial vehicles are so designed that equivalent effects are not exceeded because these greater weights are spread over large axle spacings and gross areas. In addition to the overall restriction on vehicle weights, limitations are placed on the maximum single wheel and axle loads. The design loading incorporates a 25% allowance for impact on these local loadings which is regarded as adequate in the light of suspension systems current in the UK.

Details of the requirements of BS 153 and BS 5400 regarding HA loading are presented on Data Sheets 23 and 24 respectively.

Exceptional loads

For major roads, and those giving access to certain types of industrial installation, provision has to be made for moving abnormal loads, giving rise to design loadings beyond those covered by type HA loading.

Abnormal (Type HB) loading has to be accommodated on all motorways and trunk roads. This provides for a vehicle of up to 180 tonnes gross laden weight, although the actual design load to be taken for a particular highway is specified in terms of the number of units of HB loading to be applied: 45 units gives 180 tonnes; $37\frac{1}{2}$ units, 150 tonnes; and 30 units, 120 tonnes.

Special routes are designated for vehicles in excess of these weights and in some cases bridges must be designed to deal with loads of up to 360 tonnes gross weight (Type HC loading). In fact it is found that because of the larger area and greater number of wheels, loads in the order of 300 tonnes gross weight can often be accepted on structures designed for 45 units of Type HB loading, loads of the order of 200 tonnes are possible where $37\frac{1}{2}$ units of HB loading have been allowed for, and 175 tonnes where 25 units of HB loading have been accommodated. These are very general guide lines and it is obviously necessary to check by calculation the actual structure where abnormal loads are to be carried.

Abnormal loading forms the subject of Data Sheet 25.

Local effects

The application of the normal HA line load is parallel to the supports for slab elements, regardless of what direction this may take with respect to the alignment of the traffic lane. This is because the knife-edge load does not specifically represent an axle but is a load which, when combined with the distributed loads specified for the span, gives rise to design forces appropriate to the strength requirement for an element of a deck structure.

Loading specifications have a history which goes back to well before the general use of methods of structural analysis capable of simulating plate action, and some loading specifications were drawn up to enable the strength requirements for slab elements within steel girder bridges to be evaluated by means of simple hand calculations. However, methods of analysis which evaluate the the design moments due to complex loading cases are now in widespread use, and it is therefore no longer considered necessary to enhance the distributed-load element of HA loading on short spans to give the appropriate design forces, because these can be evaluated directly from the concentrated wheel loads.

For the design of local structural elements within a bridge deck – such as the slabs spanning between longitudinal members – the requirement of a single wheel load of $11\frac{1}{4}$ tonnes is common to both HA and HB loading. There is, however, a difference in that the HA wheel includes an impact allowance of 25% whereas the HB wheel load is nett, so that such an impact factor as may arise due to local HB loading is, in effect, accepted as an overstress.

The distribution of the moments arising from concentrated wheel loads at the edges of a slab which is fixed along the line of support (as is commonly the case in a cellular or box deck) is subject to sharp peaks. Plotting the design bending moment along the length of a support will show the peak and illustrate how the area over which the load is applied becomes significant in evaluating design moments. It is therefore relevant to take the thickness of finishes and the wheel contact area into account.

Overall stability

Simple types of bridge deck rarely produce stability problems but where narrow pier arrangements are used, as is frequently the case with lengths of elevated roadway, it becomes important to check that a structure remains stable with heavy vehicles on the outer extremities of the deck. Another form of instability is for uplift to develop at the bearings under some loading conditions where there are marked differences in span on each side of a support.

Factors of safety normally applied to stability calculations are 1.1 for dead loading and 1.5 for imposed loading.

Wind

Recent design regulations governing the loading to be applied to highway structures give a great deal of attention to the evaluation of wind loading, despite the fact that this is rarely significant in small-span and medium-span bridgeworks. However, it is evident that any structure which is sensitive to stability problems will inevitably tend to be more sensitive to wind loading.

Data concerning wind loading on bridges are set out on Data Sheet 27.

Thermal effects

Thermal effects have likewise come in for closer scrutiny in recent years. It was formerly regarded as acceptable to allow these to be absorbed within the margins of safety provided when specifying allowable stresses, but the increasing complexity of structures combined with the closer tolerances worked to in design, arising from more-exact methods of analysis, have made it more important to evaluate the effects of such marginal loadings. The wider use of cast-in-situ forms of construction such as cellular decks also means that continuous spans are more commonplace, and these are subjected to greater stresses from thermal effects than simply-supported spans.

Thermal effects on bridgeworks are considered on Data Sheets 28 to 32 inclusive.

Centrifugal force

On elevated roadway structures and bridges carrying highways that have sharp horizontal curvature, centrifugal force must be taken into account. This involves making assumptions about the speed and weight of vehicles, together with the intervals between them where the loaded length allows several vehicles in line. A judgement may be made on the intervals between vehicles, based on the information about stopping distances given

in the Highway Code. BE1/77 specifies design forces to cover these conditions in anticipation of the requirements of BS 5400.

Settlement

The effects of differential settlement often need investigation unless the foundations are of a type which would not permit settlement to occur. The time scale over which settlement is likely to take place becomes an important factor in assessing the stresses which may arise in a structure, because the creep due to shrinkage has the effect of relaxing such stresses.

Loss of support

BS 5400 is likely to make recommendations regarding the investigation of the effects of a loss of support due to the damage of a pier on some highway structures. The risk of such a loss at an individual bearing due to deficiencies in the seating also merits consideration, as do the consequences that this may have on certain types of structure. This has been known to give rise to serious difficulties with torsionally stiff beams supported on a pair of bearings at each end, where the imperfect levelling of the bearings leads to the loading being taken wholly on a single bearing at one end, with the possibility that the resultant loading within one web may distress the beam.

Shrinkage and creep

The effects of shrinkage and creep can also be significant on structures which are built and loaded in stages – as in the case of serial construction. Because of the differing maturity of the concrete in various parts of the complete structure, when changes in the state of loading occur during construction, differences in the rates of creep and shrinkage arise that modify the pattern of statically-indeterminate moments, which can be significant to the design.

Reference should also be made to Data Sheet 18.

Vibration

Very slender decks may be susceptible to vibration at frequencies which could be distressing for people using the bridge. This is not usually a problem on bridge decks that are subject to highway loading, but is more likely to become a significant factor in the design of footbridges, where the light loading permits the adoption of a very slender structure with a resultant low natural frequency, to which pedestrians may be sensitive.

The evaluation of the natural frequencies of vibration within a statically-indeterminate structure is complex. It is usually regarded as sufficient to make a simplified calculation, based on the action of a simply-supported beam between the points of contraflexure.

Design regulations in the UK do not stipulate acceptable levels of vibration, but some guideline is given in an appendix to CP 117, and BE1/77 includes details of the requirements for footbridges.

Several studies have been undertaken aimed at

assessing human tolerance to vibration. Some of these results are summarized on Data Sheets 33 and 34. The subject is complex but rarely becomes an important consideration for bridge design.

Collision

Although there have been instances of major damage to bridge piers arising from the impact of vehicle collisions, this is not regarded as a major risk. However, BS 5400 does make recommendations about the resistance to impact which should be expected from a bridge pier. This is obviously more significant in a footbridge structure, where the other strength requirements for a pier are low.

Design regulations call for the provision of crash barriers in front of bridge piers in most instances, giving some measure of protection.

Other design data

To assist the designer, the bending moments, reactions and deflections at critical points on members subjected to various arrangements of loading and various types of fixity are tabulated on Data Sheets 35, 36 and 37, respectively. Requirements regarding railway clearances in the UK form the subject of Data Sheet 38.

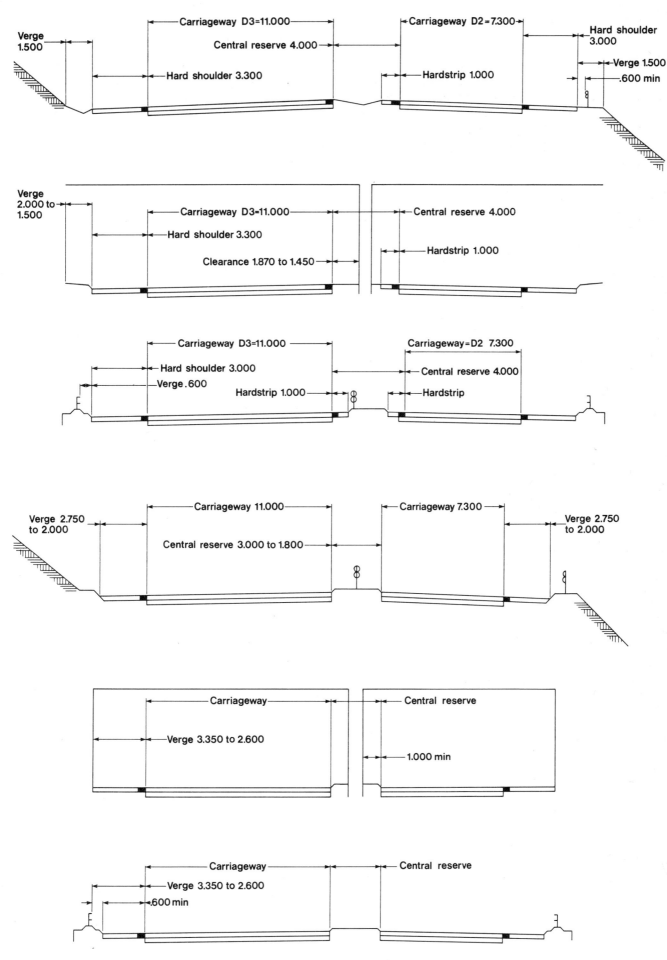

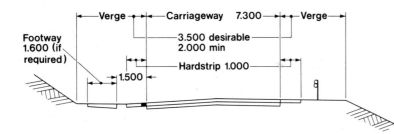

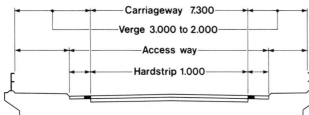

Carriageway widths are based on traffic lanes of 3.650 m nominal width: 2 lanes 7.300 m; 3 lanes 11.000 m; for all classes of road.

Verge widths vary with the class of road and whether or not pedestrians have to be catered for. In the absence of specific alternative provision for pedestrians, a minimum of 1.000 m verge width has to be provided.

Clearances to bridge substructures at overbridges may be increased where sight line requirements demand.

The headroom requirement for new construction is generally 5.100 m, although an increased headroom of 5.200 m is called for below light structures, such as footbridges, as an additional precaution against damage by vehicles. The minimum headroom to be maintained under an existing construction is 5.029 m.

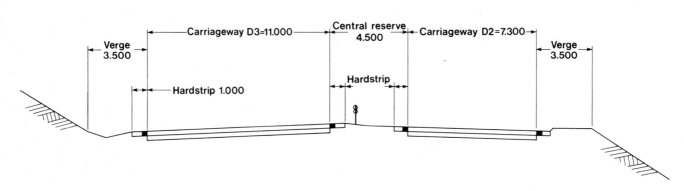

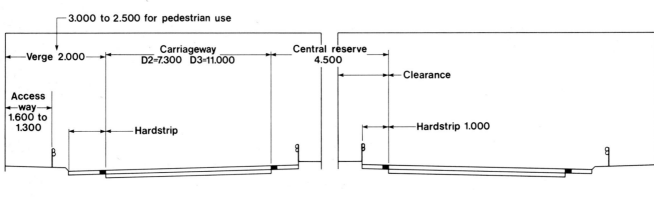

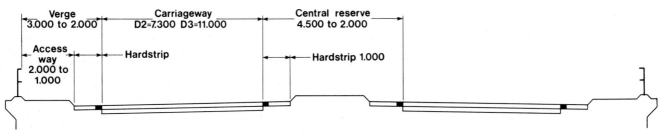

For HA loading: see Data Sheets 23 and 24.
For HB loading: see Data Sheet 25.   For HC loading: see Data Sheet 25.

Braking and traction (BS 153):

A horizontal load applied at road surface level over an area $3\,m \times 9\,m$:

HA: $100\,kN + 17\,kN$ per m of span in excess of 3 m with a maximum value of 253 kN.

HB: 450 kN (for 45 units of loading).

Horizontal loading (braking and traction) (BS 5400):

HA: 8 kN/m loaded length plus 200 kN but $\not> 700\,kN$.

HB: 25% total nominal HB load adopted.

Centrifugal force:

$\dfrac{30000}{r+150}$ kN applied over a length of 5 m in combination with a vertical load of 300 kN.

Footways and cycle tracks:

$5.0\,kN/m^2$ for local design.

$4.0\,kN/m^2$ in combination with carriageway loads, or $4 \times HA$ u.d.l./31.5 where span exceeds 23 m.

Accidental wheel loads:

This loading applies to local effects and shall not be taken into account in determining global effects on the deck. Associated carriageway loading shall be assumed to consist of full HA loading on one traffic lane and one third HA loading on remaining traffic lanes.

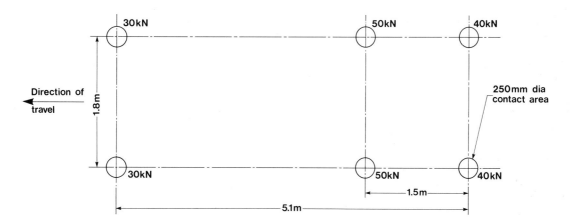

Pier impact (Technical Memorandum BE 1/77):

225 kN normal to carriageway with 75 kN parallel to carriageway at guardrail fixing level or 750 above carriageway where there is no fixing,

plus 150 kN normal to carriageway with 150 kN parallel to carriageway between 1.000 and 3.000 above carriageway.

Collision loads on supports of bridges over highways (BS 5400: Part 1):

150 kN normal to carriageway with 50 kN parallel to carriageway at guardrail fixing level or 750 above carriageway where there is no fixing,

plus 100 kN normal to carriageway with 100 kN parallel to carriageway between 1.000 and 3.000 above carriageway.

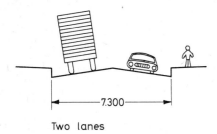

2 lanes HA + verge loading
HB + 1 lane $HA/3$ + verge loading
HC + unloaded lane + verge loading

Two lanes

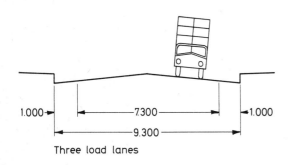

2 lanes HA + 1 lane $HA/3$ + verge loading
HB + 2 lanes $HA/3$ + verge loading
HC + unloaded lane + 1 lane $HA/3$ + verge loading

Three load lanes

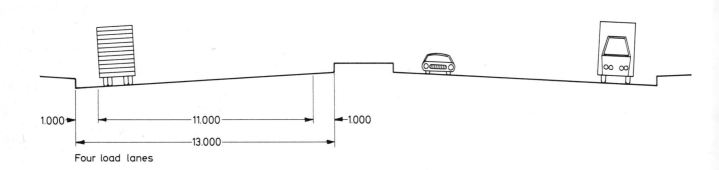

Four load lanes

2 lanes HA + 2 lanes $HA/3$ + 2 lanes HA + 2 lanes $HA/3$ + verge loading
HB + 3 lanes $HA/3$ + 2 lanes HA + 2 lanes $HA/3$ + verge loading
HC + unloaded lane + 2 lanes $HA/3$ + 2 lanes HA + 2 lanes $HA/3$ + verge loading

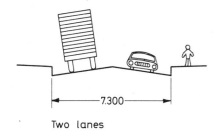

Two lanes

2 lanes HA + verge loading
HB + 1 lane HA + verge loading

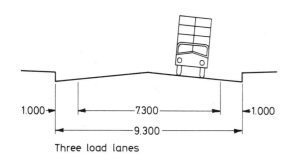

Three load lanes

2 lanes HA + 1 lane $HA/3$ + verge loading
HB + 1 lane HA + 1 lane $HA/3$ + verge loading

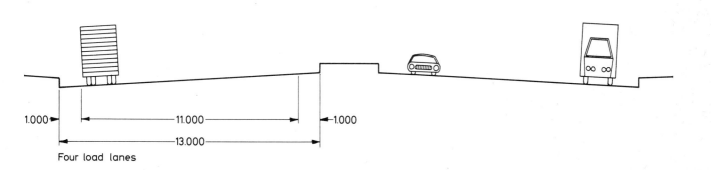

Four load lanes

2 lanes HA + 2 lanes $HA/3$ + 1 lane HA + 3 lanes $HA/3$ + verge loading
HB + 1 lane HA + 2 lanes $HA/3$ + 1 lane HA + 3 lanes $HA/3$ + verge loading

Less than 4.600: $W \div 3$ load lanes.
4.600 to 7.600: 2 lanes
7.600 to 11.400: 3 lanes
11.400 to 15.200: 4 lanes
19.000 to 22.800: 6 lanes

HA loading to BS153/Tech memo BE1/77

Data sheet No 23

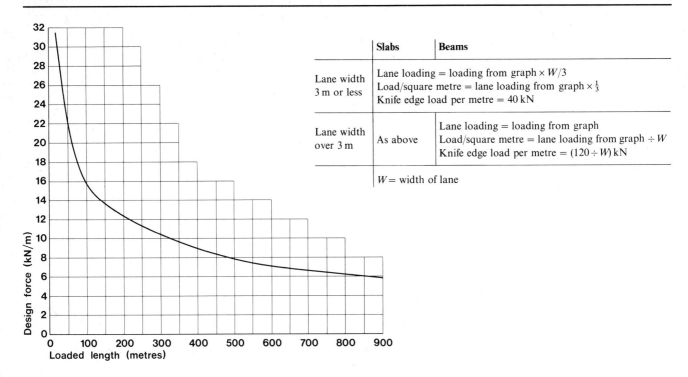

	Slabs	Beams
Lane width 3 m or less	Lane loading = loading from graph × $W/3$ Load/square metre = lane loading from graph × $\frac{1}{3}$ Knife edge load per metre = 40 kN	
Lane width over 3 m	As above	Lane loading = loading from graph Load/square metre = lane loading from graph ÷ W Knife edge load per metre = $(120 \div W)$ kN
W = width of lane		

Uniformly-distributed lane loading applied in conjunction with knife-edge load of 120 kN

Loaded length m	Load kN/m	Loaded length m	Load kN/m	Loaded length m	Load kN/m	Loaded length m	Load kN/m
Up to 23.0	31.5	51.0	22.6	79.0	17.8	200	12.7
24.0	31.2	52.0	22.3	80.0	17.7	220	12.2
25.0	30.8	53.0	22.0	82.0	17.4	240	11.7
26.0	30.4	54.0	21.8	84.0	17.2	260	11.3
27.0	30.0	55.0	21.5	86.0	17.0	280	10.9
28.0	29.7	56.0	21.3	88.0	16.8	300	10.6
29.0	29.3	57.0	21.1	90.0	16.6	325	10.1
30.0	28.9	58.0	20.9	92.0	16.4	350	9.8
31.0	28.5	59.0	20.7	94.0	16.2	375	9.5
32.0	28.2	60.0	20.6	96.0	16.1	400	9.0
33.0	27.8	61.0	20.4	98.0	16.0	425	8.6
34.0	27.4	62.0	20.2	100	15.9	450	8.4
35.0	27.0	63.0	20.0	105	15.6	475	8.2
36.0	26.8	64.0	19.8	110	15.3	500	7.9
37.0	26.6	65.0	19.7	115	15.1	525	7.7
38.0	26.2	66.0	19.6	120	14.9	550	7.4
39.0	26.0	67.0	19.4	125	14.7	575	7.3
40.0	25.7	68.0	19.3	130	14.5	600	7.1
41.0	25.4	69.0	19.1	135	14.3	625	7.0
42.0	25.2	70.0	19.0	140	14.1	650	6.8
43.0	24.9	71.0	18.9	145	14.0	675	6.7
44.0	24.6	72.0	18.7	150	13.8	700	6.6
45.0	24.3	73.0	18.6	155	13.7	725	6.5
46.0	24.0	74.0	18.5	160	13.6	750	6.4
47.0	23.8	75.0	18.3	165	13.5	775	6.3
48.0	23.5	76.0	18.2	170	13.4	800	6.1
49.0	23.2	77.0	18.1	180	13.1	850	5.9
50.0	22.9	78.0	17.9	190	12.9	900	5.8

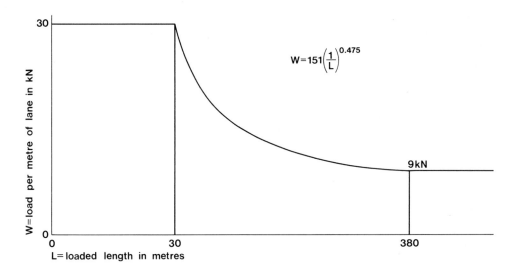

$$W = 151\left(\frac{1}{L}\right)^{0.475}$$

The loaded length is the length of the base of the positive or negative portion, as the case may be, of the influence-line diagram for the member under consideration.

Where the positive or negative portion of the base of the influence line consists of separated parts, as for continuous construction, the maximum effect shall be determined by considering any part or combination of separated parts, using the loading appropriate to the length or the total combined length of the loaded portions.

Uniformly-distributed lane loading applied in conjunction with knife-edge load of 120 kN

Loaded length m	Load kN/m	Loaded length m	Load kN/m	Loaded length m	Load kN/m
Up to 30	30.0	73	19.7	160	13.6
32	29.1	76	19.3	170	13.2
34	28.3	79	18.9	180	12.8
36	27.5	82	18.6	190	12.5
38	26.8	85	18.3	200	12.2
40	26.2	90	17.8	210	11.9
42	25.6	95	17.4	220	11.7
44	25.0	100	16.9	230	11.4
46	24.5	105	16.6	240	11.2
49	23.8	110	16.2	255	10.9
52	23.1	115	15.9	270	10.6
55	22.5	120	15.5	285	10.3
58	21.9	125	15.2	300	10.1
61	21.4	130	15.0	320	9.8
64	20.9	135	14.7	340	9.5
67	20.5	140	14.4	360	9.2
70	20.1	145	14.2	380 and above	9.0
		150	14.0		

Abnormal loads
Data sheet No 25

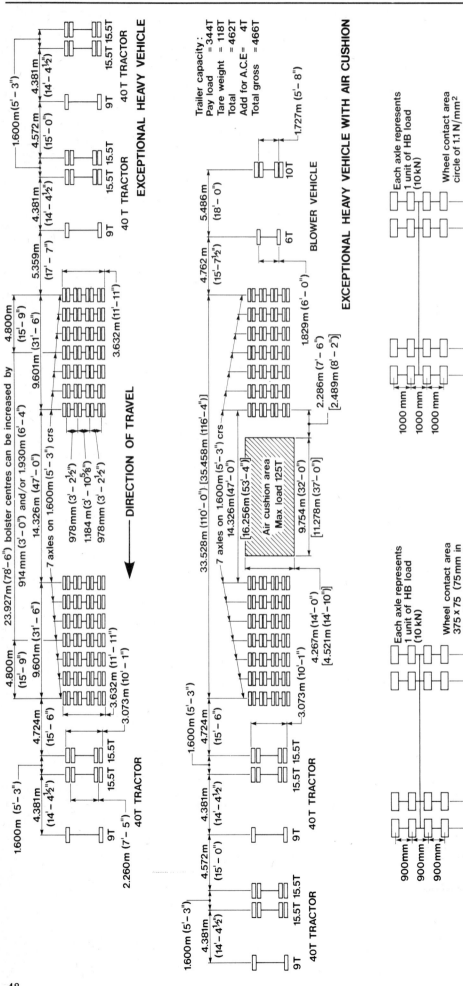

Some bridges are checked for special heavy vehicles which can range up to 466 tonnes gross weight. Where this is needed the gross weight and trailer dimensions are stated by the authority requiring this special facility on a given route.

The abnormal loading stipulated in BS 153 is applied to most public highway bridges in the UK: 45 units on motorway under-bridges, 37½ units on bridges for principal roads and 30 units on bridges for other roads.

The vehicles illustrated above are by way of example only.

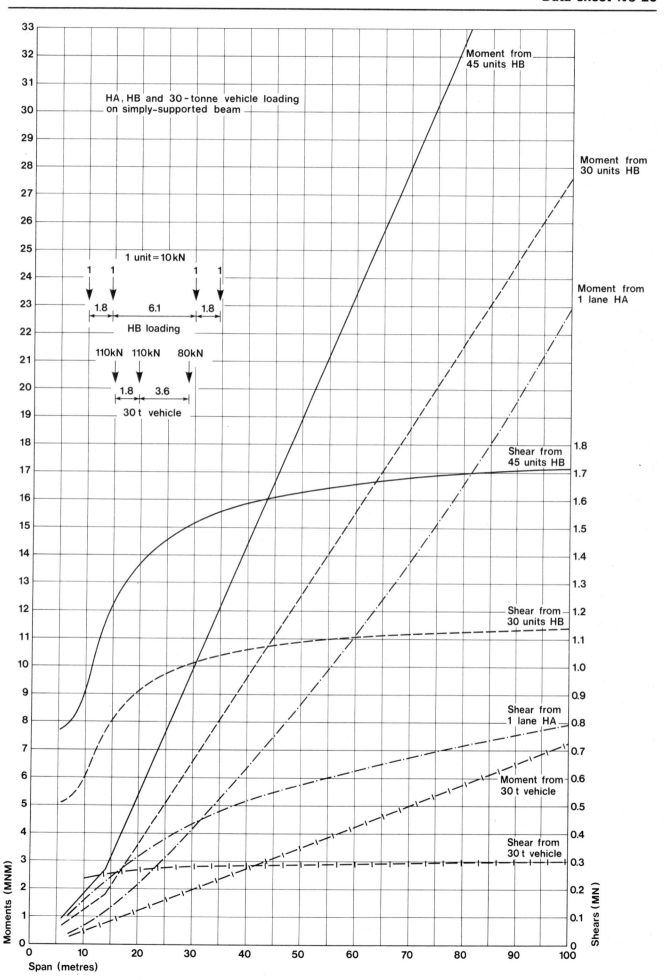

HA, HB and 30-tonne vehicle loading on simply-supported beam

1 unit = 10 kN

HB loading

30 t vehicle

Moment from 45 units HB

Moment from 30 units HB

Moment from 1 lane HA

Shear from 45 units HB

Shear from 30 units HB

Shear from 1 lane HA

Moment from 30 t vehicle

Shear from 30 t vehicle

Moments (MNM)

Shears (MN)

Span (metres)

Wind loading
Data sheet No 27

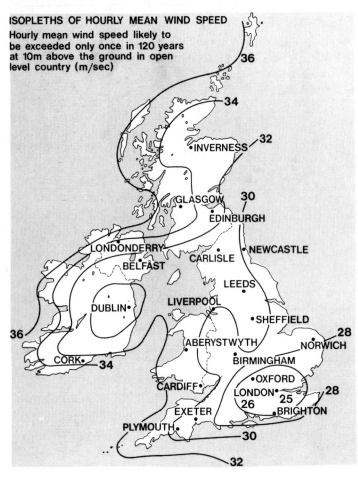

ISOPLETHS OF HOURLY MEAN WIND SPEED
Hourly mean wind speed likely to be exceeded only once in 120 years at 10m above the ground in open level country (m/sec)

Wind gust speed,

$$V_c = K V S_1 S_2 \text{ m/s},$$

where K is a coefficient relating to combinations of load. K is normally 1.0, with the exception of:

≮ 0.85 applied to loading combinations during erection unless temporary condition of up to two days duration only; and

0.3 applied where loading combination includes maximum temperature stresses.

V: Hourly mean wind speed in m/s.
S_1: Funnelling factor (1 to 1.1).
S_2: Gust factor. (Values given in accompanying table.)

Transverse wind force,

$$P_t = q C_d A_1,$$

where
q: Dynamic pressure head $= 0.613 V_c^2 \text{ N/m}^2$
C_d: Drag coefficient.
A_1: Nett exposed area.

Values of gust factor S_2 and hourly speed factor K

Height above ground level (m)	Horizontal length in metres									Hourly speed factor K
	20 or less	40	60	100	200	400	600	1000	2000	
5	1.47	1.43	1.40	1.35	1.27	1.19	1.15	1.10	1.06	0.89
10	1.56	1.53	1.49	1.45	1.37	1.29	1.25	1.21	1.16	1.00
15	1.62	1.59	1.56	1.51	1.43	1.35	1.31	1.27	1.23	1.07
20	1.66	1.63	1.60	1.56	1.48	1.40	1.36	1.32	1.28	1.13
30	1.73	1.70	1.67	1.63	1.56	1.48	1.44	1.40	1.35	1.21
40	1.77	1.74	1.72	1.68	1.61	1.54	1.50	1.46	1.41	1.27
50	1.81	1.78	1.76	1.72	1.66	1.59	1.55	1.51	1.46	1.32
60	1.84	1.81	1.79	1.76	1.69	1.62	1.58	1.54	1.50	1.36
80	1.88	1.86	1.84	1.81	1.74	1.68	1.64	1.60	1.56	1.42
100	1.92	1.90	1.88	1.84	1.78	1.72	1.68	1.65	1.60	1.48
150	1.99	1.97	1.95	1.92	1.86	1.80	1.77	1.74	1.70	1.59
200	2.04	2.02	2.01	1.98	1.92	1.87	1.84	1.80	1.77	1.66

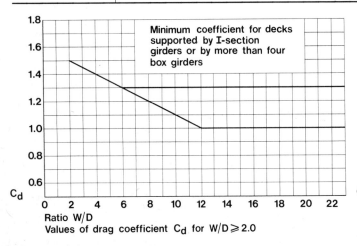

Minimum coefficient for decks supported by I-section girders or by more than four box girders

C_d

Ratio W/D
Values of drag coefficient C_d for W/D ≥ 2.0

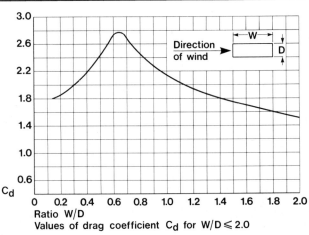

Direction of wind

C_d

Ratio W/D
Values of drag coefficient C_d for W/D ≤ 2.0

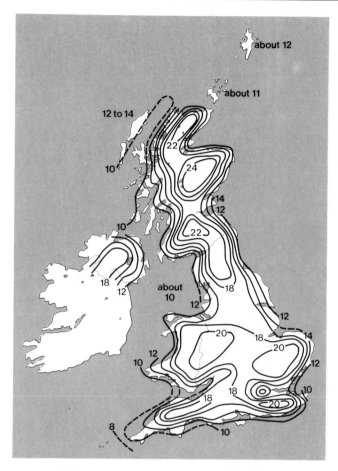

Values given are degrees Centigrade BELOW zero

Annual minimum shade air temperatures
at sea level in 120-year return period

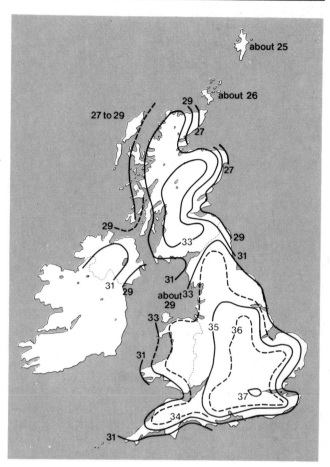

Values given are degrees Centigrade ABOVE zero

Annual maximum air shade temperatures
at sea level in 120-year return period

NOTE: For each 100 m above sea level, the minimum shade temperature reduces by 0.5°C and the maximum shade temperature reduces by 1°C.

Minimum shade air temperature	Minimum effective bridge temperature		
	Groups 1 and 2	Group 3	Group 4
−23	−27	−18	−13
−22	−26	−18	−13
−21	−25	−17	−12
−20	−23	−17	−12
−19	−22	−16	−11
−18	−21	−15	−11
−17	−20	−15	−10
−16	−19	−14	−10
−15	−18	−13	−9
−14	−17	−12	−9
−13	−16	−11	−8
−12	−15	−10	−7
−11	−14	−10	−6
−10	−12	−9	−6
−9	−11	−8	−5
−8	−10	−7	−4
−7	−9	−6	−3
−6	−8	−5	−3
−5	−7	−4	−2

Maximum shade air temperature	maximum effective bridge temperature		
	Groups 1 and 2 Steel on steel	Group 3 R. C. Slab on steel	Group 4 Concrete
24	40	31	27
25	41	32	28
26	41	33	29
27	42	34	29
28	42	34	30
29	43	35	31
30	44	36	32
31	44	36	32
32	44	37	33
33	45	37	33
34	45	38	34
35	46	39	35
36	46	39	36
37	46	40	36
38	47	40	37

In addition to the overall movement of bridge decks in response to mean bridge temperature, stresses are set up with the cross section due to changes in the temperature gradient as air temperature and solar radiation vary through the day.

This can be calculated from the data given on Data Sheet 31 by the methods described in TRRL report LR561 (see references). In the absence of such calculations the following conservative temperature gradients may be adopted:

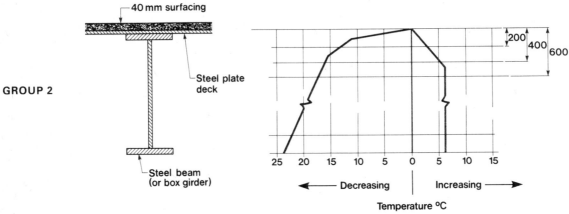

GROUP 2

Steel beam or box with steel plate deck

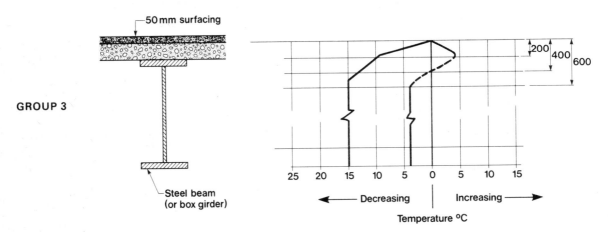

GROUP 3

Steel beams with concrete deck slab

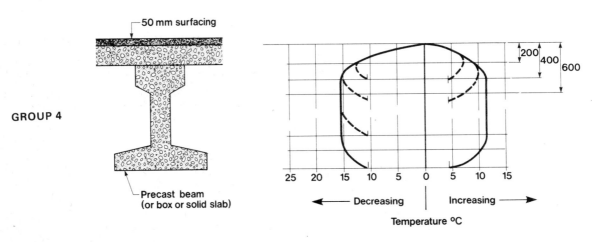

GROUP 4

Concrete deck of cast in-situ or precast construction

Simplified temperature gradients through bridge decks are shown on this Data Sheet but they relate to the use of a thickness of surfacing material rather less than that usually adopted in practice. As the thickness of finishes is very significant in arriving at the temperature distribution it is worth while calculating gradients from solar radiation and shade temperature data given on Data Sheet 31.

Representative results for a 1 m thick voided slab with 100 mm surfacing are shown below.

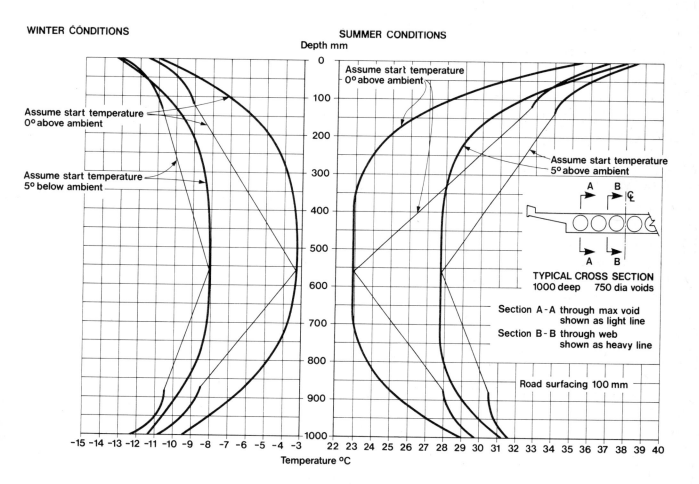

Coefficient of thermal expansion $12 \times 10^{-6}/°C$ steel or concrete, except for limestone aggregates ($7 \times 10^{-6}/°C$).

Maximum shade
temperature and
high solar radiation

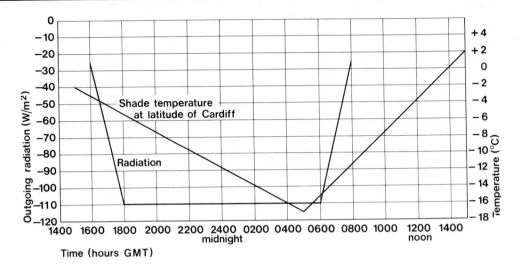

Minimum shade
temperature and
high out-going radiation

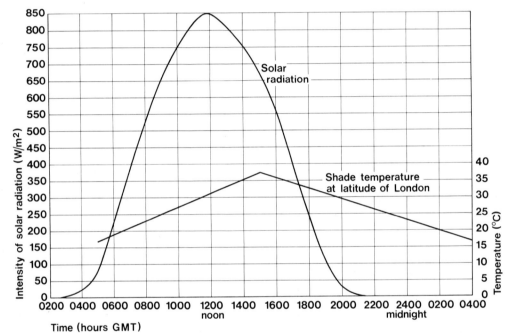

Simplified temperature
criteria for use in the
absence of temperature
gradient calculations

Group type of structure	Maximum and minimum values of mean bridge temperature in °C						Maximum difference in temperature in °C for any purpose		Maximum reverse difference in temperature in °C (i.e. when soffit is warmer than top of deck), for any purpose	
	Return period 120 years			Return period 20 years						
	Maximum		Minimum	Maximum		Minimum				
	Surfaced	Unsurfaced	Surfaced and unsurfaced	Surfaced	Unsurfaced	Surfaced and unsurfaced	Surfaced	Unsurfaced	Surfaced	Unsurfaced
Steel decks on steel truss or plate girders	50	52	−22	43	45	−17	20	25	8	9
Concrete decks on steel truss or plate girders	46	46	−19	41	41	−14	15	17	8	9
Concrete slab and concrete deck on concrete beam or box girders	38	38	−12	33	33	−7	18	21	12	14

Notes: 120-year figures are based on 10 ± 30°C shade air temperature.
20-year figures are based on 10 ± 25°C shade air temperature.
Surfaced means a surfacing not less than 28 mm in thickness on steel decks and not less than 50 mm in thickness on concrete decks.
The temperatures quoted are for altitudes up to 250 m above sea level. Lower temperatures may occur at higher altitudes.

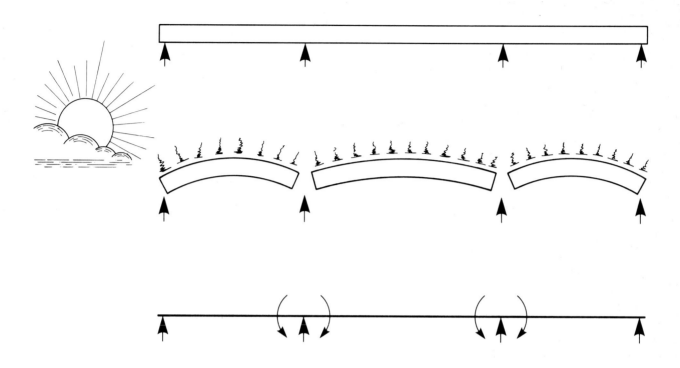

Thermal stresses

In a statically-indeterminate structure the assessment of forces arising from thermal stresses can best be approached by allowing the individual components of the structure to adopt the deformed shape suggested by the stress gradient through the thickness of the member, and then applying a force system at the joint positions to restore compatible slopes at all joints.

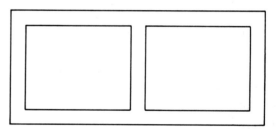

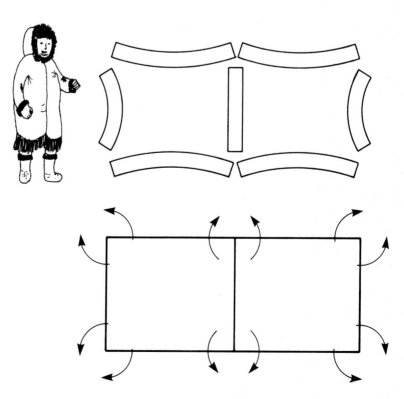

CP117:Part 2:1967 sets out the following criterion for bridge deck vibration:

The acceleration A and amplitude Δ of vibrations under the passage of a single 20-ton vehicle should desirably be such that $A\Delta$ does not exceed $5\,\text{in}^2/\text{s}^2$. The maximum increment δ of deflection, in inches, due to a static 20-ton vehicle assumed as a single point load on the centre line of the bridge, should be calculated using the fully composite rigidity EI of the full width of the bridge. The fundamental natural frequency of the bridge should then be determined from:

$$N_f = \frac{2}{L^2}\sqrt{\frac{EIg}{w_d}} \text{ c/s,}$$

where w_d = dead weight, including finishes, in tons per foot of bridge

$g = 32.2\,\text{ft/s}^2$

EI = flexural rigidy in ft/tons units of the full width of the bridge

and L = span (ft).

Where N_f is greater than 4 c/s, the maximum amplitude of vibration Δ may be taken to be 0.4δ. For lower values of N_f, the maximum amplitude should be taken to be 0.75δ.

The maximum acceleration may then be determined as

$$A = 40\Delta N_f^2 \text{ in/s}^2.$$

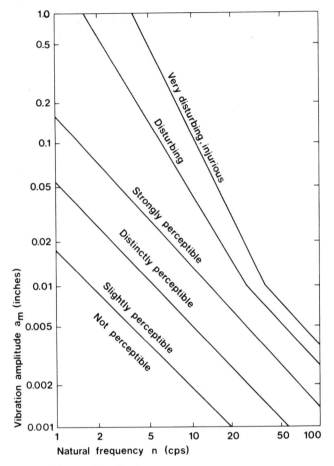

Lenzen's criteria

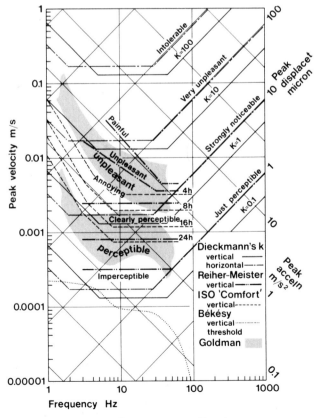

Assessment of response to vibration

The following method of assessing the vibration characteristics of prismatic, symmetrical footbridge decks, simply supported or continuous over up to three spans, and supported on bearings which may be idealised as knife-edge supports, was proposed by Technical Memorandum BE1/77, and is included in BS 5400: Part 2: Appendix C:

Max vertical acceleration $a = 4\pi^2 f^2 y_s K\psi$ m/sec²
where f = fundamental natural frequency in Hz
$\quad y_s$ = static deflection in metres under point load of 0.7kN
$\quad K$ = configuration factor
$\quad \psi$ = dynamic response factor.

Bridge configuration	Ratio L_1/L	K
△————————△	–	1.0
△————△————△	–	0.7
△ L_1 △ L △ L_1 △	1.0	0.6
	0.8	0.8
	0.6 or less	0.9

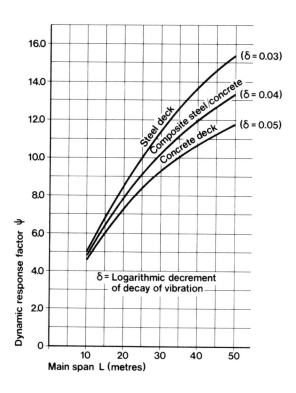

Requirements are that the natural frequency exceeds 5 Hz, or that max vertical acceleration is not greater than $\pm\frac{1}{2}\sqrt{f}$ m/sec². Where f exceeds 4 Hz, the acceleration that has been calculated may be reduced by an amount varying linearly from 0% at 4 Hz to 70% at 5 Hz.

Bending moments
Data sheet No 35

W = total load

Position	Point load at free end (→)	Central point load (≡)	Point load at a, b	Uniform load	Triangular load (increasing)	Triangular load (decreasing)
Support	$-WL$	$-\tfrac{1}{2}WL$	$-Wa$	$-\tfrac{1}{2}WL$	$-\tfrac{1}{3}WL$	$-\tfrac{1}{2}WL$
Left support	Nil	$-\tfrac{3}{16}WL$	$-\dfrac{W}{L}\left(\dfrac{a^2b}{2}+ab^2\right)$	$-\tfrac{1}{8}WL$	$-\dfrac{WL}{7.5}$	$-\tfrac{5}{32}WL$
Midspan	Nil	$\tfrac{5}{32}WL$	—	—	—	—
Max.	Nil	—	—	$\tfrac{9}{128}WL$	$\dfrac{WL}{16.7}$	$\dfrac{WL}{10.5}$
Midspan	Nil	$\tfrac{1}{4}WL$	(when $a>b$) $\dfrac{Wb}{2}$	$\tfrac{1}{8}WL$	—	$\tfrac{1}{6}WL$
Max	Nil	$\tfrac{1}{4}WL$	$\dfrac{Wab}{L}$	$\tfrac{1}{8}WL$	$\dfrac{WL}{7.81}$	$\tfrac{1}{6}WL$
Left support	Nil	$-\tfrac{1}{8}WL$	$-\dfrac{Wab^2}{L^2}$	$-\tfrac{1}{12}WL$	$-\tfrac{1}{10}WL$	$-\tfrac{5}{48}WL$
Right support	Nil	$-\tfrac{1}{8}WL$	$-\dfrac{Wa^2b}{L^2}$	$-\tfrac{1}{12}WL$	$-\tfrac{1}{15}WL$	$-\tfrac{5}{48}WL$
Midspan	Nil	$+\tfrac{1}{8}WL$	—	$+\tfrac{1}{24}WL$	—	$+\tfrac{1}{16}WL$
Max.	Nil	$+\tfrac{1}{8}WL$	—	$+\tfrac{1}{24}WL$	$+\dfrac{WL}{20.2}$	$+\tfrac{1}{16}WL$

W = total load

Support		⟶ (point load)	≡ loads	load at a, b	uniform load	triangular (increasing right)	triangular (apex left)
		W	W	W	W	W	W
Left support		Nil	$\frac{11}{16}W$	$\left(1-\frac{a}{L}\right)\left(1+\frac{a}{L}-\frac{a^2}{2L^2}\right)W$	$\frac{5}{8}W$	$\frac{4}{5}W$	$\frac{21}{32}W$
Right support		W	$\frac{5}{16}W$	$\frac{a^2}{2L^2}\left(3-\frac{a}{L}\right)W$	$\frac{3}{8}W$	$\frac{1}{5}W$	$\frac{11}{32}W$
Left support		Nil	$\frac{1}{2}W$	$\frac{Wb}{L}$	$\frac{1}{2}W$	$\frac{2}{3}W$	$\frac{1}{2}W$
Right support		W	$\frac{1}{2}W$	$\frac{Wa}{L}$	$\frac{1}{2}W$	$\frac{1}{3}W$	$\frac{1}{2}W$
Left support		Nil	$\frac{1}{2}W$	$\left(1-\frac{a}{L}\right)^2\left(1-\frac{2a}{L}\right)$	$\frac{1}{2}W$	$\frac{7}{10}W$	$\frac{1}{2}W$
Right support		W	$\frac{1}{2}W$	$\frac{a^2}{L^2}\left(3-\frac{2a}{L}\right)$	$\frac{1}{2}W$	$\frac{3}{10}W$	$\frac{1}{2}W$

W = total load

Support condition	Triangle (apex toward support)	Right triangle	Uniform (rectangle)	Point load a, b	Point load (central)	Point load (free end)
Free end	$\dfrac{11}{96}$	$\dfrac{1}{15}$	$\dfrac{1}{8}$	—	$\dfrac{5}{48}$	$\dfrac{1}{3}$
Max.	$\dfrac{1}{139.5}$	$\dfrac{1}{210}$	$\dfrac{1}{185}$	—	$\dfrac{1}{107.3}$	Nil
Max.	$\dfrac{1}{60}$	$\dfrac{1}{76.75}$	$\dfrac{5}{384}$	$\dfrac{a}{9L}\sqrt{\dfrac{1}{3}\left[1-\left(\dfrac{a}{L}\right)^{2}\right]^{3}}$ when $\alpha \not> \tfrac{1}{2}$	$\dfrac{1}{48}$	Nil
Midspan	$\dfrac{7}{1920}$	$\dfrac{1}{384}$	$\dfrac{1}{384}$	—	$\dfrac{1}{192}$	Nil
Max.	$\dfrac{7}{1920}$	$\dfrac{1}{382}$	$\dfrac{1}{384}$	—	$\dfrac{1}{192}$	Nil

Deflection = tabulated coefficient $\times \dfrac{WL^{3}}{EI}$

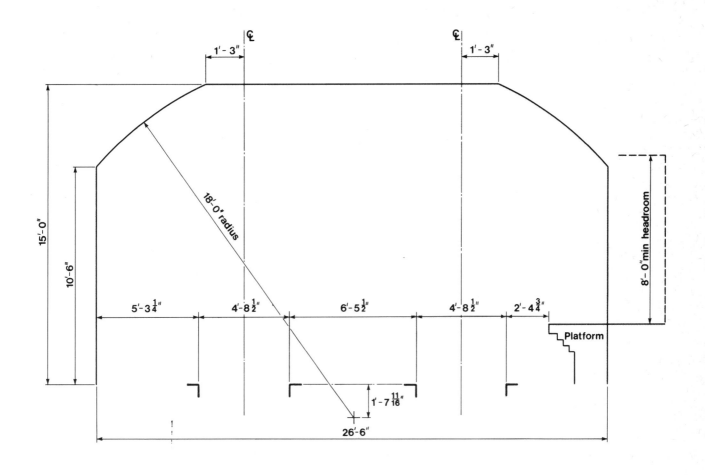

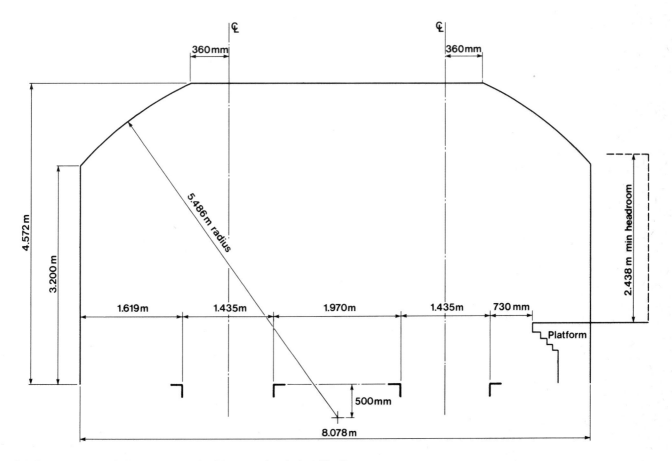

Clearances stated refer to straight track without overhead electrification

BRITISH STANDARDS INSTITUTION. BS 153:1972. *Steel girder bridges. Part 1. Materials and workmanship* and *Part 2. Weighing, shipping and erection.* pp. 16. *Part 3A. Loads.* pp. 40. *Part 3B. Stresses* and *Part 4. Design and construction.* pp. 64. London.

BRITISH STANDARDS INSTITUTION. BS 5400. *Steel concrete and composite bridges.* London. To be published.

AMERICAN ASSOCIATION OF STATE HIGHWAY OFFICIALS. Eleventh edition. *Standard specification for highway bridges.* Washington, D.C. The Association, 1973. pp. 469.

BRITISH STANDARDS INSTITUTION. CP3. *Code of basic data for the design of buildings. Chapter V: Part 2: 1972. Wind loads.* London. pp. 52.

LEONARD, D. R. *Human tolerance levels for bridge vibrations.* Crowthorne, Transport and Road Research Laboratory, 1966. Report LR 34. pp. 28.

EMERSON, M. *The calculation of the distribution of temperature in bridges.* Crowthorne, Transport and Road Research Laboratory, 1973. Report LR 561. pp. 35.

THOMAS, P. K. *A Comparative study of highway bridge loadings in different countries.* Transport and Road Research Laboratory, 1975. Supplementary Report 135 VC.

IRWIN, A. W. Human response to dynamic motion of structures. *Journal of the Institution of Structural Engineers,* Vol. 56a, No. 9. London, September 1978. pp 237–243.

HAMBLY, E. C. Temperature distribution and stresses in concrete bridges. *Journal of the Institution of Structural Engineers.* Vol. 56a, No. 5. London, May 1978. pp 143–148.

CHAPTER 5

Reinforced concrete

Even where the main structural elements of a bridge deck are prestressed, there are parts of the structure which behave as reinforced concrete.

Design regulations relating to bridgeworks prior to the appearance of BS 5400 called for design to be undertaken on an elastic basis and in the case of reinforced concrete, provided that limitations on allowable stresses were observed, there was no requirement to check ultimate resistance.

BS 5400 introduces the limit-state philosophy which means that strength calculations are approached on a load-factor basis. One step in this direction had, in effect, already been taken in earlier design requirements when limitations on deflections and crack control were introduced as additional factors to consider, over and above the limiting of the stresses in the constituent materials.

Although calculations aimed at limiting cracking often have the effect of reducing the allowable stresses in the reinforcement, there are still benefits in employing deformed bars, not only because they give better crack control than plain bars but also because there are potential economies due to the shorter lap lengths required. Differences in cost between plain and deformed bars are, in any event, usually marginal so that these benefits are well worth a minor premium in cost.

In seeking economy when proportioning reinforced concrete members it is well to remember that the most slender member does not necessarily result in the lowest cost. The relative prices of steel and concrete need to be taken into account in evaluating economic member sizes although, of course, in many instances the additional weight from the thicker sections may have an adverse effect on other elements forming the structure. An obvious example is a reinforced concrete slab as a component of a more-complex deck structure. Considering the deck slab in isolation, an economic solution may well suggest a thickness significantly greater than the minimum possible value, but the added dead load to be taken by the main structural elements of the deck would be a penalty which would more than offset the savings in the cost of the slab.

A high proportion of deck slabs spanning up to 3.5m (or 12ft) tend to be 200mm (8in.) thick. They not only need to be designed for local wheel loads and other loads imposed directly on them, but also for effects arising from the differential displacement of the members supporting the slab. This is true whether a cross-section is cellular or

in the form of open spaced beams, because each is subject to the distortion of the cross-section under localized loads.

The design moment for local wheel loads can be evaluated by using influence surfaces, such as those given by Adolf Pucher in "Influence surfaces for elastic plates." Alternatively Westergaard's analysis of concentrated loads on slabs can be used, but the method only covers simply-supported slabs so that the results must be adjusted to allow for continuity.

Pucher's charts show influence surfaces for specific sections within a slab, e.g. at midspan or at a support, each being represented by an individual chart. In many cases it is possible to judge by examination the average value of the influence surface contours over the loaded area, but where these contours are closely spaced it may become necessary to draw cross-sections of the influence surface, in the manner described in the handbook.

Any slab which forms part of the cross-section of longitudinal structural members, as in a beam-and-slab or box deck, will be subject to a combination of stresses arising from the longitudinal bending of the deck, together with the local effects of concentrated loads on the slab spanning as an individual member. These stresses are additive, but where the overall bending of the deck produces significant stresses this bending, in effect, prestresses the slab. It can therefore be considered as a prestressed member when assessing coexistent local bending stresses, provided that the whole slab section remains in compression under the combined loading.

Distribution steel is not only needed to resist local stresses but also to control cracking due to shrinkage. The extent to which this is likely to take place in a slab element depends on several factors, including the concreting sequence adopted. In fact a high proportion of what is generally referred to as "shrinkage cracking" is actually the thermal contraction which takes place during the setting and curing of the concrete due to the dissipation of the heat generated during setting. The correct choice of a curing method to assist in the dissipation of this heat at an early stage in the setting action may therefore help to control such cracking.

Nevertheless, whatever the precautions and sequence of concreting adopted, clearly some thermal contraction and subsequent shrinkage will take place, and the reinforcement provided must be sufficient to control the consequent cracking. This is particularly important at the edge of a deck, where the cracks will be more visible and exposed to weathering. Very large amounts of reinforcement are needed if an attempt is to be made to eliminate all visible cracks, and a compromise is usually necessary. Twelve-millimetre ($\frac{1}{2}$in.) high-yield bars at 150mm (6in.) centres around the perimeter should be regarded as a minimum amount for even the thinnest section. For crack control the spacing of the reinforcement is as important as the quantity provided, so that large bars spaced well apart are unlikely to be effective.

Where applicable, UK design regulations relating to bridges call for the calculations to be based on a modular ratio of 15. Other national codes call for different values, some as low a ratio as eight. The discrepancy stems from the fact that the elastic modulus for high-strength concretes is, in fact, quite high but shrinkage and creep have the effect of adjusting the relative stresses within the concrete and the reinforcement. British design regulations have taken the view that the calculations should represent the long-term effect – i.e. after shrinkage and creep have taken place – and stresses which are calculated using a modular ratio of 15 are representative of this. Lowering of the modular ratio has the effect of increasing the calculated stresses in the concrete of a reinforced concrete section, thereby tending to require slightly deeper members with marginally less reinforcement.

Concern about fatigue in reinforced concrete sections has recently led to the introduction of limitations on the total range of stress to which any given reinforcement may be subjected in the loading history of a member, as well as the limiting tensile and compressive stresses which the reinforcement may be designed to resist.

Detailing

The objective when detailing is to achieve a simple arrangement of reinforcement which provides bars where they are needed with the minimum of superfluous steel and without imposing restrictions on the formwork. A simple arrangement of reinforcement means using straight bars where possible to produce a layout of reinforcement which creates a readily identifiable pattern that a steel fixer can easily memorize, thus enabling him to work without needing to make constant reference to the details. These objectives almost inevitably mean the use of a small number of different bars within an arrangement.

Putting reinforcement where it is needed sounds obvious, but it is all too easy to detail arrangements of reinforcement which take no sensible account of tolerances that may reasonably be expected, either in bar bending or fixing. If a link passes round the full

Figure 9. Mechanical splicing of reinforcement by swaging.

perimeter of a column section and its dimensions are calculated from the column size and cover required, without making any allowance for tolerances, difficulties are likely to arise in maintaining suitable cover to the reinforcement.

There is often a conflict between the desire to adopt simple arrangements and the need to minimize superfluous reinforcement. Any attempt to restrict the reinforcement provided to the amounts theoretically required at closely spaced sections within a member would lead to an arrangement of reinforcement in which each reinforcing bar had its own individual dimensions and shape. There are, however, points within a structure where there is a tendency to duplicate reinforcement. In a cellular deck, for instance, the junction between the web and slab members suggests the adoption of a detail in which the vertical reinforcement is bent into the plane of the slab reinforcement to provide anchorage. If this is done, then that reinforcement should be arranged to contribute to the strength of the slab section, rather than simply to include it in addition to the reinforcement already provided in the horizontal plane.

For an arrangement of reinforcement to be convenient for construction it is essential that the constructional sequence and the location of construction joints are taken into account when deciding on the arrangement of steel. For example, where the head of a wall is to provide support for a slab, a simple reinforcement layout would provide an L-bar in the corner linking the wall to the slab. However, during the process of constructing the wall, the bar is projecting through the plane of the face of the wall, which restricts the height of the wall formwork, and this can prove costly. Where the members are sufficiently thick it is often possible to adopt alternative reinforcement layouts which allow the use of wall forms of any height.

Where long lengths of slab or wall are constructed without joints, cracks will inevitably develop. If it is important to control the positions of these cracks this can be attempted by creating lines of weakness. However, to be effective such lines need to coincide with the construction joints, since cracks within monolithic concrete sections usually express their own opinion as to where a plane of weakness is, regardless of what the designer does in terms of reducing the reinforcement locally or providing rebates in the face of the section.

Design data

Typical reinforced concrete details for bridgeworks are illustrated on Data Sheet 40. Some information concerning the design of diaphragms is presented on Data Sheet 41, and Data Sheet 42 deals similarly with the design of slabs linking spine beams.

Design may be undertaken either by employing elastic-strain (so-called modular ratio) theory or a limit-state analysis based on load-factor methods. The principal formulae and data necessary for the application of these alternative theories are summarized on Data Sheets 44 and 45 respectively. Modular-ratio design can be facilitated by the use of various design factors corresponding to the permissible working stresses in the concrete and the reinforcement and, for a modular ratio of 15, these factors may be read from the chart forming Data Sheet 46: brief examples of the use of the chart are given on Data Sheet 47, which also includes a chart that relates the stress in the reinforcement to the bar spacing in order to achieve adequate crack control.

The areas of various numbers and spacings of reinforcing bars of different sizes are tabulated on Data Sheet 49, while Data Sheets 50 and 51 present details of the requirements of BS 4466 for reinforcing bars of preferred shapes and other permitted shapes, respectively.

Reinforced concrete details
Data sheet No 40

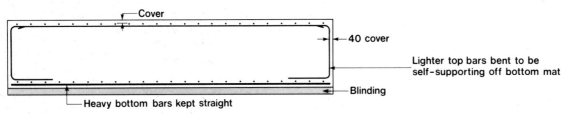

Cover

40 cover

Lighter top bars bent to be
self-supporting off bottom mat

Blinding

Heavy bottom bars kept straight

FOUNDATION

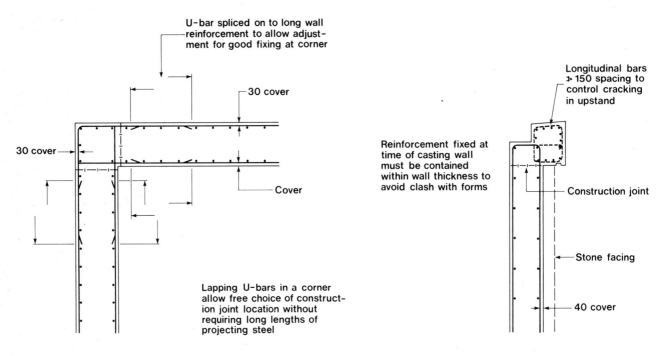

U-bar spliced on to long wall
reinforcement to allow adjustment for good fixing at corner

30 cover

30 cover

Cover

Lapping U-bars in a corner
allow free choice of construction joint location without
requiring long lengths of
projecting steel

WALL CORNER

Reinforcement fixed at
time of casting wall
must be contained
within wall thickness to
avoid clash with forms

Longitudinal bars
≯ 150 spacing to
control cracking
in upstand

Construction joint

Stone facing

40 cover

WALL CAPPING

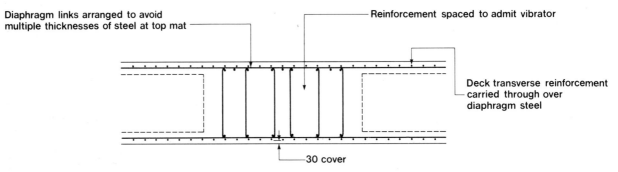

Diaphragm links arranged to avoid
multiple thicknesses of steel at top mat

Reinforcement spaced to admit vibrator

Deck transverse reinforcement
carried through over
diaphragm steel

30 cover

SKEW DIAPHRAGM

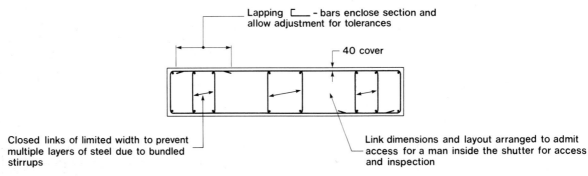

Lapping ⌐‾⌐ - bars enclose section and
allow adjustment for tolerances

40 cover

Closed links of limited width to prevent
multiple layers of steel due to bundled
stirrups

Link dimensions and layout arranged to admit
access for a man inside the shutter for access
and inspection

PLATE PIER

66

Design of diaphragm

The importance of diaphragms to the structural action of the bridge deck varies with the form of construction adopted. In some instances they act as little more than local trimmers stiffening what would otherwise be an unsupported edge of a deck slab; in other cases they stiffen the overall action of the deck, thereby improving the load-sharing characteristics of the main structural elements. In either of these cases failure of a diaphragm need not prejudice the stability of the deck. However, in some forms of construction the diaphragm is of fundamental importance to the structural integrity, and its failure would be catastrophic.

There can be dangers in relying on the results of sophisticated structural analyses to design diaphragms which come into the latter category, because any assumptions made in the analysis which are not realised in the actual structure could adversely affect the loading conditions on such an element. The independent assessment of diaphragm loading on the basis of simplified and conservative assumptions is therefore a worthwhile precaution.

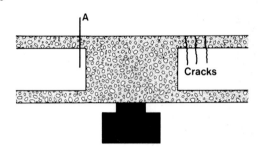

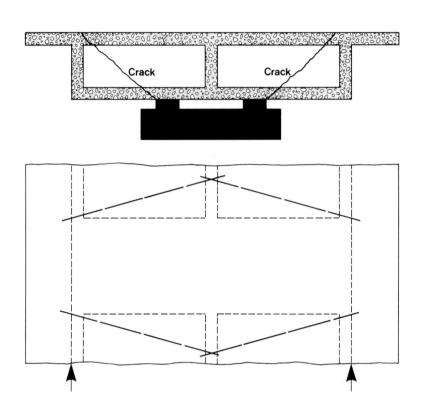

Bending in diaphragm

The development of an I-section to resist bending depends on shear lag considerations in the deck slabs. It also gives rise to horizontal shear flow in the slabs, as illustrated at A. The bottom slab at a pier will be subjected to biaxial compression at all stages in loading, and therefore well able to absorb this shear flow, but the top slab is subject to tension – particularly at loads approaching ultimate conditions – and needs significant reinforcement.

Shear in diaphragm

The pattern of shear cracking likely to develop as ultimate conditions are approached merits examination, particularly in the light of any penetrations made in the diaphragm for access or for prestressing cables.

Bending in deck

For loading cases as ultimate conditions are approached the deck section cracks, thereby reducing the proportion of the cross-section available for the effective transfer of shear from the webs to the diaphragm. Adequate reinforcement is needed to transfer the shear in this condition.

Shear in deck

The pattern of cracking developed as ultimate conditions are approached can affect the integrity of the I-section of the diaphragm where the reinforcement contributing to its action has been spread outside the net width of the diaphragm.

Torsion

Torsion adds to the shear flow in the slabs, which are also subject to I-section horizontal shear, as well as to shear in the webs.

With a load on one spine beam only the link slab is deformed by the differential deflection between the spines. This in itself leads to a transfer of shear across the link slab, thereby sharing load between the spines.

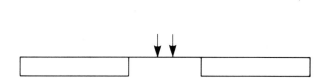

A concentrated load on the link slab not only produces local bending in that slab, but will also tend to rotate the spines, since they are subject to edge loading. The rotation relaxes the edge moments in the link slab.

The design forces in the link slab can usually be adequately assessed by considering local loading in conjunction with an evaluation of the worst distortion moments arising from unequal loading between the spines.

The latter involves the following series of calculations:

1. The deflection of one spine under unequal loads.
2. The shear in the slab per unit deflection.
3. The deflection of the spines under shear from the slab, which has a sinusoidal distribution.

The calculation is resolved by bringing the several deflections into balance.

For deep box spine beams the in-plane forces become an important consideration, making the above approach conservative.

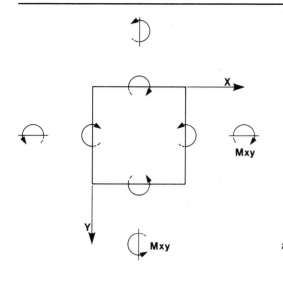

Bridge decks are often analysed by mathematical models which present the results in the form of moments and torsions on axes at right-angles to each other. For design purposes it is necessary to know the principal moments and torsions, which may not be on these same axes.

Mohr's circle provides an answer, if it is assumed that the plate is isotropic.

a) Moments on element of slab

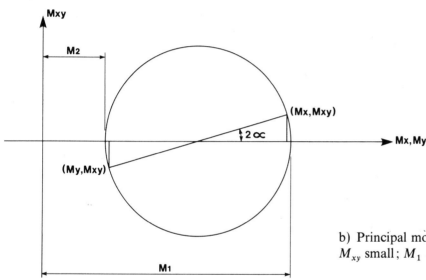

b) Principal moments,
M_{xy} small; M_1 and M_2 have same sign.

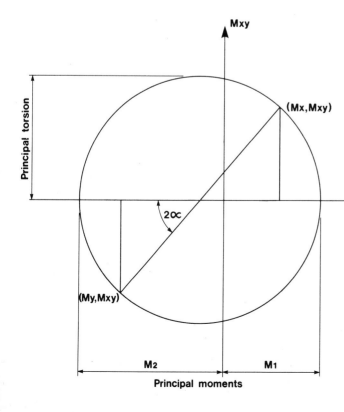

c) Principal moments,
M_{xy} large; M_1 and M_2 have opposite signs.

Note: α is the angle between the planes of the principal moments and those of M_x and M_y.

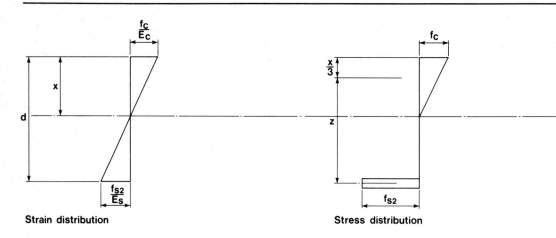

Strain distribution   Stress distribution   Cross-section

Bending
$$M = Kbd^2; \quad K = \frac{f_c}{2} \times \frac{x}{d} \times \frac{z}{d}; \quad z = d - \frac{x}{3}$$

$$x = \frac{df_c}{f_c + \dfrac{f_{s2}}{\alpha_e}}; \quad A_s = \frac{M}{zf_{s2}}$$

Shear
$$v = \frac{V}{bz}$$

$$A_s = \frac{V}{zf_s}$$

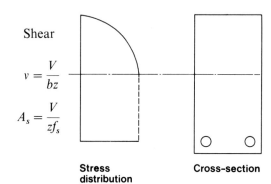

Stress distribution   Cross-section

Local bond
$$f_{bs} = \frac{V}{z\Sigma u}$$

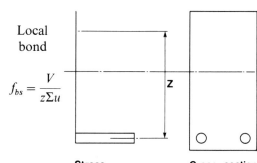

Stress distribution   Cross-section

Crack control

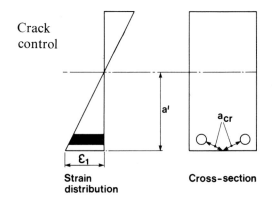

Strain distribution   Cross-section

All values in N/mm² unless otherwise stated.

Concrete:

Cube strength	30.0	37.5	45.0	
Bending stress	10.0	12.5	12.5	
Direct stress	7.6	9.5	9.5	
Shear: beams	0.87	0.87	0.87	
slabs	Related to percentage of reinforcement			
Average bond	1.00	1.00	1.00	+25% for deformed bars
Local bond	1.47	1.47	1.47	
Modulus of elasticity	28 kN/mm²	30.25 kN/mm²	32.5 kN/mm²	

Reinforcement:

	Mild steel		High-yield steel	
	≯ 40 mm dia.	> 40 mm dia.		
Tension	140	125	230	
Compression	125	110	175	Subject to
Range	265	235	325	crack
Shear reinforcement	140	125	175	control
Yield stress	200	200	330	
Characteristic stress	250	250	425	
Modulus of elasticity	200 kN/mm²	200 kN/mm²	200 kN/mm²	

Load combination	Increase in basic permissible stresses	
	HA lane loading	112 kN wheels or HB loading
1	0	25%
2	15%	30%

Crack width = $3.3a_{cr}\varepsilon_1$ for deformed bars, or $3.8a_{cr}\varepsilon_1$ for plain bars. If $a' < a_{cr}$ then substitute a' for a_{cr}.

$$M_u = 0.87 f_y A_s z \quad \text{or} \quad 0.15 f_{cu} bd^2 \text{ whichever is the lesser.}$$

$$z = d\left(1 - \frac{1.1 f_y A_s}{f_{cu} bd}\right) \ngtr 0.95d \qquad v = \frac{V}{bd} \qquad \frac{A_{sv}}{s_v} = \frac{b(v - v_c)}{0.87 f_{yv}} \qquad f_{bs} = \frac{V}{z\Sigma u}$$

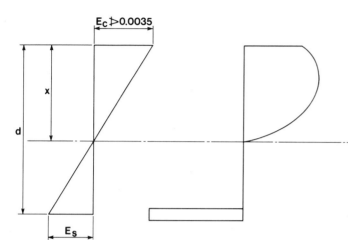

Strain distribution   Actual stress distribution   Idealised stress distribution   Cross-section

Concrete (values in N/mm²)

Characteristic strength	30.0	40 or more
Shear (ultimate-reinforced)	4.10	4.75
Local bond (ultimate)		
Plain bars	2.20	2.70
Deformed bars	2.80	3.40
Bending (serviceability)	15.0	20.0

Crack control $2.3 a_{cr} e_1$

Reinforcement (values in N/mm²)	Mild steel	High-yield steel Hot-rolled	Cold-worked ≯16 mm dia.	>16 mm dia.
Characteristic strength	250	410	460	425
Tension (serviceability)	200	328	368	340
Compression (serviceability)	200	328	368	340
Shear (ultimate)	250	410	425	425

Crack control as for elastic design.
Where more-exact calculations for M_u are required, these can be evaluated from the accompanying stress–strain curves, by employing values of γ_m of 1.5 for concrete and 1.15 for steel.

Strength of concrete (N/mm²)

Characteristic strength f_{cu}	Cube strength at an age of				
	7 days	2 months	3 months	6 months	1 year
20.0	13.5	22	23	24	25
25.0	16.5	27.5	29	30	31
30.0	20	33	35	36	37
40.0	28	44	45.5	47.5	50
50.0	36	54	55.5	57.5	60

Conditions of exposure	Nominal cover Concrete grade				Design crack width
	25	30	40	50 and over	
1. Moderate (sheltered)	40	30	25	20	0.25
2. Severe (exposed)	50	40	30	25	0.20
(Subject to de-icing salts)	N/A	50*	40*	25	0.15
3. Very severe (sea water)	N/A	N/A	60	50	0.10

* Only acceptable for entrained-air concrete.

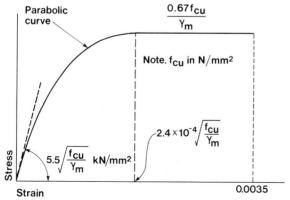

Short-term design stress-strain curve for normal-weight concrete

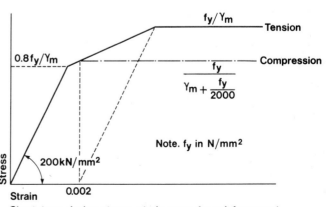

Short-term design stress-strain curve for reinforcement

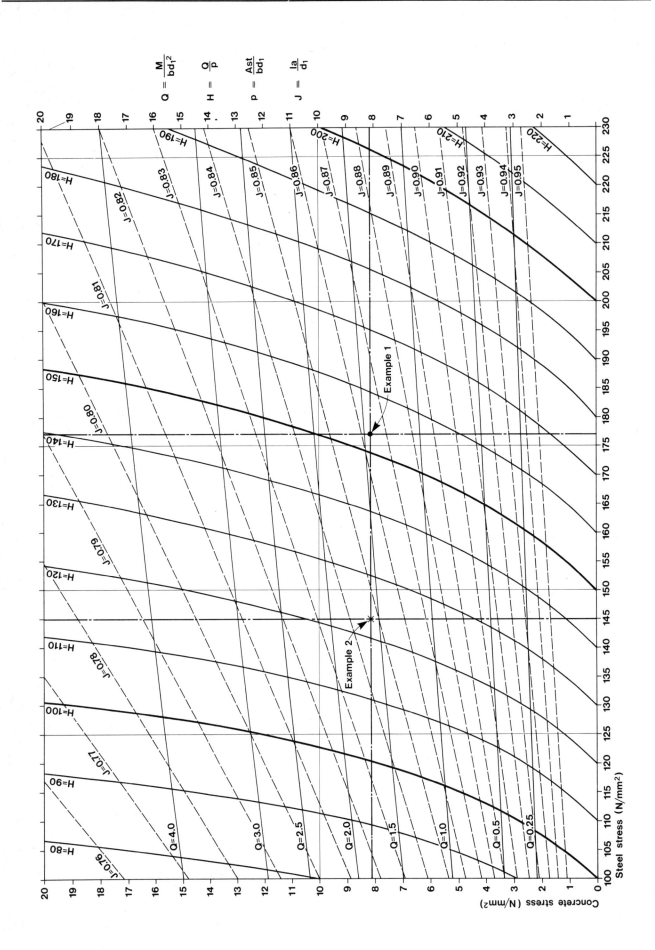

Example 1.

Since moment $= 0.80$ MN.m,

$$Q = \frac{M}{bd_1^2} = \frac{0.80}{0.6 \times 0.95^2} = 1.48.$$

From Data Sheet 46,

$$p = \frac{5500}{600 \times 950} = 9.65 \times 10^{-3}.$$

Therefore

$$H = \frac{Q}{p} = \frac{1.48}{9.65} \times 10^3 = 153.4.$$

Thus

$f_{cb} = 8.2$ N/mm² and $f_{st} = 177$ N/mm².

Also from Data Sheet 43,

$j = 0.863$, so that $l_a = 0.863 \times 950 = 820$ mm.

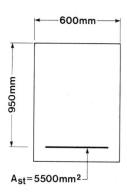

Example 2.

(Illustrating the use of the accompanying crack-control chart.)

Assuming $n = 0.4$, then

$$K = \frac{300 - 250}{(1 - 0.4)250} = 0.33.$$

Since spacing $= 150$ mm, from accompanying chart
$p_{st} = 150$ N/mm².

Moment $= 0.1$ MN m/m width. Therefore

$$Q = \frac{0.1}{1 \times 0.25^2} = 1.6.$$

For f_{st} of 150 N/mm², from chart on Data Sheet 46, $H = 127$ and
thus $p = 1.6/127$. Therefore

$$A_{st} = \frac{1.6}{127} \times 1000 \times 250 = 3149.6 \text{ mm}^2/\text{m}.$$

Provide 25 mm bars at 150 mm centres ($A_{st} = 3270$ mm²/m). Thus

$$p = \frac{3270}{1000 \times 250} = 0.01308,$$

and

$$H = \frac{1.6}{0.01308} = 122.3.$$

Therefore

$f_{cb} = 8.2$ N/mm² and $f_{st} = 145$ N/mm².

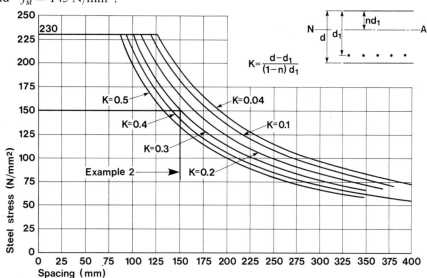

Slab moments
Data sheet No 48

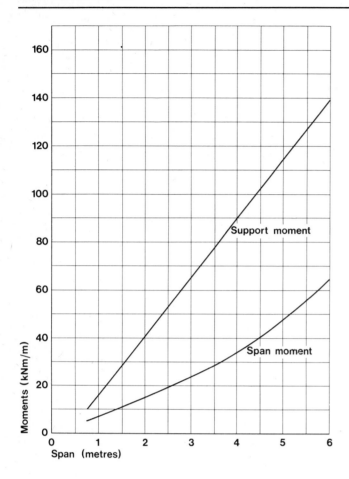

Moments (kNm/m) vs Span (metres)

Support moment

Span moment

For spans of up to 6 m the design is likely to be dominated by the effects of concentrated wheel loads.

Bending moments for encastre slab under 45 units of HB loading ($11\frac{1}{4}$-tonne wheels).

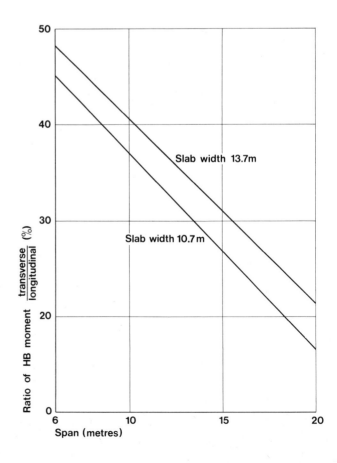

Ratio of HB moment $\frac{\text{transverse}}{\text{longitudinal}}$ (%) vs Span (metres)

Slab width 13.7m

Slab width 10.7m

For slabs less than 6 m in span, BS 153 calls for a transverse moment not less than 50% of the maximum moment due to the imposed load.

BE5/73: Transverse moments in simply-supported deck slabs.

74

Reinforcement: metric sizes and areas

Diameter		6 mm	8 mm	10 mm	12 mm	16 mm	20 mm	25 mm	32 mm	40 mm
Weight kg/m		0.222	0.395	0.616	0.888	1.58	2.47	3.85	6.31	9.81
Cross-sectional areas for specified numbers of bars (mm^2)	1	28.3	50.3	78.5	113	201	314	491	804	1257
	2	56.6	101	157	226	402	628	982	1610	2510
	3	84.9	151	236	339	603	943	1470	2410	3770
	4	113	201	314	452	804	1260	1960	3220	5030
	5	142	252	393	566	1010	1570	2460	4020	6280
	6	170	302	471	679	1210	1890	2950	4830	7540
	7	198	352	550	792	1410	2200	3440	5630	8800
	8	226	402	628	905	1610	2510	3930	6430	10100
	9	255	453	707	1020	1810	2830	4420	7240	11300
	10	283	503	785	1130	2010	3140	4910	8040	12600
	11	311	553	864	1240	2210	3460	5400	8850	13800
	12	340	604	942	1360	2410	3770	5890	9650	15100
	13	368	654	1020	1470	2610	4090	6380	10500	16300
	14	396	704	1100	1580	2820	4400	6870	11300	17600
	15	424	755	1180	1700	3020	4710	7360	12100	18800
	16	453	805	1260	1810	3220	5030	7850	12900	20100
	17	481	855	1340	1920	3420	5340	8350	13700	21400
	18	509	905	1410	2040	3620	5660	8840	14500	22600
	19	538	956	1490	2150	3820	5970	9330	15300	23900
	20	566	1010	1570	2260	4020	6280	9820	16100	25100
Cross-sectional areas of bars at specified spacings (mm^2 per metre width)	mm									
	80	353	628	982	1410	2520	3930	6140		
	90	314	558	873	1260	2240	3490	5460		
	100	282	503	786	1130	2010	3140	4910		
	110	257	457	714	1030	1830	2860	4470		
	120	235	419	655	943	1680	2620	4090		
	130	217	386	604	870	1550	2420	3780		
	140	202	359	561	808	1440	2250	3510		
	150	188	335	524	754	1340	2100	3280		
	160	176	314	491	707	1260	1970	3070		
	170	166	295	462	665	1180	1850	2890		
	180	157	279	436	628	1120	1750	2730		
	190	148	264	413	595	1060	1650	2590		
	200	141	251	393	565	1010	1570	2460		
	210	134	239	374	538	958	1500	2340		
	220	128	228	357	514	914	1430	2230		
	230	123	218	341	492	874	1370	2140		
	240	117	209	327	471	838	1310	2050		
	250	113	201	314	452	804	1260	1970		
	260	108	193	302	435	773	1210	1890		
	270	104	186	291	419	745	1160	1820		
	280	101	179	280	404	718	1120	1750		
	290	97	173	271	390	693	1080	1690		
	300	94	167	262	377	670	1050	1640		

BS4466 preferred shapes
Data sheet No 50

MINIMUM HOOK AND BEND ALLOWANCES FOR MILD STEEL BARS TO BE BS4449*

Semi-circular hooks for use with shape codes 32, 33 and 72 only

Bends forming end anchorages for use with shape codes 34, 35 and 42 only

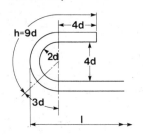

h = hook allowance = $9d$ (min.) taken to the nearest 10 mm over, or not less than 100 mm, to be added to dimension L. Hook length (min.) = $h + 3d$.

n = bend allowance = $5d$ (min.) taken to the nearest 10 mm over or not less than 100 mm, to be added to dimension L.

Bar size (mm)	d	6	8	10	12	16	20	25	32	40
Hook allowance (mm)	h	100	100	100	110	150	180	230	290	360
Bend allowance (mm)	n	100	100	100	100	100	100	130	160	200

NOTE. For intermediate sizes the dimensions and radii for the next larger size should be used.

MINIMUM HOOK AND BEND ALLOWANCES FOR HOT ROLLED HIGH YIELD BARS COMPLYING WITH BS4449* AND COLD WORKED HIGH YIELD BARS COMPLYING WITH BS4461†

Semi-circular hooks for use with shape codes 32, 33 and 72 only

Bends forming end anchorages for use with shape codes 34, 35 and 42 only

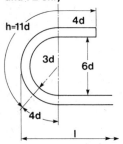

h = hook allowance = $11d$ (min.) taken to the nearest 10 mm over, or not less than 100 mm to be added to dimension L. Hook length (min.) = $h + 4d$.

n = bend allowance = $5.5d$ (min.) taken to the nearest 10 mm over, or not less than 100 mm to be added to dimension L.

Bar size (mm)	d	6	8	10	12	16	20	25	32	40
Hook allowance (mm)	h	100	100	110	140	180	220	280	360	440
Bend allowance (mm)	n	100	100	100	100	100	110	140	180	220

NOTE. For intermediate sizes the dimensions and radii for the next larger size should be used.

*BS4449, "Hot rolled steel bars for the reinforcement of concrete". (Metric units).
†BS4461, "Cold worked steel bars for the reinforcement of concrete". (Metric units)

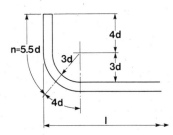
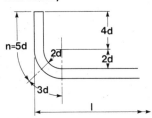

Shape code	Method of measurement of bending dimensions	Total length of bar (L) measured along centre line	Dimensions to be given in schedule
20		A	Straight
32		$A + h$	
33		$A + 2h$	
34		$A + n$	
35		$A + 2n$	
37		If r is non-standard use shape code 51 $A + B - \frac{1}{2}r - d$	
38		$A + B + C - r - 2d$ or $A + B + C - r - 2d$	
41		D shall be at least $2d$ $A + B + C$	
43		If angle with horizontal is 45° or less $A + 2B + C + E$	
51		If r is standard use shape code 37 $A + B - \frac{1}{2}r - d$	
60		$2(A + B) + 20d$	
62		If angle with horizontal is 45° or less $A + C$	
81		$2A + 3B + 22d$	A(I.D) ‖ B
83		$A + 2B + C + D - 2r - 4d$	Isometric view

INSTRUCTION. Generally an inside or outside dimension shall be indicated by the position of the bending dimensions in the sketch. If the form of the bar is such that there may be doubt as to which is the inside of the bar, arrows should be shown on the bending schedule or the dimension stated with the suffix O.D. or I.D. (outside or inside dimension).

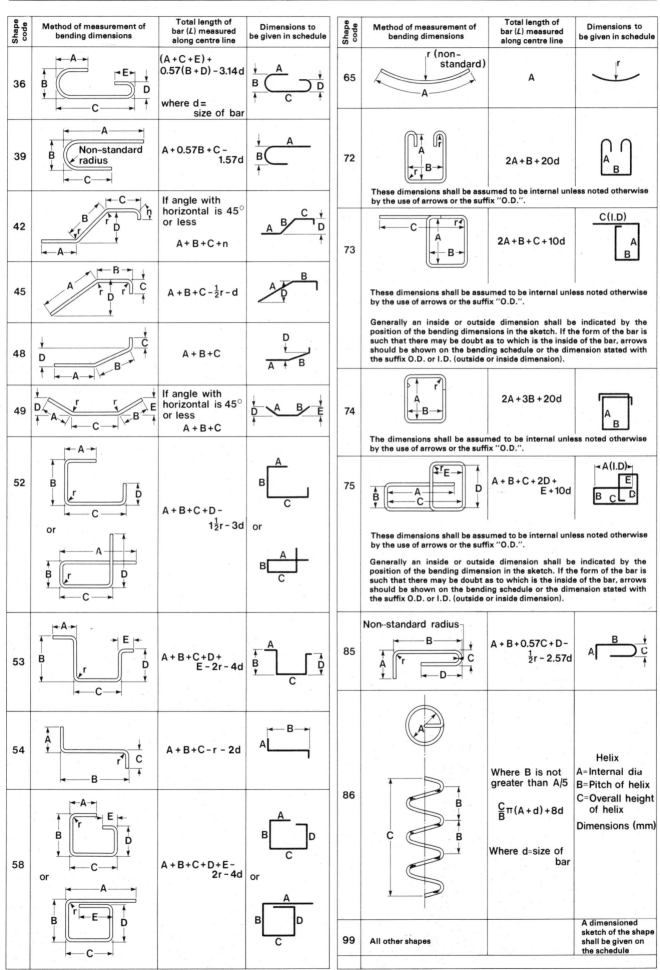

Shape code	Method of measurement of bending dimensions	Total length of bar (*L*) measured along centre line	Dimensions to be given in schedule
36		$(A+C+E)+$ $0.57(B+D)-3.14d$ where d = size of bar	
39	Non-standard radius	$A+0.57B+C-$ $1.57d$	
42		If angle with horizontal is 45° or less $A+B+C+n$	
45		$A+B+C-\frac{1}{2}r-d$	
48		$A+B+C$	
49		If angle with horizontal is 45° or less $A+B+C$	
52	or	$A+B+C+D-$ $1\frac{1}{2}r-3d$	or
53		$A+B+C+D+$ $E-2r-4d$	
54		$A+B+C-r-2d$	
58	or	$A+B+C+D+E-$ $2r-4d$	or

Shape code	Method of measurement of bending dimensions	Total length of bar (*L*) measured along centre line	Dimensions to be given in schedule
65	r (non-standard)	A	
72	These dimensions shall be assumed to be internal unless noted otherwise by the use of arrows or the suffix "O.D.".	$2A+B+20d$	
73	These dimensions shall be assumed to be internal unless noted otherwise by the use of arrows or the suffix "O.D.". Generally an inside or outside dimension shall be indicated by the position of the bending dimensions in the sketch. If the form of the bar is such that there may be doubt as to which is the inside of the bar, arrows should be shown on the bending schedule or the dimension stated with the suffix O.D. or I.D. (outside or inside dimension).	$2A+B+C+10d$	C(I.D)
74	The dimensions shall be assumed to be internal unless noted otherwise by the use of arrows or the suffix "O.D.".	$2A+3B+20d$	
75	These dimensions shall be assumed to be internal unless noted otherwise by the use of arrows or the suffix "O.D.". Generally an inside or outside dimension shall be indicated by the position of the bending dimension in the sketch. If the form of the bar is such that there may be doubt as to which is the inside of the bar, arrows should be shown on the bending schedule or the dimension stated with the suffix O.D. or I.D. (outside or inside dimension).	$A+B+C+2D+$ $E+10d$	A(I.D)
85	Non-standard radius	$A+B+0.57C+D-$ $\frac{1}{2}r-2.57d$	
86	Where B is not greater than A/5 $\frac{C}{B}\pi(A+d)+8d$ Where d=size of bar	Helix A=Internal dia B=Pitch of helix C=Overall height of helix Dimensions (mm)
99	All other shapes		A dimensioned sketch of the shape shall be given on the schedule

r = standard radius of bend unless otherwise stated

r = standard radius of bend unless otherwise stated

WOOD, R. H. The reinforcement of slabs in accordance with a predetermined field of moments. *Concrete*. Vol. 2, No. 2. February 1968. pp. 69–76. Discussion, Vol. 2, No. 8. August 1968. pp. 319–321.

CLARK, L. A. *Strength and serviceability considerations in the arrangement of reinforcement in concrete skew slab bridges.* London, Construction Industry Research and Information Association. October 1974. Report 51. pp. 15.

HUGHES, B. P. Controlling shrinkage and thermal cracking. *Concrete*. Vol. 6, No. 5. May 1972. pp. 39–42.

BRITISH STANDARDS INSTITUTION. CP 110:1972. *The structural use of concrete. Part 1. Design, materials and workability.* pp. 154. *Part 2. Design charts for singly reinforced beams, doubly reinforced beams and rectangular columns.* pp. 104. *Part 3. Design charts for circular columns and prestressed beams.* pp. 93. London.

JONES, L. L. and WOOD, R. H. *Yield-line analysis of slabs.* London, Thames and Hudson/Chatto and Windus, 1967. pp. 405.

JONES, L. L. *Ultimate load analysis of reinforced and prestressed concrete structures.* London, Chatto and Windus, 1962. pp. 248.

PUCHER, A. *Influence surfaces of elastic plates.* Fourth edition. New York, Springer-Verlag, 1973. pp. 32+93 charts.

FABER, J. and MEAD, F. *Reinforced concrete.* Revised edition. London, E. and F. Spon Ltd., 1965. pp. 534.

ASCE–ACI TASK COMMITTEE 426. The shear strength of reinforced concrete members. *Proceedings of the American Society of Civil Engineers.* Vol. 99, No. ST6. June 1973. pp. 1091–1187.

CHAPTER 6

Prestressed concrete

The idea of prestressing concrete was a natural progression following the introduction of reinforced concrete. Whereas the latter set out to overcome the lack of strength of concrete in tension by providing steel bars in those areas of the concrete susceptible to tensile stresses, the purpose of prestressing is to induce compression in the concrete which will oppose the tensile stresses that arise due to applied loading, thus ensuring that the whole concrete section remains in compression at all the stages of its working life. Recommendations for the limiting concrete stresses in precast and site-cast prestressed concrete are tabulated on Data Sheet 53.

One of the early motivations of the idea of prestressing came from the thought of producing a simulated arch. Whereas the cross-section of a natural arch remains in compression due to the natural thrust which develops at the arch springings, prestressed concrete artificially replaces the force line, which occurs naturally in an arch, by a curved steel tendon which is under stress, thus giving rise to a comparable force system in the member.

Several types of prestressing tendon have been employed. Steel bars and drawn wire were early materials, while in more recent years helically-spun stranded cables built up from cold-drawn wire have become the most commonly used type of tendon.

Provided that the tendon force is effectively transmitted to the concrete section, nothing dictates that the tendon must be contained within the cross-section of the member. Internal tendons are more common but the use of external tendons can allow reduced dimensions to be adopted for the concrete member in circumstances where the size of the section is dictated by the need to accommodate the tendons themselves.

Many patented anchorage systems are marketed for each type of prestressing tendon. Where rolled steel bars threaded at the ends are used a nut bearing against an anchor plate makes a simple anchorage assembly. One of the earliest types of anchorage for multiple-wire cables was that developed by Freyssinet. This is based on a tapering hollow cylinder within which the wires are secured by a conical metal wedge designed to anchor, simultaneously, each of the wires around its periphery. The method leads to the wires forming a natural circular grouping in cross section, thus fitting conveniently into a circular duct. Magnel developed a system in which each prestressing wire is independently wedged by a series of tapering plates. This allows the formation of a cable of almost any

size, contained within a rectangular duct. The system developed in the UK by Gifford, anchors each strand independently using its own metal barrel and wedge grip. It is this principle which forms the basis of the majority of systems marketed for anchoring strand or wire cables today.

One departure from the wedge principle for anchoring wire is that in which the end of the wire is deformed into a button head, having a shape rather like the head of a knitting needle. This method is now marketed as the BBRV system in the UK.

One disadvantage of the threaded-bar and button-head types of anchorage is the need to precalculate the length of each tendon accurately in order to prepare the anchorage. Exponents of these systems discount this complaint as a minor chore, however.

A fundamental requirement for prestressing tendons is that they must be protected against corrosive attack in order to maintain the integrity of the structure. Where the cables are contained within ducts inside a concrete section this protection is provided by pumping cement grout into the duct after prestressing has taken place. Where the tendons are external to the section other options become available, including providing an added casing of concrete directly around the tendons, or using a polyvinylchloride coating to enclose the cable which has been prepacked with grease.

The anchorage is a significant part of the cost of a prestressing tendon and where a substantial number of similar units are to be fabricated there can be advantages in stressing between anchorages that are external to the members themselves, tensioning the tendons prior to casting the concrete in direct contact with them and thereby forming an immediate bond. This technique is known as pretensioning. On releasing the anchorages the force in the tendon is transmitted to the concrete section by the bond which is developed between the tendon and the concrete. This approach to construction obviously requires the use of a permanent prestressing bed where the re-usable anchorages are established, and therefore involves precast concrete construction. The method only becomes economic where the number of units to be produced is sufficient for the saving in the cost of anchorages (which would otherwise be built into each individual unit) to offset the cost of handling precast units, any loss of economy in the structural form of the members, the establishment costs at the pretensioning bed,

Figure 10. Equipment for grouting prestressing cable ducts under pressure. High-speed mixer and storage bin with continuous agitation.

and the structural limitations of pretensioning as opposed to post-tensioning in terms of design. To be worthwhile, substantial quantities of similar units must be required, and this pretensioning technique is at its best in the fabrication of small, repeatable units such as lintols for buildings, or railway sleepers, where the cost of providing individual anchorages in each unit would represent a significant proportion of their total cost. For large units such as bridge beams the balance of these factors is more difficult to predict.

Because of the changes in stress induced by the application of loading at different sections along a beam, the optimum use of prestressing requires that the position of the tendons should change within the section from one point to another along the length. In post-tensioning this is achieved without difficulty by fixing the cable ducts to the required profile before concreting. Where pretensioning is used this obviously cannot be done, since the tendon is stressed prior to concreting. The tendon can be pulled or deflected out of a straight line to approximate to the ideal profile but this "harping" adds complexity to the stressing procedure and is only reckoned as appropriate for large units. An alternative technique for simulating the effect of a profile is to break the bond between selected tendons and the surrounding concrete near the ends of the unit. This "debonding" is achieved by placing sleeves over the selected tendons and thus rendering them ineffective at

that point. Plastics hosepipe is commonly used for this purpose. Further information regarding debonding is given on Data Sheet 54.

Parasitic forces

In statically-indeterminate structures, parasitic forces are set up by the prestressing force in addition to the moments induced by the eccentricity of the prestressing cable (measured from the centroid of the section) at points along the beam. An exception to this occurs where the shape of the cable profile is such that it would not modify the support reactions – a so-called concordant profile – which is rarely achieved in practice.

Parasitic forces develop because the structure is not free to deform as the prestressing forces alone would dictate. The deformation of the structure is constrained by the supports, and constraining forces therefore develop at these supports, modifying the reactions to external loading and inducing a pattern of moments in the structure: i.e. parasitic moments. This is illustrated on Data Sheet 55.

For design purposes it is necessary to assess the "effective" eccentricity of the cable at points along the structure, this eccentricity not necessarily being equal to the eccentricity of the cable measured from the centroid of the section. The effective eccentricity can be assessed by treating the forces exerted on the structure due to the prestressing force as a loading case, thus producing bending-moment and shearing-force diagrams. The bending moment at any section, divided by the prestressing force, then gives an effective eccentricity at that point.

An alternative approach is to plot a diagram of Pe/EI for the structure, the eccentricity e being measured from the centroid of the section in the first instance. The diagram is then balanced at the points of continuity by adjusting the indeterminate moments to give a compatible "moment-area" diagram, showing zero relative displacement at the points of support in accordance with "moment-area" methods.

Combination of prestressing force and dead load

Although consideration of the stresses at known critical cross-sections (e.g. at midspan and at the supports) may show satisfactory stresses at all stages; where prestressing cables are subject to reverse curves it is necessary to check the stresses throughout the span. This is best ensured by drawing a stress profile for the combined effects of the prestressing force and the self-weight. For a prismatic deck, the stress diagram for the prestressing force will follow the profile of the prestressing cable so that, having evaluated the stresses at the pier sections and at midspan, this diagram is readily constructed. An example is shown on Data Sheet 56.

Difficulties can arise in calculating the stresses produced by prestressing forces and applied loading on a voided slab deck at the pier diaphragms. Sectional properties are well defined within the span. At the supports, however, the situation is complicated by shear lag and by the presence of a diaphragm which is solid over the pier. The effect of shear lag is to remove the side cantilevers from the effective section resisting the bending moments. For prestressing calculations the gross area – i.e. including the cantilevering slabs – still applies to the average stress induced by prestressing forces.

At the face of the diaphragm member the section is again well defined. Any tapering of the voids that is adopted to assist in providing shearing resistance or a more gradual distribution of stress between the fully voided section and the solid pier section at the centre-line must, of course, be reflected in the sectional properties taken at this point.

At the centre-line of the pier the real section is solid, but the uniform stress due to the prestressing force requires a certain distance to redistribute itself over the solid section in place of the voided section for the rest of the deck. It is therefore questionable whether stress calculations that are based on the solid section give valid answers. As the size of void increases it becomes clearer that stresses evaluated at the face of the diaphragm are those which are most relevant for design purposes.

An additional effect of the diaphragm is to modify the longitudinal bending moments because the support reactions are distributed through the width of the diaphragm, rather than acting at a point, as is usually assumed when calculating moments and shearing forces on the deck. This means that any stress calculations that are based on peak values of the bending moments tend to

be academic, and do not reflect a real stress situation in the bridge. This shortcoming is generally accepted as a contribution towards conservatism in design, but where calculations for severe temperature stresses must also be taken into account, demanding substantial residual stresses under applied loads, it seems appropriate to consider this width of support.

Serial construction

Some of the difficulties incurred when employing serial construction are discussed on page 3, and illustrated on Data Sheet 57.

Loss of prestress

Although the force transmitted to a structure at the anchorage points may be well defined at the time stressing of the tendons takes place, these stresses will be modified by the subsequent behaviour of the structure. The prestressing tendons and the concrete are sustaining each other in an equilibrium state of stress, arising from the strains locked in by the stressing operations. Steel subjected to locked-in strain experiences some loss of stress with time, this phenomenon being known as relaxation. Concrete is subject to shrinkage and to minor changes in the stress/strain relationship with time, these effects being known as creep. In the process of stressing, the loads imposed by successive tendons as they are stressed cause the structure to deform elastically, thereby modifying the locked-in strain in those tendons that have previously been tensioned. All of these effects reduce the locked-in forces, thus resulting in a loss of prestress. An additional loss of prestress in post-tensioned tendons arises from the friction between the cable and the duct, which leads to a progressive reduction in the actual force in the cable as the distance from the jacking point increases.

The total loss of prestress is usually substantially greater with pretensioning than with post-tensioning because the whole prestressing force is applied to the member simultaneously in pretensioning, and the demand for rapid fabrication usually leads to the stress being transferred into the member while the concrete is still relatively "green" and thus more susceptible to losses due to creep. Also, pretensioning is affected by the entire shrinkage of the concrete, whereas in the case of post-tensioning some of this shrinkage takes place prior to the commencement of prestressing, and does not therefore affect the prestressing force.

Data Sheet 58 gives specimen design charts for the loss of prestress, based on selected coefficients for shrinkage, creep and modulus of elasticity.

Anchor blocks

At the point where a prestressing cable is anchored the full prestressing force in that cable is transmitted to the structure. This represents a substantial force concentrated on a very small area, and early prestressed concrete design and construction produced examples of failure in the region of anchorages, due to the splitting of the

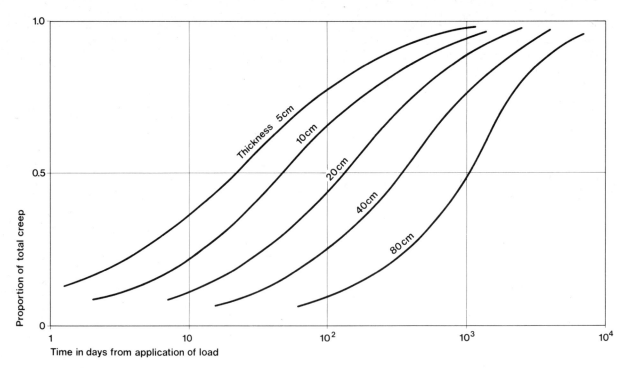

Figure 11. Relationship between creep and time.

concrete. Similar problems can still overtake the unwary designer. The effect of these large anchorage forces is not unlike that of driving a wedge into the structure, and the shape of many prestressing anchorages encourages the analogy.

Several theories were developed as a basis for the design of anchorages (Freysinnet, Guyon, Magnel, Bortsch, Bleich, Siever, Morsch, etc), producing significant differences in the results. The Cement and Concrete Association (C & CA) undertook a substantial series of tests, presenting its findings in two research reports, the first dealing with single anchorages and the second with group effects. These have formed a basis for most prestressed anchor-block design in the UK since that time.

The prime requirement resulting from the calculations derived from these research reports is the need for heavy reinforcement perpendicular to the axis of the prestressing cable and immediately behind the anchorage, to withstand the splitting forces arising from the wedge-like action of the anchorage.

An additional requirement in the region of prestressing anchorages is the need to examine the way in which the forces disperse into the full section of the deck. For example, in a box-section deck groups of anchorages are usually concentrated in concrete "anchor blocks" formed by an enlargement of the web. The dispersal of these large concentrated forces into the full cross-section gives rise to shearing and tensile stresses around the blocks. Each case requires individual assessment, assumptions being made as to the flow of the forces, and reinforcement being provided to cater for the shearing and tensile stresses that result. Within the anchor blocks themselves the design approach can be based on deep-beam theory.

The substantial amounts of reinforcement often necessary in the region of anchorages call for particular care in detailing. It is all too easy to adopt an arrangement of reinforcement which fits well on a drawing but proves quite impossible to assemble on site. If there is a conflict between the need to provide the theoretical amount of reinforcement required and the resulting production of an arrangement so congested as to prevent good concreting in that region, it is obviously even more important that well-compacted concrete should support an anchorage than that the calculated area of reinforcement should be present.

The fixing of closely-spaced reinforcement can usually be facilitated by detailing the steel in such a way that the reinforcement required in the bottom of the deck to deal with slab or diaphragm action can be fixed first. Anchorage-block reinforcement is then assembled on top of this mat, followed by the top surface reinforcement for the diaphragm or slab, which is assembled on top of the bursting steel. The system of stirrups adopted must permit this sequence.

For bursting steel itself many designers favour the use of a spiral immediately around the anchorage. This follows from the development of an early form of anchorage for small prestressing systems, which was constructed with fine-aggregate concrete inside a contiguously wound helix. The attraction of the spiral is its unquestionable effectiveness in all directions within the plane of the splitting force, and the fact that it unites a significant lump of concrete with the anchorage. Only in smaller stressing systems is this spiral adequate on its own, however, and a system of links, U-bars and straight bars will often be needed to supplement the spiral. Where conventional links are used care should be taken to detail reinforcement to a shape which avoids a double thickness of steel at the overlap closing the link. The close spacing of reinforcement needed in an anchorage zone can be prejudiced by employing avoidable laps of this kind.

The design of anchor blocks forms the subject of Data Sheet 59 while Data Sheet 60 deals with anchor blocks for external cables. Various types of anchorage for strand are illustrated on Data Sheet 61 and appropriate design data are tabulated on Data Sheet 62. Data Sheet 63 illustrates some of the anchorage systems that are available for prestressing methods that use wire, and details of strand couplers are presented on Data Sheet 64.

Shear

The capacity of a prestressed concrete member to resist shear depends on the amount of bending moment acting in conjunction with shearing force at the section. This is best appreciated by considering the case of a simply-supported beam subject to concentrated loads at third points, as shown on Data Sheet 65. Adjacent to the supports the limiting shear capacity of a beam depends on its ability to sustain the diagonal compressive force arising from the shearing force, without causing buckling of the section.

Moving away from the supports into the area where the pattern of shearing stresses is fully developed (clear of the influence of the support reaction), but where bending stresses are modest, any distress arising from excessive shear will be shown by the formation of diagonal cracks near the neutral axis of the member — where the shearing stresses are a maximum — and extending towards the boundaries of the section as the load increases, until failure occurs either by the shear stirrups yielding or the web buckling in compression.

In the vicinity of the two applied loads is a region of shearing stress associated with high bending stresses. In this area failure of the section will be heralded by the formation of cracks beginning at the extreme tensile fibre and extending upward into the member as the load increases. The propagation of these cracks impinges on the cross-sectional area available to provide effective shearing resistance, and thus reducing the shear capacity. Once a critical point is reached, the shearing and bending effects combine to extend the crack to the point where failure occurs. In the case of a continuous beam it is normal to find areas of high shearing stresses and high bending stresses together, so that this mode of failure becomes critical in such cases.

Between the two applied loads, nominal shearing stress will be combined with high bending stresses. Failure in this zone would occur as a result of pure bending.

The approach necessary to calculate the shear capacity differs according to the zone concerned. Inclined prestressing cables have a marked effect on the principal stresses in a web subjected to shear and are therefore significant in assessing the shear capacity where bending does not produce flexural cracks. The moment at which flexural cracks commence to form is unaffected by the

inclination of the stressing cables so that, where the shear capacity is limited by flexural cracking, inclined tendons do not help.

Ultimate moment of resistance

The basic aim in prestressed concrete design is to maintain the section in compression under all conditions of loading. However, where overload does occur tensile stresses can develop to such an extent that the section begins to crack, and the whole basis of evaluating the capacity of the section to resist load changes.

There are fundamental differences between the behaviour of bonded and unbonded tendons in ultimate-load conditions. Since a bonded tendon is united with the concrete section at all points along its length, the concrete and the prestressing tendon will continue to act together, responding to the same strain-distribution curve at each section, until failure takes place. With unbonded tendons, whereas the concrete section will be responding to the varying systems of force and distributions of strain at individual sections, the tendon is stressed by a strain that is locked into it by being held at points far removed from each other along the length of the member. It is therefore insensitive to particular distributions of strain of individual sections so that, although the concrete at a particular section may be strained to a point approaching its ultimate capacity, the prestressing tendon crossing the section may only be stressed to a level approximating to its normal working load.

The general approach to assessing the ultimate resistance of a prestressed concrete member is to seek, by trial and adjustment, a balance between the internal and external forces based on an assumed distribution of strain. For sections having a simple geometric shape, this analysis can be reduced to the solution of a formula based on simplified assumptions regarding the distribution of strain.

Data Sheet 67 summarizes the assessment of the ultimate moment of resistance of section.

Other design data

The remaining Data Sheets relating to the chapter give additional material that is useful in prestressed concrete design. Calculations for interface shear are illustrated on Data Sheet 66. Information relating to prestressing ducts is presented on Data Sheet 68, while Data Sheet 69 describes the procedure to be followed when calculating differential shrinkage. The various properties of strand are tabulated on Data Sheet 70 and data relating to strand relaxation are collated on Data Sheet 71.

The following mixes are selected as being the most appropriate for precast and cast-in-situ work, respectively. Variations may be appropriate in particular jobs.

Factory-made precast concrete

$52\frac{1}{2}$ N/mm^2 at 28 days ($E = 34\frac{1}{2}$ kN/mm^2)

Working stresses: (Group I loading)

Compression in bending:

For HA loading	17.3 N/mm^2
For HB loading	22.0 N/mm^2
Tension (applied load)	0
Tension (prestress/dead load)	1 N/mm^2
Shear: (see BE2/73 flow chart)	

At transfer: Compression in bending

$\begin{cases} 0.5 \text{ Ultimate} \\ 0.4 \text{ Ultimate} \end{cases}$

Tension	1 N/mm^2

For shear: See BE2/73, Clause 8

Site concrete

45 N/mm^2 at 28 days ($E = 32\frac{1}{2}$ kN/mm^2)

Working stresses: (Group I loading)

Compression in bending:

For HA loading	14.85 N/mm^2
For HB loading	18.6 N/mm^2

Other stresses as above.

Where parts of prestressed structures having $37\frac{1}{2}$ kN/mm^2 or higher 28-day concrete strength are acting as reinforced concrete, the following stresses can be adopted.

Working stresses:

Compression in bending	$12\frac{1}{2}$ N/mm^2
Direct compression	$9\frac{1}{2}$ N/mm^2
Shear, bond, etc., as for 30 N/mm^2 concrete.	

Debonding/deflecting

One of the limitations on the design of pretensioned units is that the arrangement of prestress which is most effective at midspan, where some of the stresses induced by prestressing are offset by the self-weight of the unit, may produce unacceptable distributions of stress at the support positions.

One solution to this problem is to break the bond between selected prestressing strands and the concrete near the ends of the unit, thus rendering these tendons ineffective towards the ends of the units. This arrangement thereby modifies the prestressing force and may produce acceptable stresses.

The debonding is usually achieved by providing a sleeve of p.v.c. piping which is slipped over the strand.

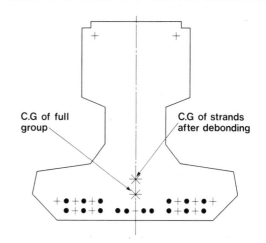

C.G of full group

C.G of strands after debonding

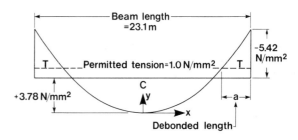

Beam length =23.1 m

Permitted tension=1.0 N/mm²

−5.42 N/mm²

+3.78 N/mm²

Debonded length

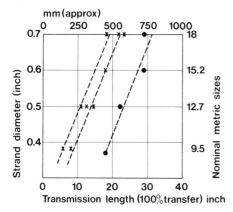

mm (approx)

x C. and C.A. Tests on ordinary strand (70% initial stress)

x Tests on ordinary strand (75% initial stress)

● Average values for Dyform strand (75% initial stress)

Curve is parabolic, i.e. $y = fx^2$, i.e.

$$9.20 = f \times 11.55^2 \quad \text{and thus} \quad f = \frac{9.20}{11.55^2}.$$

The concrete reaches a tension of 1.0 N/mm² at $(11.55 - a) = b$. Therefore

$$4.78 = \frac{9.20}{11.55^2} \, b^2,$$

and thus

$$b = \sqrt{\frac{4.78}{9.20}} \times 11.55 = 8.3 \text{ m},$$

i.e., $\quad a = 11.55 - 8.3 = 3.25 \text{ m}.$

Deflected tendons An alternative to debonding is to pull selected prestressing cables out of their normal straight line between the anchorages after applying calculated preloading, thereby simulating the profile of a ducted tendon.

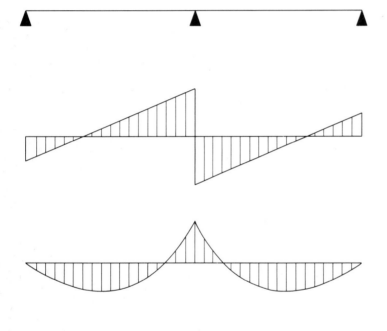

If an unrestrained beam is subjected to eccentric prestressing forces it will tend to deform.

Assuming unyielding supports, the same member acting as a continuous beam would give rise to the shearing-force and bending-moment diagrams illustrated, when subjected to uniformly distributed loads.

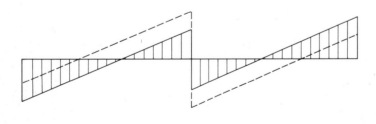

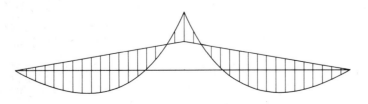

Any tendency for the beam to deform under the prestressing forces will modify the reactions, change the shearing forces and hence the bending moments

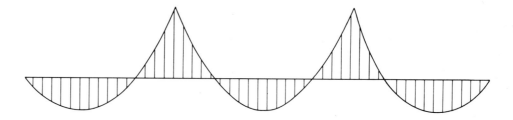

Moments and stresses
due to self weight

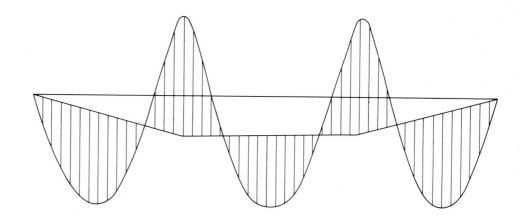

Effective eccentricity
of prestress

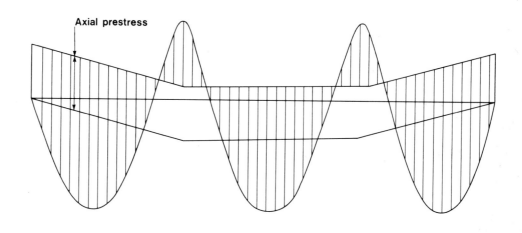

Stresses due to prestress
(axial + moments)

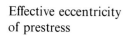

Stresses due to
prestress + self weight

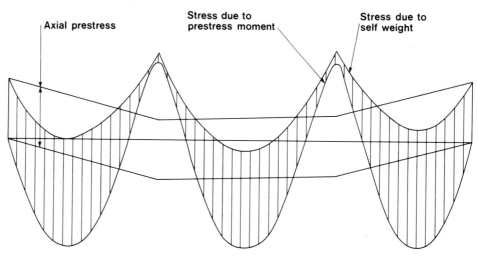

It is essential to consider the loading conditions at all stages of construction where serial construction is adopted. The design forces arising from self-weight and prestress can be significantly different from those calculated for the completed "fully-continuous" state. Creep and shrinkage also modify the statically-indeterminate forces.

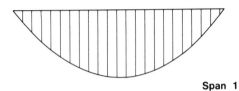

Span 1

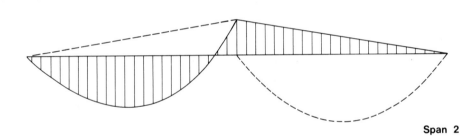

Span 2

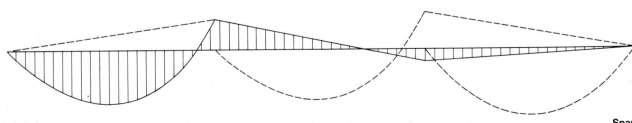

Span 3

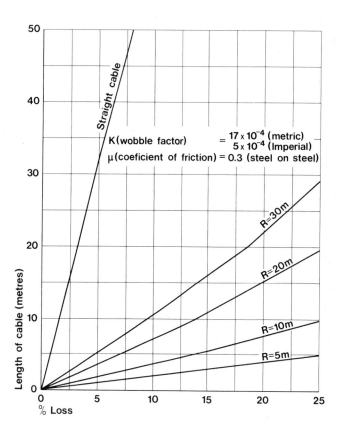

Losses indicated for post-tensioning assume several cables per beam, and that each cable is fully stressed in turn. This means that 50% of the elastic shortening in the concrete applies.

Additional losses arise due to friction in the jack, and anchorage slip at lock-off. These are normally accounted for by raising the jacking force.

Loss of prestress due to friction.

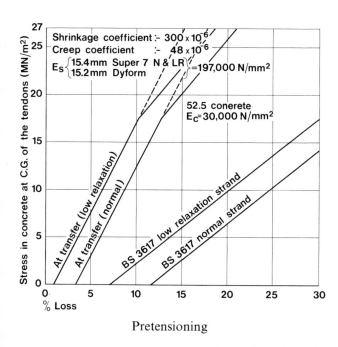

Pretensioning

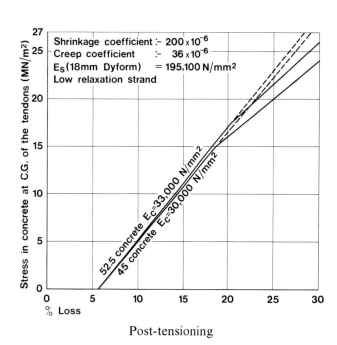

Post-tensioning

Loss of prestress due to relaxation, shrinkage, creep and elastic shortening.

Anchor block design
Data sheet No 59

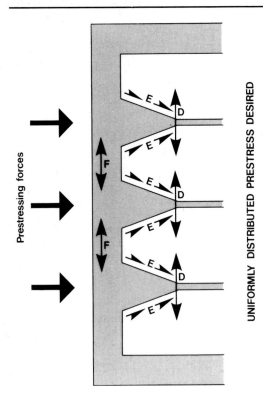

Prestressing forces

UNIFORMLY DISTRIBUTED PRESTRESS DESIRED

The design forces to be taken into consideration in the design of anchor blocks include the following.

A. Anchorage bursting forces, requiring reinforcement in the immediate vicinity of the prestressing anchorage.

B. "A"-frame tension arising from deep-beam action, distributing prestressing forces into the full depth of the section.

C. Shear developing between the anchor block and the top and bottom slabs of the cellular deck.

D. Tensile forces arising from the lateral distribution of the prestressing force across the width of the deck, akin to "A"-frame action in plan.

E. Shear between the anchorage blocks and the top and bottom slabs of a cellular deck.

F. Tensile forces similar to those in D above, but at the extremity of the deck.

Forces "D" and "F" might be visualized as akin to the tensile forces developing in a beam for which the prestressing forces act as reactions and the distributed prestress in the deck acts as the load. The depth of this beam is then equal to the depth from the end of the deck to the furthest end of the anchor block.

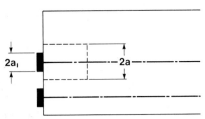

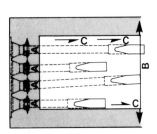

ANCHOR BLOCK

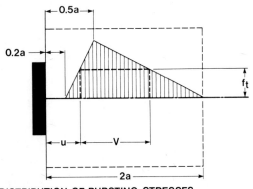

DISTRIBUTION OF BURSTING STRESSES

Anchor block

Prestressing force $= P_0$.

Crushing stress $\quad f_c = \dfrac{P_0}{2a^2}$.

Tensile stress in concrete

$$f_y = f_c\left[0.4625\left(\frac{a_1}{a}\right)^2 - 1.3\frac{a_1}{a} + 1.1\right].$$

Bursting force $\quad T = P\left(0.5 - 0.4\dfrac{a_1}{a}\right).$

Permitted tensile stress in concrete $\quad f_t = 0.39\sqrt{u_t}.$

Bursting reinforcement $\quad A_{st} = \dfrac{T}{f_{st}}\left[1 - \left(\dfrac{Kf_t}{f_y}\right)^2\right]$

where $\quad K = 0.5\dfrac{a_1}{a} + 1.12.$

Location of bursting steel:

$$u = \left(0.2 + \frac{0.3Kf_t}{f_y}\right)a \quad \text{and} \quad V = 1.8a\left(1 - \frac{Kf_t}{f_y}\right).$$

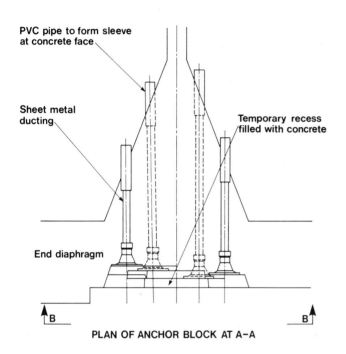

PVC pipe to form sleeve at concrete face

Sheet metal ducting

Temporary recess filled with concrete

End diaphragm

B   B

PLAN OF ANCHOR BLOCK AT A-A

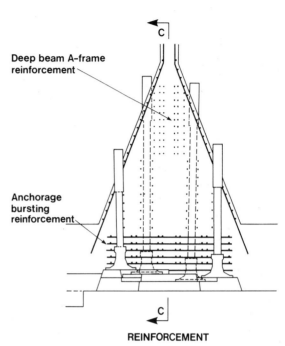

Deep beam A-frame reinforcement

Anchorage bursting reinforcement

C   C

REINFORCEMENT

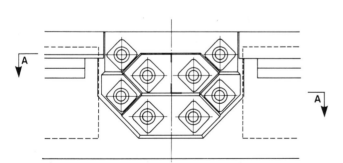

A   A

ELEVATION OF ANCHOR BLOCK (B-B) ON END OF BRIDGE DECK

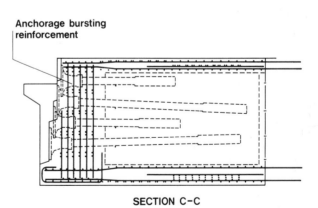

Anchorage bursting reinforcement

SECTION C-C

Below: Jack for simultaneous stressing of all strands in a cable.

Above: Design details must admit access for heavy jacking equipment if simultaneous stressing is to be adopted.

Below: Individual stressing of strands in a cable.

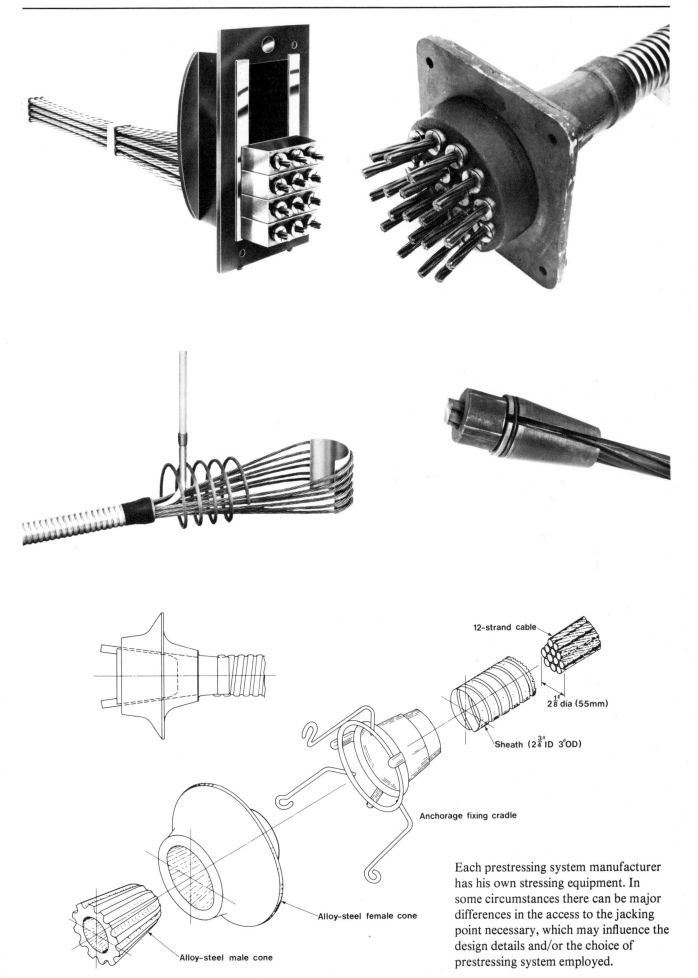

12-strand cable

$2\frac{1}{8}''$ dia (55mm)

Sheath ($2\frac{3}{4}''$ ID 3"OD)

Anchorage fixing cradle

Alloy-steel female cone

Alloy-steel male cone

Each prestressing system manufacturer has his own stressing equipment. In some circumstances there can be major differences in the access to the jacking point necessary, which may influence the design details and/or the choice of prestressing system employed.

Tendon				Force	
Strand size mm	Type	Number of strands	Cross-sectional area	Specified characteristic load in kN	
				100%	70%
12.7	DYF	7	784	1463	1024
18.0	DYF	4	892	1520	1064
15.2	STD	7	970	1589	1112
15.4	SUPA	7	1002	1750	1225
12.5	STD	12	1130	1980	1386
15.2	DYF	7	1155	2100	1470
12.9	SUPA	12	1206	2208	1545
12.7	DYF	12	1344	2508	1755
18.0	DYF	7	1561	2660	1862
15.2	STD	12	1664	2724	1906
15.4	SUPA	12	1718	3000	2100
12.5	STD	19	1789	3135	2194
15.2	STD	15	2080	3405	2383
12.9	SUPA	19	1909	3496	2447
15.2	DYF	12	1980	3600	2520
15.2	DYF	13	2145	3900	2730
12.5	STD	25	2355	4125	2887
15.2	STD	19	2635	4313	3019
12.9	SUPA	25	2512	4600	3220
15.4	SUPA	19	2720	4750	3325
12.5	STD	31	2920	5115	3580
15.2	DYF	19	3135	5700	3990
12.9	SUPA	31	3115	5704	3992
18.0	DYF	19	4237	7220	5054

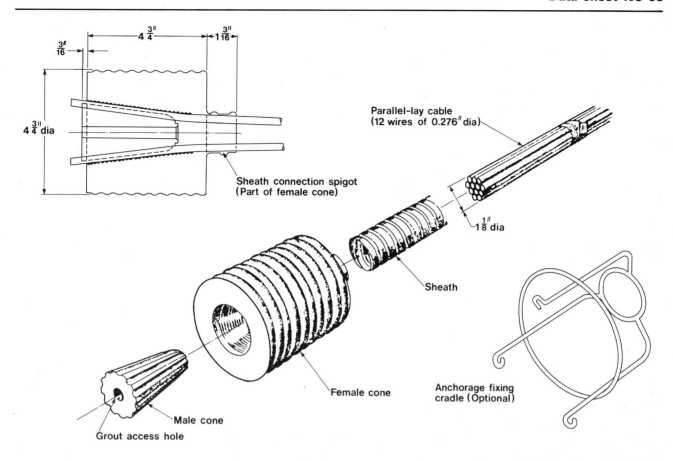

Sheath connection spigot
(Part of female cone)

$4\frac{3}{4}$ dia

$\frac{3}{16}''$

$4\frac{3}{4}''$

$1\frac{3}{16}''$

Parallel-lay cable
(12 wires of 0.276" dia)

$1\frac{1}{8}''$ dia

Sheath

Anchorage fixing
cradle (Optional)

Female cone

Male cone

Grout access hole

Preformed cable with
button-head wire anchorages.

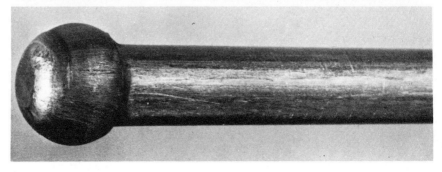

A button-head.

Strand couplers
Data sheet No 64

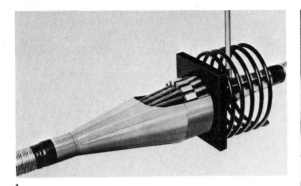

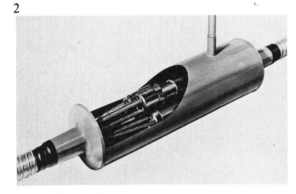

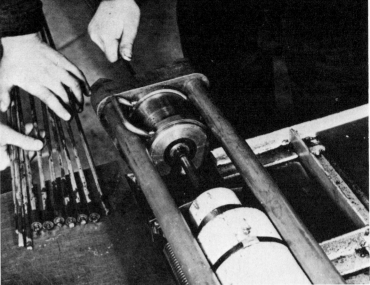

5

1 Temporary anchorage–coupler assembly.

2 Form of coupler for joining stranded cables at point where no intermediate stressing is required.

3 Alternative form of coupler, suitable for use with temporary anchorage, and allowing simultaneous stressing of all strands in cable.

4 Extrusion fittings for anchoring strand at a point remote from the jacking position.

5 Rig for on-site assembly of extrusion fitting strand anchorages.

6 Strand cable coupler allowing stressing of first-stage cable prior to extension and stressing for subsequent spans, based on single-strand stressing.

6

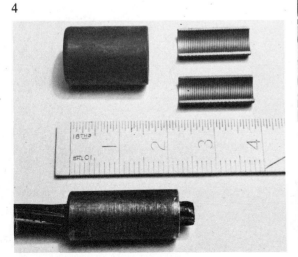

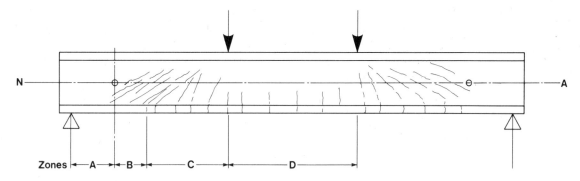

Zones |← A →|← B →|← C →|← D →|

Methods of calculation for assessing the shear capacity of prestressed concrete members vary according to the combination of forces acting. These are generally identified as the four sets of conditions illustrated in zones A, B, C and D.

Zone A: High shear with nominal bending

Cracks do not develop up to failure, which may involve crushing or buckling of the web.

$$V \not> 0.92bd\sqrt{f_{cu}}.$$

Zone B: High shear with moderate bending

Cracks develop in the web due to the principal tension exceeding the tensile strength of the concrete. They extend toward the flanges with increases in load. Failure can occur due to shear-tension failure, or by buckling of the web in compression.

$$V_c = 0.67bd\sqrt{(0.24\sqrt{f_{cu}})^2 + 0.8f_{cp}0.24\sqrt{f_{cu}}} + 0.8V_p.$$

Since inclined prestressing tendons help to reduce the principal tension in the web the component of the prestress V_p is taken into account for this condition.

Zone C: High bending and shear

Cracks commence in the tension flange and extend up into the web with increasing load. This can lead to bending-shear failure as the reduced area of concrete in compression is crushed. Shear cracks accelerate the reduction of the effective concrete section.

$$\text{Critical moment } M_0 = (0.37\sqrt{f_{cu}} + 0.8f_{pt})\frac{I}{y}.$$

$$V_c = 0.037\, bd\sqrt{f_{cu}} + \frac{VM_0}{M}.$$

Zone D: High bending with low shear

If $V \leqslant \frac{1}{2}V_c$, provide nominal reinforcement.
If $V > \frac{1}{2}V_c$, design stirrups.

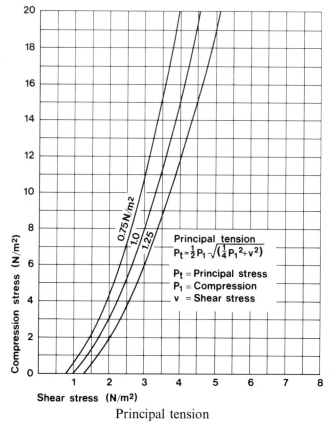

Principal tension

Principal tension
$$P_t = \frac{1}{2}P_1 - \sqrt{(\frac{1}{4}P_1^2 + v^2)}$$

P_t = Principal stress
P_1 = Compression
v = Shear stress

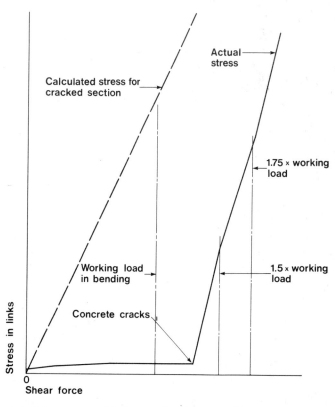

Stirrups provided to resist shear at ultimate load are only nominally stressed until cracks develop

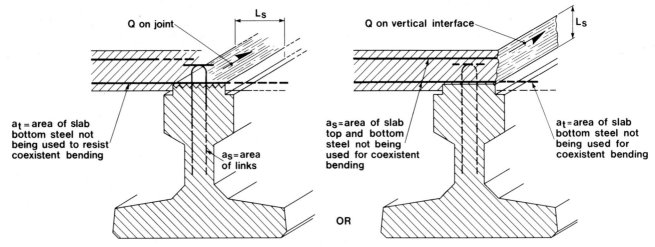

Forms of construction involving composite precast and cast-in-situ concrete have to be checked for shear at the interface between cast-in-situ and precast components. The following specimen calculation is based on the requirements of DoE Technical Memorandum BE2/73:

Specimen calculation
Load case: 4   Beam section: Node 13

Shearing force per web	$S = 0.26\,\text{MN}$
Overstress	$= 25\%$

Sectional properties:

Interface width	$L_s = 150\,\text{mm}$
Slab area	$A = 0.493\,\text{m}^2$
Height of slab c.g. above n.a.	$y = 0.300\,\text{m}$
Moment of inertia of section	$I = 0.086\,\text{m}^4$

Longitudinal shearing force

$$Q = \frac{SAy}{I} \qquad = 447\,\text{N/mm}$$

Material properties:

Lesser cube strength of slab or beam ($\not> 37.5$)	$U_w = 37.5\,\text{N/mm}^2$
Permissible tensile strength of shearing reinforcement	$f_s = 175\,\text{N/mm}^2$
Characteristic strength of reinforcement ($\not> 425$)	$f_y = 410\,\text{N/mm}^2$
(Use 410 for high-yield steel, unless good reason)	
Tensile stress at top of slab in hogging region (assuming concrete uncracked)	$f_{fc} = \text{——}\,\text{N/mm}^2$

Rules:

(i) Limiting longitudinal force
$$= \tfrac{5}{12}L_s\sqrt{u_w} \times \text{overstress} \qquad = 478\,\text{N/mm}$$
Rule (i) satisfied if $> Q$

(ii) Required steel in slab bottom excluding that for coexistent bending

$$a_t \geqslant \frac{Q}{2f_y \times \text{overstress}} \qquad = 436\,\text{mm}^2/\text{m}$$

Area of bottom reinforcement provided $\qquad = 900\,\text{mm}^2/\text{m}$
Required steel cutting interface excluding that for coexistent bending

(iii) Sagging region

$$a_s \geqslant \frac{(Q - \tfrac{1}{12}L_s\sqrt{u_w} \times \text{overstress})}{f_s \times \text{overstress}} \qquad = 1606\,\text{mm}^2/\text{m}$$

(iv) Hogging region

$$a_s \geqslant \frac{\left(Q - \left[1 - \dfrac{10}{u_w}f_{tc}\right]\tfrac{1}{12}L_s\sqrt{u_w} \times \text{overstress}\right)}{f_s \times \text{overstress}} \qquad = \text{——}\,\text{mm}^2/\text{m}$$

Area of interface reinforcement provided $\qquad = 1790\,\text{mm}^2/\text{m}.$

Under working loads the concrete section remains in compression. The total tension in the prestressing steel is balanced by the total compression in the concrete. Stress and strain are assumed to be distributed linearly.

Equivalent force in concrete →

← **Tension in steel**

As the loading passes the point where tension develops in the concrete, the section is assumed to crack. As that crack extends past the untensioned reinforcement the tensile strain adds to the effective prestress. The additional tensile strain in the prestressing steel also increases the tensile force — assuming the cable to be effectively bonded at the section.

Total force in concrete →

← **Tension in steel**

The strain is considered to be linear at all stages of loading, but stress–strain relationship under ultimate conditions is not linear, and the stress distribution is assessed from typical stress–strain curves.

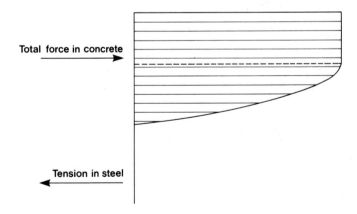

Total force in concrete →

← **Tension in steel**

In the case of unbonded cables, the tension in the steel is not affected by the tensile strains developing in the concrete at the critical section. However, any normal reinforcement cast into the concrete section will be so affected.

For the relationship between stress and strain, see Data Sheet No. 45.

The assumed distribution of stress-strain must be plotted on the design section and resultant forces evaluated to meet the following basic requirements:

Total forces in concrete and tensile steel must be equal and opposite.

Strain in concrete $\not> 0.0035$.

The most commonly used form of
ducting for prestressing cables is made
up from sheet metal, spirally wound
to give some measure of flexibility
along its length combined with a
robust section.

Recommended minimum radius of curvature

Diameter	105 mm	95 mm	85 mm	75 mm	65 mm	50 mm	40 mm
Radius	7.0 m	6.0 m	6.0 m	5.5 m	4.5 m	4.0 m	3.5 m
Diameter	$4\frac{1}{8}''$	$3\frac{3}{4}''$	$3\frac{3}{8}''$	$3''$	$2\frac{9}{16}''$	$2''$	$1\frac{5}{8}''$
Radius	$23'0''$	$20'0''$	$20'0''$	$18'0''$	$15'0''$	$13'0''$	$11'0''$

Ducts for prestressing cables must be
held securely in position at frequent
intervals. The forces exerted during
the placing of the concrete are severe
and the consequences of displacement
are disastrous. The stresses in a
prestressed section are sensitive to
tolerances relating to location of the
cable, so that accurate positioning is
important.

Bars supporting ducts should prefer-
ably be curved in sympathy with
the duct. Straight-bar supports give
rise to local indentations which must
increase the friction when the cable is
stressed.

Spot welding can be used to secure
the duct supports to the adjoining
reinforcement, but weld splatter is
liable to affect the formwork surfaces
nearby.

Prestressing saddles need mechanical strength to resist the forces imposed by the prestressing cable. Their design is also influenced by the need to limit the bearing stresses imposed on the concrete. Length and curvature should allow for tolerances arising in location and setting-out as well as in saddle manufacture. Where pre-applied coatings are used on the strand on the saddle length it is even more important to avoid tearing and splitting the coating.

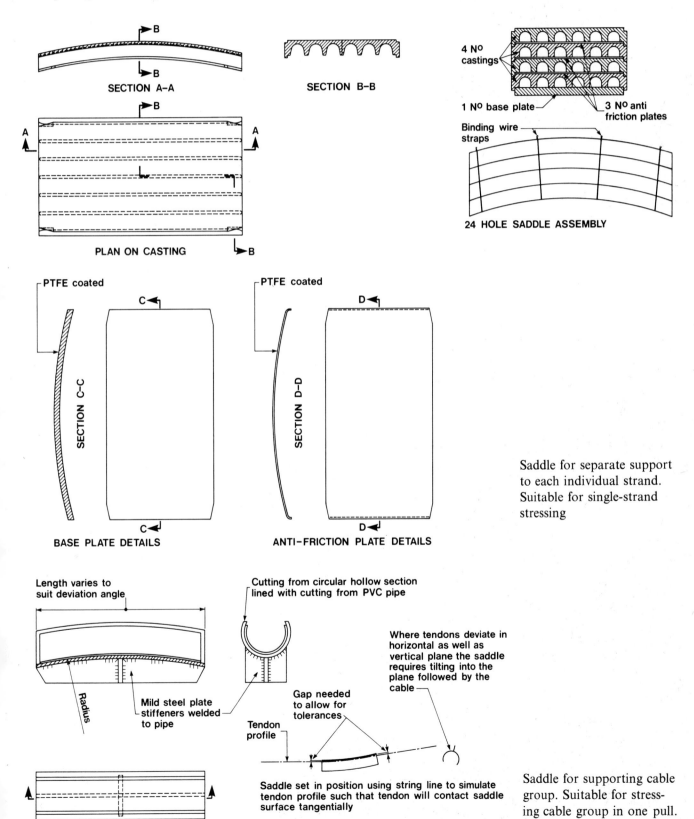

SECTION A-A

SECTION B-B

4 No castings

1 No base plate

3 No anti friction plates

24 HOLE SADDLE ASSEMBLY

Binding wire straps

PLAN ON CASTING

PTFE coated

SECTION C-C

BASE PLATE DETAILS

PTFE coated

SECTION D-D

ANTI-FRICTION PLATE DETAILS

Saddle for separate support to each individual strand. Suitable for single-strand stressing

Length varies to suit deviation angle

Radius

Mild steel plate stiffeners welded to pipe

Cutting from circular hollow section lined with cutting from PVC pipe

Where tendons deviate in horizontal as well as vertical plane the saddle requires tilting into the plane followed by the cable

Gap needed to allow for tolerances

Tendon profile

Saddle set in position using string line to simulate tendon profile such that tendon will contact saddle surface tangentially

Saddle for supporting cable group. Suitable for stressing cable group in one pull.

Differential shrinkage
Data sheet No 69

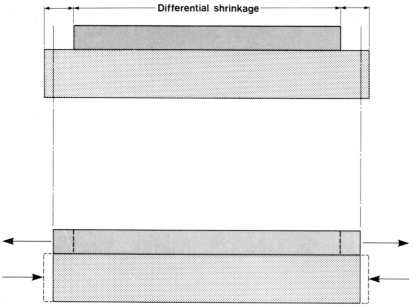

Where a concrete section is constructed in two stages involving the placing of fresh concrete against already mature material, differential shrinkage will set up stresses in the section, which may be significant. The most obvious example of this is a beam-and-slab deck.

When a cast-in-situ slab is cast on top of precast concrete beams, the shrinkage in the slab subsequent to casting will be greater than in the beam.

Since the joint between the beam and the slab ensures that no slipping takes place between them, it is evident that a tensile force must develop in the slab and a compressive force in the beam, to keep them the same overall length. Statics demand that these two forces must be equal and opposite.

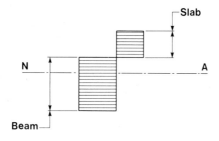

This tension and compression action suggests the accompanying stress diagram.

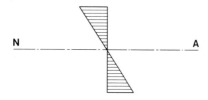

But the distribution of stress produces a moment, and as there is no system of external forces to maintain equilibrium, a further set of internal stresses arises to absorb the moment.

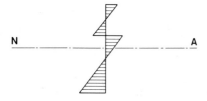

Adding the two foregoing diagrams together then gives the shrinkage stresses.

These stresses are in turn modified by creep.

BS3617   Normal-relaxation strand

Nominal diameter of strand	Nominal area of steel	Nominal mass per 1000 m run	Specified charac-teristic load	Minimum 0.2% proof load	Minimum elongation	Maximum relaxation after 1000 hours from initial load of 70% of the specified characteristic load	Maximum relaxation after 1000 hours from initial load of 80% of the specified characteristic load
mm	mm²	kg	kN	kN	%	%	%
9.3	52.3	411	93.5	79.5 ⎫			
10.9	71.0	564	125.0	106.3 ⎬ 3.5		7	12
12.5	94.2	744	165.0	140.3			
15.2	138.7	1101	227.0	193.0 ⎭			

BS3617   Low-relaxation strand

Nominal diameter of strand	Nominal area of steel	Nominal mass per 1000 m run	Specified charac-teristic load	Minimum 0.2% proof load	Minimum elongation	Maximum relaxation after 1000 hours from initial load of 70% of the specified characteristic load	Maximum relaxation after 1000 hours from initial load of 80% of the specified characteristic load
mm	mm²	kg	kN	kN	%	%	%
9.3	52.3	411	93.5	84.1 ⎫			
10.9	71.0	564	125.0	112.5 ⎬ 3.5		2.5	3.5
12.5	94.2	744	165.0	148.5			
15.2	138.7	1101	227.0	204.3 ⎭			

Dyform L-R prestressing strand

Nominal diameter of strand	Nominal area of steel	Nominal mass per 1000 m run	Specified characteristic load		Minimum load at 1% relaxation Normal-relaxation strand	Minimum load at 1% relaxation Low-relaxation strand
mm	mm²	kg	kN	lbf	kN	kN
12.7	112.0	890	209.0	46985	—	181
15.2	165.0	1300	300.0	67443	—	260
18.0	223.0	1750	380.0	85427	—	330

Bridon SUPA-7 prestressing strand

Nominal diameter of strand	Nominal area of steel	Nominal mass per 1000 m run	Specified characteristic load		Minimum load at 1% relaxation Normal-relaxation strand	Minimum load at 1% relaxation Low-relaxation strand
9.6	56.0	440	102.5	23043	87.1	92.3
11.3	76.0	600	138.0	31024	117.3	124.2
12.9	100.5	800	184.0	41365	156.4	165.6
15.4	143.2	1130	250.0	56202	212.5	225.0

Relation between metric and other values

Nominal diameter of strand	Specified characteristic load Specified	Specified characteristic load Practical equivalents	
mm	kN	kgf	lbf
9.3	93.5	9530 (9534)	21000 (21020)
10.9	125.0	12750 (12747)	28100 (28101)
12.5	165.0	16820 (16825)	37100 (37094)
15.2	227.0	23150 (23148)	51000 (51032)

NOTE. The values in brackets are exact conversions.

There are several grades of prestressing strand available. All prestressing strands are stress relieved, but further processes are often employed to reduce the losses arising from the relaxation of the steel. These processes involve a combination of applied heat and stress, carried out under such varying trade names as Thermalising, Normalising, etc.

Compact strand is pulled through a die after being spun as a stranded cable, which not only physically modifies the cross-sectional shape, but also enhances the strength characteristics of the stranded cable as a result of the further cold working.

For the purposes of assessing prestressing strand extensions, calculations should be based on values of E taken from tests on specimens of the actual strand used. For design purposes a figure of $200 \, \text{kN/m}^2$ may be used.

Strand relaxation

Data sheet No 71

For prestressed concrete the accepted procedure for design purposes is to allow for the relaxation of prestressing steel on the basis of tests, taking the value at 70% of the ultimate tensile strength and 20°C after 1000 hours. Relaxation is sensitive to stress and temperature, as is illustrated by the accompanying graphs relating to British Ropes Dyform strand.

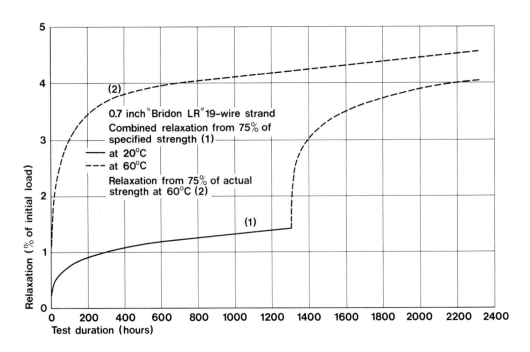

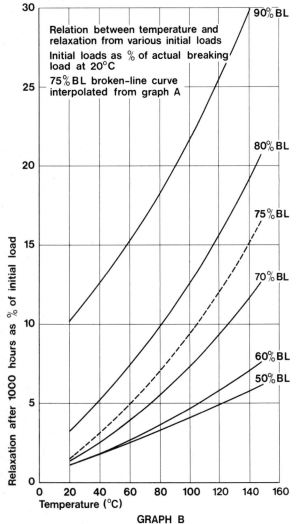

GRAPH B

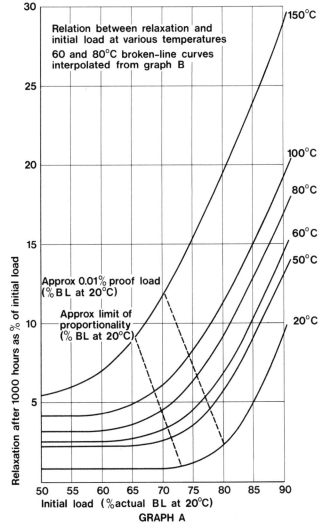

GRAPH A

FEDERATION INTERNATIONALE DE LA
PRECONTRAINTE and COMITE EUROPEEN DU BETON.
*International recommendations for the design and construction of
concrete structures.* London, Cement and Concrete Association,
1970. *Vol. 1: Principles and Recommendations.* pp. 80. *Vol. 2:
Appendices.* pp. 47.

BRITISH STANDARDS INSTITUTION. BS 3617:1971.
Seven-wire steel strand for prestressed concrete. London. pp. 16.

BRITISH STANDARDS INSTITUTION. BS 4757:1971.
Nineteen-wire steel strand for prestressed concrete. London.
pp. 16.

MANTON, B. H. and WILSON, C. B. *MoT/C & CA standard
bridge beams.* Wexham Springs, Cement and Concrete
Association, 1975. pp. 20. Advisory Publication No. 46.012.

LEONHARDT, F. *Prestressed concrete: Design and construction.* Berlin, Wilhelm Ernst and Sohn, 1964. pp. 677.

CHAPTER 7

Development of structural form

If man has always been as preoccupied with creature comforts as he is today it seems likely that his earliest efforts at producing a structure to span between supports would have been aimed at providing a roof over his head, rather than at bridging a gap. Timber, vegetation and animal skins are likely materials to have formed his earliest attempts at a roof covering. Because of the limited life of these materials the best evidence that remains as to these earliest techniques of construction is in the methods still adopted by primitive peoples today.

A tree deliberately felled to provide a dry crossing of a stream is presumed to have formed the first man-made bridge. As problems of transportation led to the adoption of established routes and the heavy use of such crossings, stone offered the prospect of a more durable material. Its first application probably followed the use of structural forms pioneered by heavy timbers; some members standing on end (or stacked) to act as posts, while others were laid to span between these closely-spaced supports.

Stone imposes severe limitations as to the distances that it will span in this way, not because of its tensile strength but because of the practical limitations in the size of a single stone which can be cut and handled. The surviving heritage of Greek and Egyptian architecture contains ample examples of what has been achieved with this simple structural form. Columns had to be closely spaced to restrict beam action to short spans, and this had a constricting effect on the layout of buildings, making it impossible to achieve wide open spaces under the covering of a stone canopy. The nearest approach was to adopt a colonnade of closely-spaced columns in two directions in the form of a grid. Wide spaces could only be covered by using timber, so that the development of techniques for jointing timbers controlled progress in that respect.

Despite their limitations, stone columns and architraves formed the basic structure for many magnificent buildings. Their durability cannot be questioned in the light of examples that survive until today. Even in the UK, which claims no special place in that architectural era, the well-known bridge at Tarr Steps in Devon represents a simple example of stone slab construction reputed to have been in service for up to 3,000 years (see Frontispiece).

The development of the arch was a major breakthrough for construction using stone, now making it a material suitable for use in the construction of bridges as well as for prestigous buildings. It might be appropriate to go to the expense and special effort of cutting and transporting very large stones to create impressive public buildings, but when it came to more utilitarian structures, such as bridges, a form of construction had been needed which made use of the more-readily-available small stones.

The circular arch form used by the Etruscans and Romans demanded a fixed relationship between rise and span. These peoples built barrel roofs as well as free-standing arches, to give long covered areas. It was also possible to form an intersection between barrel arches crossing each other, but only where the intersecting barrels were of similar dimensions – otherwise problems of stability would arise at the intersection. The circular arch therefore imposed severe limitations on the layout and appearance of buildings.

Much Roman architecture still adhered to the traditions of columns and architraves adopted by the Greeks. The arch seems to have been more extensively used in bridge construction and in the creation of particular spectacles: triumphal arches and public buildings. The fact that great men and national victories were commemorated by building arches reflects the importance of such arches in the technology of the empire, almost amounting to the status of a national symbol.

It was not until the 12th century that the concept of the Gothic arch was introduced, breaking away from the semi-circle, to adopt a form embodying a pointed apex. This change introduced flexibility into the relationship between the span and the height of an arch, so that transepts could be created having a span differing from the intercepted aisle. This gave a new degree of freedom in the planning of structures.

Pointed-arch forms also allowed greater spans, because the horizontal thrust at the arch springing is of a lower magnitude than with the semi-circular form. This trend was further aided by the development of flying buttresses which help to balance the horizontal forces. In this context the innovation of adding pinnacles to the buttresses might be regarded as an early example of prestressing – by adding deadweight – aimed at stabilizing these complex structural forms. Although these features were given elaborate decorative treatment by way of carving, their prime function was (in most cases) structural rather than ornamental.

When the processing of metals developed to the stage at which it could be applied to the construction of large structures, its first use was based on the structural form of an arch, reflecting the technology which had developed from centuries of construction using stone.

Iron Bridge in Shropshire is the first example of a metal bridge, which still stands as a monument to the skill and craftsmanship of those who built it in 1799. The bridge at Coleport, built in 1818, is a further example. Both are of arch construction, which is not the form best suited to metals.

Cast iron, being weak in tension, tended to be used primarily in compression members with only a limited use for beam members. The development of wrought iron, with its superior tensile qualities, opened the way for further developments in structural form.

The influence of earlier materials and the structural forms to which they were applied have created pitfalls for the designer as well as inhibiting the way in which a new material is first applied. The notorious weakness of cast iron in tension lured engineers into faulty design in that, when early structures in wrought iron were built, great care was taken to test the strength of members in tension but the phenomenon of buckling in long struts was not appreciated until accidents took place.

The capacity of wrought iron to accept tensile stresses opened the door to several new structural forms. Suspension cables became the tensile complement to the all-compression arch. Frameworks were developed in which some members acted in compression and others in tension. The well-known characteristics of the arch form were exploited in some framed girders by giving the compression boom an arch shape, the springings of the arch being tied together by a straight tensile member – the lower boom. Stephenson's design for the Conway Bridge represents an early suspension bridge, which was subjected to model testing as a means of proving the design.

It was when mild steel was developed, offering a wide range of rolled sections and plates, that truss and plate girder forms were fully developed. Each of these forms found its best application within particular ranges of span.

The early use of concrete shows yet another repetition of the cycle associated with the introduction of new materials, which start with the disadvantage of being applied to structural forms better suited to their predecessors. It was inevitable that concrete should initially be regarded as reconstituted stone and used in that context. People now knew the limitations of compression-only materials, and thus concrete had obvious applications if the arch form were adopted.

Reinforced concrete presented an opportunity to adopt structural forms in parallel with those used for steel sections, and the I-beam has become an established structural form utilized in reinforced and prestressed concrete structures. Some attempts were also made to build concrete structures of lattice girder form.

Because steel is produced by a rolling process, which gives long lengths of continuous members, the structural forms that were created in steel were inevitably based on linear structural action. To provide adequate support for an area of floor or bridge deck it was necessary to create a grid with a primary, secondary, and sometimes tertiary members spanning at right-angles to one another to cover

Figure 12. Temple of Bacchus. A remnant of the magnificence achieved with the simplest structural forms.

Figure 13. Braidley Road Bridge, Bournemouth.

the area. But the potential merit of concrete is its ability to form shapes which can have a bi-directional structural action, and to be moulded to give economy to suit those two complementary actions. The voided slab or hollow box can be tailored to suit the varying requirements of relative longitudinal and transverse strengths at different points in a bridge deck, representing the effective use of concrete in structural forms which are peculiarly its own and making optimum use of its inherent qualities.

The earliest efforts at building in concrete using box forms were substantially influenced by earlier efforts at building boxes in steel, where transverse stiffening members and diaphragms are essential to prevent the box buckling. In the case of concrete, however, experience has shown that a satisfactory box structure can be achieved without such stiffening diaphragms being needed, resulting in substantial economies.

The rate at which new materials become available for construction, and the parallel development of structural forms is accelerating rapidly. The column and architrave and the arch each developed through a period somewhat in excess of a millenium. Metal structures have been with us for little more than a century and reinforced concrete has barely celebrated its jubilee. If this acceleration continues, structural engineers will have to foster a new flexibility in thought about structural form as they handle new materials.

Future development

It is, of course, a good deal easier to review the past than to predict the avenues along which future development is likely to take place. There is a natural tendency to feel that our methods of construction are well developed in the context of the materials we have available. This has doubtless been the view of engineers of each generation. In fact the foregoing review seems to suggest that it is the availability of new materials which has paved the way for each break-through in constructional techniques, and that designers have been relatively slow to respond to each new material, and to find the best use for it.

There is limited scope for the exploitation of concretes having significantly higher strengths than those available at present. The prime effect of utilizing substantially stronger concrete would seem to be that limitations on design would then be imposed by the requirements of stiffness rather than of strength. Fibre-reinforced concrete is at present receiving a great deal of attention, but it

seems likely that the impact of this material would be to increase the range of application of cement-bound materials, rather than to extend the capability of existing structural applications. Even if fibre reinforcement were applied to conventional structural concrete construction, its impact on the dimensions of beams and slabs would be only marginal. However, fibre reinforcement makes it possible to create very thin concrete sections compared with those which can be formed with conventional reinforcement. This opens up new possibilities for cement-bound facing panels which can be light in weight.

A good deal of attention has also been given to the possibility of developing prestressing tendons from non-corrosive materials. Although this might be useful in removing one cause for anxiety over the life of a prestressed structure, it would make no great impact on the design concept.

Turning attention to the structural forms adopted, it is apparent that box construction has greatly increased in popularity over recent years. Now that we have outgrown the tendency to provide complicated and unnecessary stiffeners at frequent intervals throughout a span, boxes are becoming progressively lighter in construction and this is likely to extend their range of application.

The ribbon bridge has appeared on the scene in recent years. This is a catenary of prestressed concrete forming what is, in effect, a stiff suspension cable. It has been applied to footbridge construction, but although a ribbon

Figure 14. Precast concrete track for experimental tracked hovercraft.

109

Figure 15. Erecting beam for hovercraft track.

highway bridge is theoretically possible, its appearance is likely to be distressing. The marked sag is too suggestive of imminent collapse to be acceptable.

Some interesting work has been done on the possible applications of triaxial prestressing. We know that the weakness of concrete as a material is due to its limited tensile strength, so that if it can be maintained in a compressive state on all axes, its potential strength is very high. A cylindrical element of concrete can be maintained in a state of triaxial precompression by winding a tensioned wire around it, or by enclosing the concrete within a steel tube. This results in a member that is capable of resisting very much higher axial forces than would be acceptable on a comparable cylinder of concrete not reinforced in one of these ways. Some work carried out in the USSR has considered the theoretical possibilities of building trusses of concrete maintained in triaxial compression by a spiral winding of wire. It is hard to believe that a structure of this form would be competitive with the alternative steel structure, however.

If we are to speculate on the future development of structural forms, it is perhaps easier to imagine the potential impact of new types of problem. The tracked hovercraft is a case in point: the requirement for long lengths of elevated structure, narrow in width and demanding very high standards of tolerance to admit the anticipated speed of vehicles of this type imposes severe demands on constructional tolerance. The experimental track erected on the fens in East Anglia was based on pretensioned precast concrete box construction, for which a very high standard of tolerance was achieved.

There is a good deal of excitement in being involved with new developments, but this is not a goal to be pursued for its own sake. The rôle of the designer is to produce an economic and pleasing solution rather than a novel one. Concrete is firmly established as the principal material for bridge construction in the short-span to medium-span range. The prime effort of designers should be directed toward ensuring that the structures we build do not detract from their environment.

CHAPTER 8

Structural analysis of bridge decks

Analytical methods

A five-year research programme was recently carried out by the Construction Industry Research and Information Association (CIRIA) in conjunction with the Cement and Concrete Association to evaluate the various methods of analysis available for the design of bridge decks. It was concluded that the following four analytical tools could be appropriate in given circumstances.

The load-distribution method.
Grillage analysis.
The finite-strip method.
Finite-plate elements.

Load-distribution method

The use of the load-distribution method has been well documented by the C & CA. Its range of application is limited: it is only applicable to slab, pseudo-slab and beam-and-slab types of construction having prismatic cross-sections, the spans being simply supported, with line supports and right spans only. In practice this analytical tool is of much wider use than these limitations first imply. Its results can generally be accepted for skews of up to 20°, and a series of discrete supports can be accepted as representing a line support, provided that there is no significant overhang beyond the outer bearings and that the spanning effect between the bearings does not become dominant in terms of the behaviour of the deck.

Even where it is felt that the load-distribution method would not provide a suitable final analysis for a deck it can be a useful tool for making a reasonable approximation of the load-distribution characteristics at an early stage in design calculations.

Until recently this has been a method that could be undertaken by hand calculation, but the theory has now been reformulated in a manner which lends itself to computerized calculation, with the resulting benefit of improved accuracy.

Grillage analysis

Grillage analysis is perhaps the most versatile, and certainly the most widely used, method of analysing bridge decks. Its attraction lies in the fact that a system of interconnecting beams forming a grillage, gives a pictorial analogy of the structure which most designers feel they

can readily comprehend. There are also ample programmes available that are capable of solving the resulting grillage equations. There are no restrictions on support conditions, the cross-section need not be constant, and skew can be accommodated provided that a grillage can be generated which is representative of the deck shape.

Because this is the most widely used method of analysis a more lengthy explanation is given in the following sections of this chapter.

Finite-strip method

This is a particular version of finite-element technique. The bridge deck is divided into strips which may all be in the horizontal plane for a plate deck, or in a three-dimensional arrangement, as would be required for box construction, with the strips in the horizontal plane representing the slabs, and those in a vertical (or inclined) plane the webs.

This is a very useful method, economical in computer time and giving good solutions for those structures which lie within its limitations. It can only represent bridge decks having constant cross-sections and with right end supports. Irregular intermediate supports, can, however, be catered for by the technique of superimposing results to give zero deflections at the points of support on a beam originally considered as spanning between the end supports.

Finite-plate elements

This analytical method is reputed to be very versatile, and is capable of representing complex structures acting in a complex manner. This flexibility inevitably leads to complex computer programs which do not always behave as anticipated. It is expensive to use compared with the other methods, and its complexities mean that it is not the method for a design engineer who has not been steeped in computer lore and in the mathematics involved in the behaviour of plates.

The method was developed for the design of aircraft structures, where design and development costs dominate the total cost of a project. In that context such sophisticated methods make sense. For the design of bridgeworks – which are normally "one-off" designs – the relevance of its application is open to debate.

Approach to analysis

To design a structure which will give good service an engineer needs to evaluate the forces and stresses developed within its various components under service conditions. This requires an appreciation of how the structure is behaving, which may be aided by analogies with structures which will lend themselves to mathematical solution.

It is important for the designer to maintain the realization that any mathematical analysis carried out is an analogy that is not always truly representative of the way in which the real structure would behave. Too great a reliance on the quantitative answers arising from some form of mathematical analysis may be indicative of a lack of engineering judgement.

Methods of analysis are evaluated by comparing the results with those given by laboratory tests carried out on models. Considerable progress has been made towards making models representative of prototype structures, but heavy reliance is still placed on measuring the deflected shape under load because of the difficulties in attempting to measure strains, which may be more directly related to the stresses developed. The fact that a good comparison is achieved between the displacements obtained on a laboratory model and on an analytical mathematical model does not, in itself, mean that they are both predicting the same pattern of stresses. So the results of mathematical analyses still need to be approached with caution.

Grillage analysis is the most widely used mathematical model, and the type of deck structure most difficult to represent in this way is a cellular deck, whether this is a voided slab or a box form of construction. The difficulties arise from the fact that the grillage is two-dimensional only, whereas a cellular deck behaves in a three-dimensional manner. A consideration of these differences can be a valuable aid to understanding both the cellular deck and the analytical limitations of a grillage.

Torsion

There are fundamental differences between a grillage and a cellular bridge deck in relation to the forces and stresses which arise due to torsion. Elementary considerations of equilibrium demand that a shearing stress in one plane can only co-exist with a shearing stress of equal intensity in the complementary plane. In the case of a simple beam this means that shearing stresses of equal intensity are present over a vertical cross-section and in the complementary horizontal plane. In the case of the top or bottom slab of a cellular deck, the implication is that shear flow arising from torsion is of equal intensity over both transverse and longitudinal sections through the deck, at any one point. By contrast with this there is no interdependence between the longitudinal and transverse torsional moments within a grillage. Balanced results can only be achieved by carefully evaluating the sectional properties. To obtain accurate values for torsion using a grillage, which might be directly applied to the real structure, it is necessary to re-assess the torsional stiffnesses of the component members for each individual loading case, in the light of the pattern of deformation that is anticipated.

The torsional resistance of a cellular deck results from two primary components, shear flow in the webs and shear flow in the top and bottom slabs. A rectangular cell subjected to torsion develops shear flow of a pattern which means that the vertical (web) members make a contribution to the torsional resistance which is equal to that afforded by the top and bottom slabs.

A grillage subjected to torsion develops a system of reacting forces consisting of three components.

A torsional shear in the longitudinal members in association with torsion in the transverse members.

A differential flexural shear in the longitudinal members, due to non-uniform load sharing.

Torsional moments in the longitudinal members with associated flexure of the transverse members.

The torsional moments evaluated in the longitudinal members by using a grillage are inevitably underestimated: assuming the stiffnesses of transverse members have been correctly evaluated, an appropriate amount of shear flow will develop in the webs. To this will be added the differential flexural shear reflecting the load-sharing pattern of the longitudinal members. A grillage will only use the torsional stiffness of the longitudinal members to make up the deficiency in equilibrium. If use is made of these longitudinal torsions to evaluate the flow of shear in the top and bottom plates, this will inevitably give a value which is less than that in the vertical webs, which must be equal in terms of force per unit perimeter.

Stiffnesses assigned to transverse members of the grillage have a two-fold effect: they give rise to torsional moments which can be used to evaluate the flow of shear in the top and bottom slabs, and they modify the bending moments in the longitudinal grillage members, inducing shears which represent the flow of shear within the webs of the box. It is this which gives the grillage bending-moment diagrams their characteristic saw-toothed shape.

In a grillage representing a multi-celled box the pattern of torsion in the transverse members within the various "bays" of the grillage shows the build-up of torsion from the edges of the box inward. Intermediate longitudinal members are influenced only by the change in torsion along a transverse member, on each side of the node at which they intersect.

In considering a particular cross-section of deck, the transverse members reflect the torsion on the basis of the twist along that line. But the shear flow in the webs will be a product of the twist in the adjoining transverse members also, which may be some distance away and possibly subject to a significantly different twist, because of the deflected shape of the deck. To this extent the shear flows evaluated are misrepresented.

It follows that the transverse members are the better source of values for the torsion within a grillage. However, if shear flexibility has been incorporated in the grillage sectional properties this will have the effect of increasing the differential deflection between the longitudinal members and, therefore, correspondingly increasing the twist in the longitudinal members connecting them. The torsion in the transverse members is therefore overstated.

It has long been realized that grillages are not particularly sensitive to torsion, in that variations in the torsional stiffnesses assigned to the members make no dramatic impact on the predicted behaviour of the grillage in flexure – provided that the local "saw-tooth" effects are ironed out when interpreting the results. This is just as well, because the grillage gives a poor representation of the torsional moments present. Fortunately, these moments are not difficult to evaluate by another means. This is less true when variations in the plan geometry take place, either in the form of introducing skewed or non-symmetrically arranged supports. In these cases it is more important to fit the torsional stiffnesses to the results.

Clearly, the prime contributors to torsional stiffness are the top and bottom slabs. Where diaphragms are present within the depth of a deck, a consideration of membrane analogy for torsion will readily show that the flow of torsional shear in a diaphragm member is only the difference in the flow of shear in the top and bottom slabs as they cross the diaphragm.

Grillage mesh

Where a bridge deck is formed of a small number of cells, it is appropriate to place the longitudinal grillage members along the axes of the web members. Where there are sloping webs, the grillage members should be placed along the lines of intersection between the web and the top or bottom slab.

Excessive preoccupation with torsion might lead to the conclusion that longitudinal members would best be placed along the centre-lines of the cells, but in fact it is better to place such members along the web axes to obtain the best representation of the transverse flexural characteristics of the deck. The torsional values included in the output are rarely directly applicable, in any case.

For a multi-celled deck which approaches the characteristics of an orthotropic plate in its behaviour, there is no need to align the grillage members with individual webs. Suggested guide-lines for the selection of the number of longitudinal grillage members are that five or more members should be considered, and that the spacing of the longitudinal members should not exceed one-half of the width of a traffic lane, or one-and-a-half times the overall depth of the deck, whichever is the lesser.

Transverse grillage members must be placed along the line of each diaphragm in a structure. Additional transverse members are also needed to reflect the load-sharing characteristics of the deck. The frequency of these members should be such that the differences between the analytical model and the real structure do not dominate the output, and thereby obscure interpretation. West* has suggested that transverse members should be placed at intervals not exceeding twice the spacing of the longitudinal members. In any event, the adoption of less than five intermediate transverse members produces results in which the interpretation of the values at the intersection points of the grillage members could obscure the results.

* See reference on Data Sheet 76.

Sectional properties

In assigning stiffnesses to the grillage members it can appear for many decks that the arbitrary division of the deck into separate members by intersection lines at the mid-points between the members will give an adequate result. In the case of a deck having sloping webs, however, it is apparent that such an intersection line would result in the outer members having very low moments of inertia, with the position of the neutral axis changing abruptly from one member to another, whereas it has been demonstrated that such changes in the level of the neutral axis do not actually take place. Obviously the total stiffness should be correct, and this stiffness could be distributed in proportion to the respective areas of the members or purely as a matter of judgement.

Depending on the proportions of a structure, it may be necessary to take shear lag into account in assigning stiffnesses to grillage members.

The torsional stiffness is evaluated from the opposing shearing action of the top and bottom slabs, giving a torsional constant of one-half of that which arises from considering the closed section as a thin-walled box. This halving was found many years ago to best fit the experimental results, but no satisfactory explanation has been given as to why this should be the case for a cellular deck when the full calculated figure is used for other forms of construction. The explanation may be in the equal contributions of torsion in the members, and the adjusted shears in the intersecting members.

Shear lag

According to the basic assumptions of simple beam theory – where cross-sections remain plane after flexure – the distribution of stress across the top flange of a beam is constant. In a broad-flanged T- or I-section, this assumption is not true except for sections which are far from a point of contraflexure. At a point of contraflexure the section is subjected to shearing force but no bending moment. Zero moment implies that there is no direct stress in the flanges, while shear on the section indicates that there are horizontal shearing stresses reducing in intensity toward the extremities of the section. In the case of a broad flanged I-section this means that the horizontal shear flow diminishes to zero at the outer edges of the flange. Away from the point of contraflexure direct stresses are present because of the moment on the section, and the shearing stresses are modified. As with the case of simple bending theory for beams, the horizontal shear flow and direct stresses are inter-related, and what is happening may be visualized in terms of the shear flow injecting direct stresses into the flange. The build-up of these direct stresses resulting from the shear flow is not uniform across the width of the wide flange, but produces stresses which tail off toward the extremities, until a distance is attained that is far enough from the point of contraflexure for the pattern of stresses to have reached a balance which produces uniform direct stress. The effects associated with this change of distribution of direct stress are known as "shear lag."

In order to assess the peak stresses in such a section,

the commonly adopted procedure is to calculate the sectional properties on the basis of a reduced (so-called "effective") flange width. CP 110 and CP 117 recommend methods of assessing this reduced width. An exact assessment of the effects of shear lag involves recourse to plate theory, because the effect is a function of each particular loading case as well as of the plate dimensions.

With continuous bridge decks the effects of shear lag are most significant at the intermediate supports. The recommendation of CP 110 (i.e. that the effective flange widths are assessed on the assumption of points of contraflexure at distances of 0.7 of the span apart) can produce substantial errors at the support section. A reasonable compromise is to evaluate the effects of shear lag on the basis of the points of contraflexure which arise on a given structure under a uniformly distributed load although, strictly speaking, these positions should be re-evaluated for each loading case.

Since shear lag reduces the effective stiffness of a member in addition to modifying the distribution of stresses across it, improved accuracy can be obtained from a grillage analysis if the "effective" sectional properties, arising from shear lag, are used in the grillage. This may redistribute some moment away from those sections modified by shear lag, thereby reducing the resultant stresses.

Where it is needed, a good picture of the distribution of stresses across the width of a plate can be obtained by plotting those stresses which arise from the net "effective" sectional properties, together with those arising from the gross sectional properties. The curved distribution of stress across the flange can then be sketched.

When applying shear lag to a box deck, the sectional properties of the reduced section can imply a different neutral-axis position to that which applies to the gross section. For a prestressed beam having varying sectional properties, it is well known that if the neutral axis changes in level this, in itself, modifies the moment applied by the prestress. However, in the case of a change in the position of the neutral axis due to shear lag, this is not the case.

The forces produced by the prestress can be considered as two separate elements: the horizontal force applied to the deck and the bending moments produced by the cable profile. In the case of a beam with varying sectional properties a change in the position of the neutral axis modifies the stresses produced by the horizontal force in the same way that a direct load on a column produces varying stresses if the sectional properties change — because of the changing eccentricity of the load at each section. This analogy cannot be adopted in shear-lag calculations because differing rates of shear lag apply to the horizontal load due to the prestress, and to the bending moments. For the horizontal load, shear lag affects only those regions adjacent to the anchorages where the horizontal force is applied. The fact that the stresses induced by bending moments arising from the vertical forces applied by changes in direction of the prestressing cable are subject to shear lag does not, in itself, modify the stresses produced by the horizontal force.

No adjustment is therefore needed to the stresses arising from axial prestress, even though the shear lag

phenomena suggests a change in the position of the neutral axis when considering moments.

Distortion

When a concentrated load is applied over a single beam within the width of an open-spaced beam-and-slab deck, some load-sharing clearly takes place with adjacent beams, but the member directly under the load obviously deflects more than the others, and the slab which provides the transverse link between beams is therefore deformed. With a multi-celled box, similar deformations occur to the cross-section when the loads are applied over a single web, but the cross-section is now a closed frame and the webs of a multi-celled box are not free to rotate in the way that is possible in a beam-and-slab deck, because they are tied laterally, top and bottom. The pattern of deformation and the resulting force system are akin to those of a Vierendeel girder.

The term "distortion" which is applied to this pattern of deformation can be misleading because it inevitably becomes associated with torsion, which is not necessarily the case. In fact, by considering a twin-celled box subjected to distortion by a concentrated load over the central web it is evident that the force system which develops can be in equilibrium without imparting any torsional rotation to the deck. Distortion is therefore essentially the effect of differential deflection between adjacent longitudinal "members".

Because of distortion, a cellular deck has a dual stiffness transversely. Circular bending across the deck results in direct tension and compression in the top and bottom slabs, thereby forming a couple to resist the bending moments. No distortion is involved. On the other hand, where there is a transfer of shear across the deck, this gives rise to distortion and the stiffness of the deck is now totally different from that which applies to circular bending. Most real loading cases produce a combination of these two effects. It is therefore essential that a grillage should be capable of handling this duality of stiffness.

In calculating the deflections of a beam, it is normal to consider only those deformations which arise due to bending. A full mathematical expression of the deflection in a beam includes the deformations arising as a result of shear, in addition to those due to flexure. But shear deformations are normally neglected because they are very small by comparison with those due to bending. To enable the transverse members of a grillage to take account of the dual stiffnesses applicable to bending and to shear, grillage programs have been written that include the full deflection equations, including shear. It is therefore possible to take account of the dual stiffness of a cellular section by calculating a shear area for the transverse members which would give the same rate of deformation as that which, in reality, arises from distortion.

The calculation of this "effective shear area" is based on assumptions of how the cross-section deforms. This will, in fact, differ according to the loading case applied. In the case of a heavy load applied at one edge of a deck, all the cells deform in a similar manner, including the flexure of the webs themselves. In contrast, a heavy load placed in the middle of the deck, which is such that the force systems are in balance on each side of the point of application, means that the web under the load does not flex (because there is no moment in it).

In the case of thin-webbed boxes, the presence or otherwise of flexure in the webs may significantly affect the stiffness of the cell. The shear area assigned to the transverse members can therefore only approximate the distortional stiffness, but in most practical bridge-deck sections the top and bottom slab elements are considerably more flexible than the webs so this error is not serious.

Where there are variations in the shape of the cross-section, such as sloping webs, which complicate the assessment of the distortional flexibility, this can be assessed with the aid of a frame representing the cross-sectional shape. The deformation of the frame under the load provides a basis for assessing the "effective shear area".

Having obtained the grillage output, the force system arising from deformation is calculated by assuming that points of contraflexure develop midway between the webs, and that the total shear from the grillage is shared between the top and bottom slabs in proportion to their stiffnesses.

In designing reinforcement or determining the prestress required to cater for the forces developing around the cross-section, the values are dominated by those forces which arise from local wheel loads. These are best evaluated by applying Pucher's* or a similar design method for concentrated loads. The distortional stresses are significant, but they are small in comparison with the results of local wheel loads.

In cases where cellular construction is used in separate sections within the cross-section of a deck, the sections being linked together by slabs which are made monolithic with the adjoining cellular elements, the distortional stresses arising in these linking slabs are also obtainable from a grillage analysis. In such cases the distortional stresses can be very much more prominent in the total design figures (see Data Sheet 42).

Voided slabs

When the method of "effective shear area" is applied to a slab having circular voids, it is sufficient to assess the deformation of the cross-section on the assumption of a simplified cross-section which has rectangular voids that give slab and web thicknesses that are slightly greater than the actual minimum thicknesses at these locations.

Skew

Because of the difficulties which arise in evaluating torsional parameters, the values obtainable for a grillage with members intersecting other than at right-angles are subject to error. The skewed deck should therefore be constructed with an orthogonal grillage, apart from the need to show the diaphragms in their real location.

In many instances it is likely that the dominant difference in stiffness between the diaphragm and the other parts of the deck is the increased shearing stiffness. Although difficulties inevitably arise from overlapping

* See reference on Data Sheet 52.

members within a skewed deck, it is often sufficient to allow the orthogonal grillage members to represent the stiffness of the cellular section, and to superimpose on this a diaphragm – usually in a skewed direction – which is assigned a flexural stiffness equal to its own nett dimensions, and a shear area equal to its actual cross-sectional area.

It is within a skewed deck that the accurate assessment of the torsional stiffness becomes more significant as otherwise the torsions introduced in the areas of skew support will not be evaluated realistically.

Variations in the plan geometry of a deck can introduce problems of tapering cells, which make the adoption of an orthogonal grillage impossible.

In a majority of cellular structures diaphragm members are contained within the depth of the deck. The force systems resulting from the grillage at the intersections between the diaphragm and the web members are not necessary directly applicable to these members themselves. They represent the force field in the total deck and, in most instances, the web diaphragm members will not be significantly affected by the torsions, which will be resisted by the top and bottom slabs. Any attempt to design an intersection between such members for the torsion which a grillage analysis implies is transmitted through the connection is therefore a mis-directed effort.

Loading cases

In any structure which is prestressed the forces developed by the prestressing force are intended to oppose those arising from applied loading. Whenever the geometry of the deck is such that it will induce a complex system of forces, the intensity of these resultant forces in the real structure will be reduced by the opposition between the prestress and the applied loading. It is therefore of fundamental importance to include the prestress as a loading case in any analysis.

In bridge decks having simple geometry it can be sufficient to use the grillage merely to get a picture of the distribution of moments across the width of the deck, and then to resort to continuous-beam calculations to obtain the actual design figures.

In many instances the optimum value can be obtained from a grillage analysis by applying axle loads at intervals along the span as individual loading cases which then form the basis of influence lines. The benefit to be obtained from this, as opposed to employing a full HB vehicle as a loading case, is that any local effects can be more closely identified and evaluated.

In all cases it is recommended that the loads should be applied to the longitudinal members forming the grillage only, so that the transverse members reflect the forces arising from distortion, without adding the complication of the effects of local loads.

Data sheets

The force system employed in grillage analysis is illustrated on Data Sheet 73, while Data Sheet 74 is devoted to the use of a grillage to analyse a cellular deck. The interpretation of the results obtained from an analysis using a grillage is illustrated on Data Sheet 75.

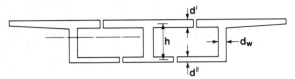

(a) Deck cross-section

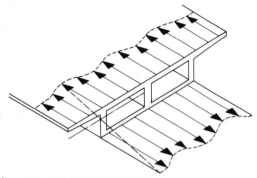

(b) Longitudinal bending stresses

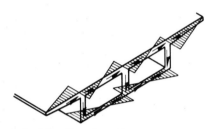

(c) Longitudinal bending shear flow

(d) Transverse bending

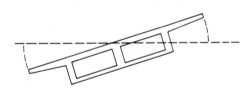

(e) Torsion

(f) Distortion

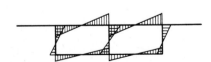

(g) Transverse moments in slabs and webs due to distortion (f)

FORCE SYSTEM IN A TWIN-CELL BOX

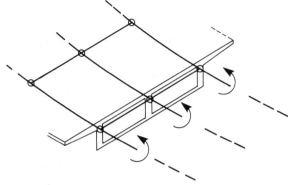

(b) Longitudinal bending moments

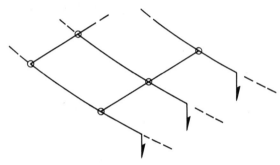

(c) Longitudinal bending shear forces

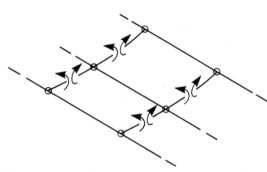

(d) Transverse bending

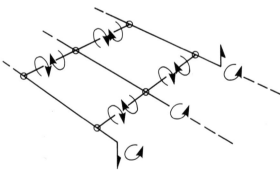

(e) Torsion torques and shear

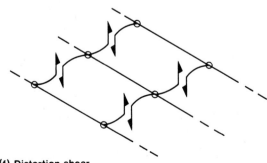

(f) Distortion shear

GRILLAGE FORCE SYSTEMS

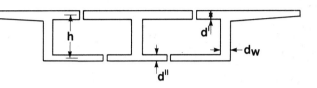

The bending stiffness of grillage beam elements making up the cross-section of a cellular deck must be based on a division of the section which maintains the neutral axis at a constant level. The sum of the stiffnesses of the beam elements must equal that of the gross deck section.

The influence of shear lag is greatest where the cell width is large in relation to the span. Shear lag not only influences the distribution of stress at various points in a cross-section, but also modifies the effective stiffness of the section. The accuracy of grillage results may be improved by taking shear lag into account in assigning bending stiffness to the grillage elements. This can only be worthwhile, however, where shear lag has a major influence on the distribution of stress.

$$\frac{f}{y} = \frac{M}{I} = \frac{E}{R} \qquad (1)$$

$$r = \frac{S_M A \bar{y}}{I} \qquad (2)$$

$$S_M = \frac{dM}{dx} \qquad (3)$$

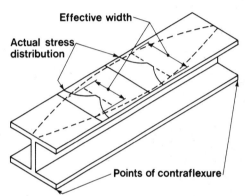

EFFECTIVE FLANGE WIDTH REDUCED BY SHEAR LAG

Transverse bending action of a cellular deck involves distortion. Two stiffness parameters are therefore needed to represent the dual action of transverse bending/shear. They are as follows.

1. For bending about the common neutral axis of the top and bottom slabs:

$$I_t = \frac{h^2 d' d''}{(d' + d'')} \text{ per unit length} \qquad (4)$$

2. For shear deformation of the cross-section the relationship between the shear and the displacement ω_s, across a rectangular cell can be taken as

$$S \simeq \frac{(d'^3 + d''^3)}{l^3} \left\{ \frac{d_w^3 l}{d_w^3 l + (d'^3 + d''^3)h} \right\} E\omega_s \text{ per unit width} \qquad (5)$$

Since the beam theory gives the relationship between the shearing force and the shear displacement as

$$S = \frac{A_s G \omega_s}{l} \qquad (6)$$

an "equivalent shear area" for transverse members crossing a rectangular cell can be given as

$$A_s = \frac{(d'^3 + d''^3)}{l^2} \left\{ \frac{d_w^3 l}{d_w^3 l + (d'^3 + d''^3)h} \right\} \frac{E}{G} \text{ per unit width} \qquad (7)$$

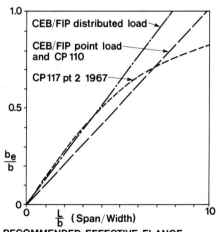

RECOMMENDED EFFECTIVE FLANGE WIDTHS FROM CODES OF PRACTICE

117

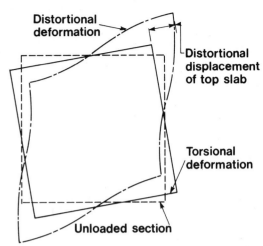

TORSIONAL DEFORMATION OF A BOX CELL

The torsional stiffnesses to be included in a grillage representing a cellular deck must be those calculated from the opposing action of the top and bottom slabs only. Although the webs contribute to the torsional stiffness their contribution is already taken into account by the interaction between torsion and shear.

$$C = 2(h'^2 d' + h''^2 d'') = \frac{2h^2 d' d''}{(d' + d'')} \text{ per unit width} \qquad (8)$$

The main limitation regarding grillage representation of the structural action of a cellular deck arises from the fact that the grillage has no means of representing the relative lateral displacements of the top and bottom slabs other than that arising from pure torsion. In fact, the distortion of the cross-section modifies the relative lateral displacements of the top and bottom slabs, but the grillage is unable to take account of this because of its two-dimensional limitation.

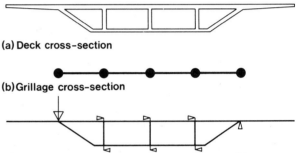

(a) Deck cross-section

(b) Grillage cross-section

(c) Plane frame for assessing transverse shear stiffness
GRILLAGE REPRESENTATION OF SLOPING WEB BOX

In the case of a deck having a cross-section that incorporates non-rectangular cells, the "equivalent shear area" for the transverse members cannot be assessed properly by means of Equation 7.

The solution may be approached on the basis of portraying the cross-section as a plane frame, applying a uniform shearing force across the full width of the frame and equating the resulting shear deformation to

$$S = \frac{A_s G \omega_s}{l} \qquad (9)$$

In the case of a cellular deck with circular voids an assessment can be made by replacing the circles by an equivalent rectangle.

Relative stiffness of shaped voids demonstrated by foam-plastics models.

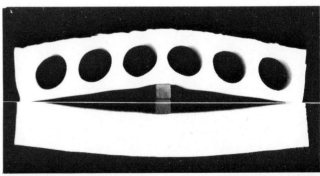

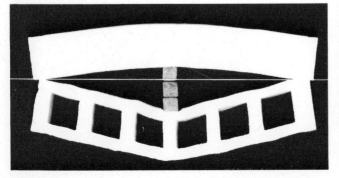

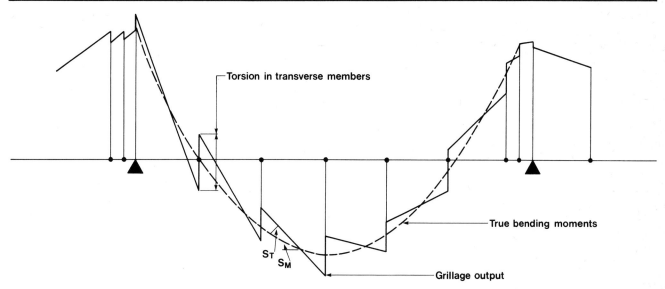

Design shear = Bending S_M + Torsion S_T
= Grillage output

(a) PART OF GRILLAGE BENDING-MOMENT DIAGRAM FOR LONGITUDINAL MEMBER

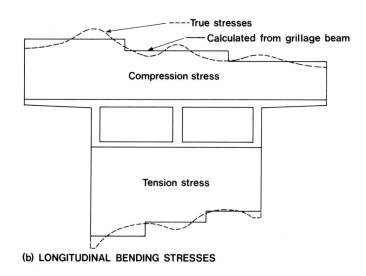

(b) LONGITUDINAL BENDING STRESSES

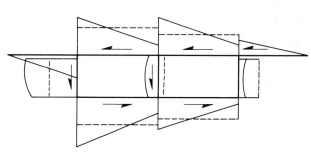

(e) COMBINED SHEAR FLOW (c+d)

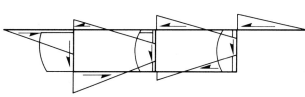

(c) BENDING SHEAR FLOW

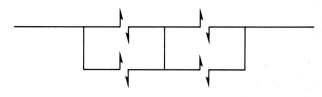

(f) TRANSVERSE SHEAR FORCES DISTRIBUTED TO TOP AND
BOTTOM SLABS IN PROPORTION TO STIFFNESSES

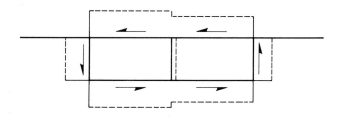

(d) TORSION SHEAR FLOW

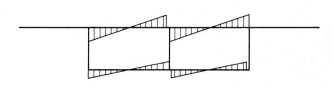

(g) SLAB TRANSVERSE MOMENTS FROM SHEAR FORCES (f)

HAMBLY, E. C. *Bridge deck behaviour*. London, Chapman Hall, 1976. pp. 272.

HAMBLY, E. C. and PENNELLS, E. Grillage analysis applied to cellular bridge decks. *The Structural Engineer*. Vol. 53, No. 7. July 1975. pp. 267–275.

CUSENS, A. R. *Load distribution in concrete bridge decks*. London, Construction Industry Research and Information Association. December 1974. Report 53. pp. 38.

CUSENS, A. R. and PAMA, R. P. *Bridge deck analysis*. London, Wiley-Interscience, 1974. pp. 278.

BEST, B. C. *Methods of analysis for slab-type structures*. London, Construction Industry Research and Information Association. December 1974. Technical Note 62. pp. 96.

MAISEL, B. I. and SWANN, R. A. *The design of concrete box spine-beam bridges*. London, Construction Industry Research and Information Association. November 1974. Report 52. pp. 52.

MAISEL, B. I., ROWE, R. E. and SWANN, R. A. Concrete box girder bridges. *The Structural Engineer*. Vol. 51, No. 10. October 1973. pp. 363–376. Discussion: Vol. 52, No. 7. July 1974. pp. 257–272.

WEST, R. *Recommendation on the use of grillage analysis for slab and pseudo-slab bridge decks*. Wexham Springs, Cement and Concrete Association, 1973. pp. 24. Advisory Publication 46.017.

TERRINGTON, J. S. *Combined bending and torsion of beams and girders*. London, British Constructional Steelwork Association, 1970. pp. 132. Publication No. 31.

SAWKO, F. Recent developments in the analysis of steel bridges using electronic computers. *Proceedings of the Conference on Steel Bridges*. London, British Constructional Steelwork Association, 1968. pp. 39–48.

CHAPMAN, J. C. and TERASZKIEWICS, J. S. Research on composite construction at Imperial College. *Proceedings of the Conference on Steel Bridges*. London, British Constructional Steelwork Association, 1968. pp. 49–58.

JONES, L. L. and WOOD, R. H. *Yield-line analysis of slabs*. London, Thames and Hudson/Chatto and Windus, 1967. pp. 405.

ROWE, R. E. *Concrete bridge design*. London, Applied Science Publishers, 1962. pp. 372.

MORICE, P. B. and LITTLE, G. *The analysis of right bridge decks subjected to abnormal loading*. London, Cement and Concrete Association. July 1956. Db 11. pp. 43. Publication No. 46.002.

ROBINSON, K. E. *The behaviour of simply supported skew bridge slabs under concentrated loads*. London, Cement and Concrete Association. November 1959. Research Report 8. pp. 184. Publication No. 41.008.

MEHMEL, A. and WEISE, H. *Model investigation on skew slabs on elastically yielding point supports*. London, Cement and Concrete Association. December 1963. Library Translation 123. pp. 88. Publication No. 61.123.

RÜSCH, H. and HERGENRÖDER, A. *Influence surfaces for moments in skew slabs*. London, Cement and Concrete Association, 1964. pp. 174. Publication No. 624.073.

MORICE, P. B., LITTLE, G. and ROWE, R. E. *Design curves for the effects of concentrated loads on concrete*. London, Cement and Concrete Association. August 1955. pp. 29. Publication No. 42.202.

CHAPTER 9

Electronic calculators

The use of computers to undertake calculations is usually associated with the need to process large quantities of numerical data, as in the case of accounting systems, or to carry out complex mathematical manipulations using large quantities of data. For these reasons, in the initial development of computers much emphasis was placed on size and speed of operation. The complexity of the equipment and its mode of operation tended to restrict the use of computers to large problems only, where it was economic to make use of staff with very specialized knowledge of computer systems. However, computer languages have now become more orientated towards the non-specialized user, making computerized calculation increasingly attractive for certain types of engineering problems. Even so, this has generally been restricted to a basic structural analysis for a bridge deck, for example, rather than the normal routines of engineering calculations.

One inherent disadvantage in using a computer is the inevitable delay between preparing the data relating to the problem and getting the result. Many organizations employ the basis of sending data away to a computer bureau and are thus inevitably subjected to postal and processing delays before the answers are received. Another point is that programs available through bureaux have generally been designed for widespread use or to tackle a series of associated problems, and a particular program is therefore inevitably not written with the specific needs of an individual user in mind. Indeed, in some instances, programs leave much to be desired in terms of convenience for the user.

The increasing popularity in the use of terminals that are linked from remote points to a single computer, on a time-sharing basis, has removed some of the delay in processing results, but available programs are still of the generalized type with the inevitable limitations that this imposes. The opportunity to write specific programs is available when such terminals are used, but in practice this is not an attractive proposition for anything more complex than minor calculations. Also the bulk of the data that must be entered can often require long periods of time to be spent at the terminal by personnel whose training and skills would be better used in other ways.

Desk-top computers are now reaching levels of capability which make them adequate to process many of the calculating requirements of a design office. The first reaction may be to feel that a desk-top computer is therefore expected to carry out those analytical tasks previously undertaken by equipment remote from the office. However, the time required to prepare programs to deal with problems of such magnitude, and the potential restrictions imposed by the limited capacity of desk-top machines, can make that approach difficult. A better way to utilize such a machine is to explore the potential of having at hand equipment that is capable of dealing with programs specifically written to tackle the problems encountered within a particular office, and to present the results in a format convenient to that office. One advantage of a programmed calculation is that it gives output of a consistent format, however many times the calculations are carried out, whereas hand calculations may tend to become rather sketchy after a number of repetitions. Simple diagrams can also be created as part of the output, as aids to the interpretation of results or to check the input data.

In this way the desk-top calculator represents a computer which can be made to handle problems in the way that we choose, rather than one that has to take advantage of whatever facilities happen to exist, as is the case with bureaux programs. Data can be stored as a problem progresses, and re-entered or modified for subsequent stages in processing a problem. Methods of entering data to run a program can be modelled to suit the particular needs of the user. A certain interaction between the machine and the user can be established by arranging for the input data to be called for by a series of questions from the machine, rather expecting the user to be schooled in a particular sequence and format for entering data. This can be an aid to intelligent thought as the calculations proceed, as opposed to the blind entering of digits in a mechanical sequence.

Given these facilities, decisions must be made as to what types of problem should best be computerized to give the maximum productive benefits. To be beneficial, a program must deal with calculations which either involve a great deal of repetition (so that the machine relieves the engineer from the tedium of repetitive arithmetical calculations), or of a complexity not readily dealt with by hand.

Because design involves a large element of trial and error, there is ample scope for relieving the designer of the tedium of repetitive calculation. For example, in designing a prestressed concrete beam it is necessary to calculate the stresses in various sections at all stages of loading. In

Individual results plotted to scale

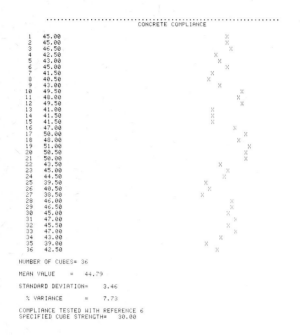

Statistical analyses of concrete Cube results and their comparison with various specifications is readily carried out by computer.
Presenting results graphically makes interpretation easier and aids the identification of trends in strength which may call for remedial action.

"Cumulative sum" plots

Histogram of

Figure 16. Concrete cube results.

Pier loading

```
.............................................................
                    CALCULATIONS

    ↑   +Y
    !
    !       +MY
    .----->
    . !
   -!-
    !            +DY
        FY ↑  +HY
    !
    !
    !<--- --- --- X --- --- --->!
    !-----------------!
    !                 !
    !     +           !        V  (+VE = COMPRESSION)
    !     1           ! - - - - *
    !                 !
    !                 !     FX
    !                 !    ----->
    !                 !     +DX
    !                 ! Y   +HX
    !                 !
    !     +           !      ↑ +MX
   -X --- --O----------!--- ---!-!----> +X
   <- - -!O-----------------!--- --- --!--->
    !                   !. .
    V  -Y
```

```
COORDS.          IN M
DISPLACEMENTS IN MM
FORCES           IN MN
MOMENTS          IN MN.M
ALL LOADING DATA GIVEN IN TERMS OF : SYMBOL,VALUE (EG: MX,0.97)

PIER DIMENSIONS  0.600  *  5.500  M

LEVEL AT COLUMN FOOT  = 10.000  M
LEVEL AT COLUMN TOP   = 15.500  M
```

For a simply-shaped reinforced concrete member, calculations can be extended beyond analysis of stresses in the section, to assessing the detailed reinforcement requirements and the associated reinforcement schedule.

Diagrammatic reinforcement layout

```
.............................................................
                    CALCULATIONS

    PIER WITH 4.12    % REINFORCEMENT
        ---------------
   1    !  . . . . .
        ! . 444
        ! .
        ! .
   2    ! . 444
        ! .
   3    ! . 444
        ! .
        ! . . . . .
        ! .
   4    ! . 444
        ! .
   5    ! . 444
        ! . . . . .
        ! .
        ! .
        ! .
        ! .
        ! .
   6    ! . 444
        ! .
   7    ! . 444
        ! . . . . .
        ! .
        ! .
        ! .
        ! .
        ! .
        ! .
   8    ! . 444
        ! .
   9    ! . 444
        ! . . . . .
        ! .
        ! .
```

Figure 17. Plate pier design.

Program listing

```
1040 MAT P=ZER
1050 K1=B*D↑3/12
1060 K2=D*B↑3/12
1070 FORMAT 8X,2F9.3
1080 FORMAT 8X,2F8.3
1090 DISP "LEVEL AT COLUMN FOOT";
1100 INPUT L1
1110 PRINT TAB8"LEVEL AT COLUMN FOOT    ="L1"M"
1120 DISP "LEVEL AT COLUMN TOP";
1130 INPUT L2
1140 PRINT TAB8"LEVEL AT COLUMN TOP     ="L2"M"
1150 DISP "PINNED AT TOP";
1160 INPUT L3
1170 PRINT
1180 STANDARD
1190 N=J=1
1200 IF L3=0 THEN 1230
1210 DISP "NUMBER OF BEARINGS";
1220 INPUT N
1230 FOR I=1 TO N
1240 X2=B/2
1250 Y2=D/2
1260 P[4]=2+4*L3
1270 GOSUB 20
1280 IF L3=0 THEN 1380
1290 PRINT TAB8"BEARING"I
1300 DISP "COORDS OF BEARING: X , Y     M";
1310 INPUT P[1,I],P[2,I]
1320 WRITE (15,1080)"COORDS OF BEARING    "P[1,I];P[2,I]
1330 X2=P[1,I]
1340 Y2=P[2,I]
1350 DISP "FRICTION COEFFICIENTS:FX,FY";
1360 INPUT P[4,I],P[3,I]
1370 WRITE (15,1080)"FRICTION COEFFICIENTS"P[4,I];P[3,I]
1380 DISP "DEAD LOAD , ADDED D.L.";
1390 INPUT P[5,I],P[6,I]
1400 WRITE (15,1070)"DEAD LOAD :"P[5,I]
1410 WRITE (15,1070)"ADDED D.L.:"P[6,I]
1420 PRINT
1430 S=P[5,I]+P[6,I]
1440 GOSUB 2490
1450 NEXT I
1460 X2=B/2
1470 S=B*D*0.024*(L2-L1)
1480 Y2=D/2
1490 GOSUB 2520
1500 FOR I=7 TO 12
1510 FOR J=2 TO 6
1520 P[I,J]=P[I,1]
1530 NEXT J
1540 NEXT I
1550 P[4]=2
1560 GOSUB 20
1570 PRINT TAB8"WHEN DATA COMPLETE PRESS SPECIAL FUNCTION KEY F4-END DATA"
1580 PRINT
1590 J=0
1600 J=J+1
1610 IF J#7 THEN 1640
1620 J=J-1
1630 GOTO 2470
1640 I=0
1650 P[4]=3
1660 GOSUB 20
1670 PRINT
1680 PRINT TAB10"LOADCASE"J
1690 PRINT
1700 I=I+1
1710 DISP "LOAD DATA"I"SYMBOL , VALUE";
1720 INPUT A$
1730 IF A$="999999" THEN 2440
1740 A1=POS(A$,",")
1750 P[4]=1
1760 GOSUB 20
1770 S=VAL(A$[A1+1])
```

123

Data input for one span

```
.............................................................
                        CALCULATIONS

BEAM LOADING
============

  LOAD CODES
  ----------

      1.  UDL ALL SPANS
      2.  DISTRIBUTED LOADS
      3.  TRAPEZOIDAL LOADS
      4.  POINT LOADS
      5.  APPLIED MOMENTS
      6.  SETTLEMENTS

  TYPE 2 LOADING
  --------------

                        WWWWWWW
          ---------------------------------------
          ↑                          ↑
          *-   A   -*-   B   -*

     SPAN 5    W =   0.032   A =   0.000   B =  24.450

  TYPE 4 LOADING
  --------------

                       ! P
                       V
          ---------------------------------------
          ↑                          ↑
          *-   A   -*

     SPAN 5    P =   0.120   A =  12.000

  SUP.    SHEAR LH      SHEAR RH      MOMENT        REACTION
  ----    --------      --------      ------        --------

    1      0.000        -0.003         0.000         0.00255
    2     -0.003         0.007         0.031        -0.00960
    3      0.007        -0.018        -0.102         0.02554
    4     -0.018         0.066         0.341        -0.08411
    5      0.066        -0.450        -1.255         0.51584
    6      0.440        -0.049        -1.157         0.48877
    7     -0.049         0.000         0.000        -0.04881
```

Program listing (part)

```
320 FOR N=1 TO C
330 DISP "ENTER LENGTH OF SPAN"N;
340 INPUT D[N,56]
350 PRINT TAB12"SPAN"N" = "D[N,56]
360 PRINT
370 NEXT N
380 F[4]=3
390 GOSUB 1470
400 PRINT TAB10"CROSS-SECTIONS"
410 PRINT TAB10"--------------"
420 PRINT
430 GOSUB 1270
440 FOR N=1 TO C
450 DISP "IS SPAN"N"PRISMATIC";
460 INPUT X
470 IF X=0 THEN 630
480 DISP "ENTER I,A,N/A,ZT,ZB FOR SPAN"N;
490 INPUT D[N,1],D[N,12],D[N,23],D[N,34],D[N,45]
500 FOR I=1 TO 45 STEP 11
510 FOR J=1 TO 10
520 D[N,I+J]=D[N,I]
530 NEXT J
540 NEXT I
550 F[4]=2
560 GOSUB 1470
570 IF F[3]#F[4] THEN 590
580 GOSUB 1270
590 WRITE (15,600)N,D[N,1],D[N,12],D[N,23],D[N,34],D[N,45]
600 FORMAT 13X,F2.0,3X,"P",5F10.3
610 PRINT
620 GOTO 740
630 F[4]=12
640 GOSUB 1470
650 IF F[3]#F[4] THEN 670
660 GOSUB 1270
670 FOR I=1 TO 11
680 DISP "ENTER I,A,N/A,ZT,ZB FOR POINT"I;
690 INPUT D[N,I],D[N,I+11],D[N,I+22],D[N,I+33],D[N,I+44]
700 WRITE (15,710)N,I,D[N,I],D[N,I+11],D[N,I+22],D[N,I+33],D[N,I+44]
710 FORMAT 13X,F2.0,1X,F3.0,5F10.3
720 NEXT I
730 PRINT
740 NEXT N
750 DISP "ENTER YOUNG'S MODULUS";
760 INPUT E
770 F[4]=2
780 GOSUB 1470
790 PRINT
800 PRINT TAB10"YOUNG'S MODULUS FOR THE BEAM ="E
810 GOTO 1000
820 G=1
830 GOTO 870
840 G=2
850 GOTO 870
860 G=3
870 DISP "WANT TO DELETE A LOAD CASE";
880 INPUT X
890 IF X=0 THEN 1000
900 FOR N=1 TO 20
910 TRANSFER L[N,1] TO X$[1,20]
920 IF X$[1,1]=" " THEN 980
930 DISP "DELETE "X$[1,20];
940 INPUT X
950 IF X=0 THEN 980
960 X$[1,20]=" "
970 TRANSFER X$[1,20] TO L[N,1]
```

Figure 18. Continuous beam.

Specimen stress output

```
.............................................................
                        CALCULATIONS
                 TRANSFER STRESS SPAN 3

POINT  BTM                                            TOP

   1    8.608          !        B*********T          18.959
   2   12.948          !          B**T               16.129
   3   16.935          !        T*****B               11.241
   4   18.113          !        T********B             7.811
   5   17.352          !       T*********B             6.190
   6   16.949          !       T*********B             5.654
   7   17.519          !       T**********B            6.001
   8   18.691          !       T***********B           7.407
   9   17.977          !         T******B             10.801
  10   14.286          !            B+T               15.938
  11   10.338          !        B********T            18.768

                 TRANSFER STRESS SPAN 4

POINT  BTM                                            TOP

   1    9.076          !        B*********T          18.542
   2   13.417          !          B**T               15.636
   3   17.937          !        T******B              9.956
   4   19.007          !       T***********B          5.985
   5   17.396          !       T***********B          4.118
   6   16.755          !      T***********B            3.151
   7   17.215          !       T***********B           3.064
   8   18.775          !       T**************B        3.951
   9   20.937          !        T**************B       6.064
  10   19.256          !          T*******B           10.598
  11   16.169          !            T*B               14.388
```

Schedule page

```
..........................................................
      BENDING SCHEDULES TO BS 4466:1969-ALL DIMENSIONS MM
   !    !    !            !    !    !
 BAR!TYPE!N  U  M  B  E  R ! CUT !SHPE!    D I M E N S I O N S
MARK!&DIA!MEMS!PER.M!TOTAL !LENGTH!CODE!  A      B      C      D    E/R

PIERS & FOUNDATIONS NORTH BRIDGE

1001!Y 10!  1!  19!  19!  8750! 86 !  1175   150    350

2501!Y 25!  1!  48!  48!  6575! 38 !   400  5900

3201!Y 32!  1!  48!  48!  6550! 38 !   400  5900

3202!Y 32!  1!  23!  23!  6525! 37 !   600

3204!Y 32!  1!  11!  11!  2025! 37 !   600

4001!Y 40!  1!  23!  23!  5500! 37 !   600

2001!Y 20!  1!   6!   6!  3050! 83 !   600  1100   225

MEMBER WEIGHT SUMMARY...KG.

DIA:   10    20    25    32    40
  Y:  103    45  1216  3073  1248    TOTAL:  5685
  R:    0     0     0     0     0    TOTAL:     0

PIERS & FOUNDATIONS SOUTH BRIDGE

1001!Y 10!  1!  19!  19!  8750! 86 !  1175   150    350

2501!Y 25!  1!  48!  48!  6575! 38 !   400  5900

3201!Y 32!  1!  48!  48!  6550! 38 !   400  5900

3202!Y 32!  1!  23!  23!  6525! 37 !   600

3203!Y 32!  1!  11!  11!  2250! 37 !   600

4001!Y 40!  1!  23!  23!  5500! 37 !   600

2001!Y 20!  1!   6!   6!  3050! 83 !   600  1100   225

MEMBER WEIGHT SUMMARY...KG.

DIA:   10    20    25    32    40
  Y:  103    45  1216  3089  1248    TOTAL:  5701
  R:    0     0     0     0     0    TOTAL:     0
```

The preparation of reinforcement bending schedules involves a great deal of simple arithmetic. Most people find this tedious, and the level of accuracy in their work can be poor as a result.

Programmed calculations for cut length of bars, and for summing weights of bars under the various headings required in Bills of Quantities, can relieve much of this tedium, and give more reliable results. This is only worthwhile where the program produces printed schedules in a format which can be issued direct to the site.

Weight summary

```
..............................................................
      BENDING SCHEDULES TO BS 4466:1969-ALL DIMENSIONS MM



              SUMMARY OF WEIGHT OF BARS IN SCHEDULE...TONNES
   BAR DIA:      10      20      25      32      40

   HIGH YIELD STEEL....STRAIGHT BARS:
   <12M   LONG:  0.000   0.000   0.000   0.000   0.000    TOTAL:  0.000
   12-15M LONG:  0.000   0.000   0.000   0.000   0.000    TOTAL:  0.000
   >15M   LONG:  0.000   0.000   0.000   0.000   0.000    TOTAL:  0.000

   HIGH YIELD STEEL....BENT BARS:
   <12M   LONG:  0.205   0.090   2.432   6.162   2.496    TOTAL: 11.386
   12-15M LONG:  0.000   0.000   0.000   0.000   0.000    TOTAL:  0.000
   >15M   LONG:  0.000   0.000   0.000   0.000   0.000    TOTAL:  0.000

   MILD STEEL....STRAIGHT BARS:
   <12M   LONG:  0.000   0.000   0.000   0.000   0.000    TOTAL:  0.000
   12-15M LONG:  0.000   0.000   0.000   0.000   0.000    TOTAL:  0.000
   >15M   LONG:  0.000   0.000   0.000   0.000   0.000    TOTAL:  0.000

   MILD STEEL....BENT BARS:
   <12M   LONG:  0.000   0.000   0.000   0.000   0.000    TOTAL:  0.000
   12-15M LONG:  0.000   0.000   0.000   0.000   0.000    TOTAL:  0.000
   >15M   LONG:  0.000   0.000   0.000   0.000   0.000    TOTAL:  0.000


        TOTAL REINFORCEMENT ON THIS SCHEDULE =    11.386 TONNES
```

Figure 19. Bending schedules.

Data check

```
...........................................................
                         GRILLAGE

YOUNGS MODULUS = 31800

MEMBER PROPERTIES
  NO   END 1 END 2     L        SIN       COS      GC/E         I
```

NO	END 1	END 2	L	SIN	COS	GC/E	I
1	1	2	1.89400	0.00000	1.00000	0.0056840	0.0174740
2	2	3	1.89400	0.00000	1.00000	0.0056840	0.0174740
3	3	4	1.89400	0.00000	1.00000	0.0056840	0.0174740
4	4	5	1.89400	0.00000	1.00000	0.0056840	0.0174740
5	5	6	1.89400	0.00000	1.00000	0.0056840	0.0174740
6	6	7	1.89400	0.00000	1.00000	0.0056840	0.0174740
7	8	9	1.89400	0.00000	1.00000	0.0159540	0.0255880
8	9	10	1.89400	0.00000	1.00000	0.0159540	0.0255880
9	10	11	1.89400	0.00000	1.00000	0.0159540	0.0255880
10	11	12	1.89400	0.00000	1.00000	0.0159540	0.0255880
11	12	13	1.89400	0.00000	1.00000	0.0159540	0.0255880
12	13	14	1.89400	0.00000	1.00000	0.0159540	0.0255880
13	15	16	1.89400	0.00000	1.00000	0.0159540	0.0255880
14	16	17	1.89400	0.00000	1.00000	0.0159540	0.0255880
15	17	18	1.89400	0.00000	1.00000	0.0159540	0.0255880
16	18	19	1.89400	0.00000	1.00000	0.0159540	0.0255880
17	19	20	1.89400	0.00000	1.00000	0.0159540	0.0255880
18	20	21	1.89400	0.00000	1.00000	0.0159540	0.0255880
19	22	23	1.89400	0.00000	1.00000	0.0159540	0.0255880
20	23	24	1.89400	0.00000	1.00000	0.0159540	0.0255880
21	24	25	1.89400	0.00000	1.00000	0.0159540	0.0255880
22	25	26	1.89400	0.00000	1.00000	0.0159540	0.0255880
23	26	27	1.89400	0.00000	1.00000	0.0159540	0.0255880
24	27	28	1.89400	0.00000	1.00000	0.0159540	0.0255880
25	29	30	1.89400	0.00000	1.00000	0.0159540	0.0255880
26	30	31	1.89400	0.00000	1.00000	0.0159540	0.0255880
27	31	32	1.89400	0.00000	1.00000	0.0159540	0.0255880
28	32	33	1.89400	0.00000	1.00000	0.0159540	0.0255880
29	33	34	1.89400	0.00000	1.00000	0.0159540	0.0255880
30	34	35	1.89400	0.00000	1.00000	0.0159540	0.0255880
31	36	37	1.89400	0.00000	1.00000	0.0159540	0.0255880
32	37	38	1.89400	0.00000	1.00000	0.0159540	0.0255880
33	38	39	1.89400	0.00000	1.00000	0.0159540	0.0255880
34	39	40	1.89400	0.00000	1.00000	0.0159540	0.0255880
35	40	41	1.89400	0.00000	1.00000	0.0159540	0.0255880
36	41	42	1.89400	0.00000	1.00000	0.0159540	0.0255880
37	43	44	1.89400	0.00000	1.00000	0.0159540	0.0255880
38	44	45	1.89400	0.00000	1.00000	0.0159540	0.0255880
39	45	46	1.89400	0.00000	1.00000	0.0159540	0.0255880
40	46	47	1.89400	0.00000	1.00000	0.0159540	0.0255880
41	47	48	1.89400	0.00000	1.00000	0.0159540	0.0255880
42	48	49	1.89400	0.00000	1.00000	0.0159540	0.0255880
43	50	51	1.89400	0.00000	1.00000	0.0159540	0.0255880
44	51	52	1.89400	0.00000	1.00000	0.0159540	0.0255880
45	52	53	1.89400	0.00000	1.00000	0.0159540	0.0255880

The limited capacity of desk top computers restricts their ability to deal with complex structural analysis, but a machine with 4K words storage has proven capable of dealing with a grillage, or plane frame, of about 100 nodes.

Displacements

```
...........................................................
                         GRILLAGE
                                       SPRING LOADS
```

JOINT NO.	X-ROTATION (RADIANS)	Y-ROTATION (RADIANS)	VERTICAL DEFLEXION	X-ROTATION MOMENTS	Y-ROTATION MOMENTS	VERTICAL FORCE
1	0.0003537	-0.0006339	0.0000103	0.00000	0.00000	0.01048 *
2	0.0004222	-0.0005210	-0.0010886			
3	0.0003865	-0.0002727	-0.0018423			
4	0.0002577	0.0000353	-0.0020663			
5	0.0000731	0.0003124	-0.0017329			
6	-0.0001081	0.0004901	-0.0009699			
7	-0.0002352	0.0005432	0.0000103	0.00000	0.00000	0.01047 *
8	0.0003703	-0.0007258	-0.0000396	0.00000	0.00000	-0.04034
9	0.0004369	-0.0005951	-0.0013192			
10	0.0004012	-0.0003099	-0.0021927			
11	0.0002680	0.0000447	-0.0024479			
12	0.0000767	0.0003631	-0.0020468			
13	-0.0001142	0.0005616	-0.0011507			
14	-0.0002514	0.0006135	0.0000168	0.00000	0.00000	-0.01715
15	0.0004120	-0.0008405	-0.0000603	0.00000	0.00000	-0.06155
16	0.0004892	-0.0006896	-0.0015467			
17	0.0004519	-0.0003608	-0.0025643			
18	0.0003009	0.0000508	-0.0028662			
19	0.0000826	0.0004222	-0.0024021			
20	-0.0001388	0.0006532	-0.0013592			
21	-0.0003031	0.0007103	-0.0000389	0.00000	0.00000	-0.03966
22	0.0004707	-0.0009646	-0.0000761	0.00000	0.00000	-0.07762
23	0.0005512	-0.0007982	-0.0017928			
24	0.0005121	-0.0004230	-0.0029809			
25	0.0003409	0.0000562	-0.0033411			
26	0.0000870	0.0004909	-0.0028062			
27	-0.0001698	0.0007610	-0.0015918			
28	-0.0003581	0.0008275	-0.0000515	0.00000	0.00000	-0.05256
29	0.0005206	-0.0010816	-0.0000930	0.00000	0.00000	-0.09483
30	0.0005854	-0.0009139	-0.0020395			
31	0.0005442	-0.0004997	-0.0034246			
32	0.0003590	0.0000581	-0.0038647			
33	0.0000716	0.0005678	-0.0032525			
34	-0.0002133	0.0008796	-0.0018461			
35	-0.0004139	0.0009563	-0.0000642	0.00000	0.00000	-0.06548
36	0.0005410	-0.0011600	-0.0001020	0.00000	0.00000	-0.10406
37	0.0005533	-0.0010146	-0.0022219			
38	0.0004828	-0.0005909	-0.0038076			
39	0.0002886	0.0000425	-0.0043636			
40	-0.0000045	0.0006387	-0.0036900			
41	-0.0002858	0.0009931	-0.0020962			
42	-0.0004703	0.0010815	-0.0000802	0.00000	0.00000	-0.08180
43	0.0005268	-0.0011693	-0.0000974	0.00000	0.00000	-0.09932
44	0.0004540	-0.0010573	-0.0022641			
45	0.0003020	-0.0006663	-0.0039663			

Figure 20. Grillage.

Forces

```
...........................................................
                         GRILLAGE
```

MEMBER BETWEEN JOINTS		TORSION	BENDING MOMENTS END 1	END 2	SHEAR VERTICAL
1	2	0.0163844	0.0210824	0.1710610	0.1014420
2	3	0.0290403	-0.1524720	0.2345070	0.0423166
3	4	0.0328629	-0.2362700	0.2418490	0.0029423
4	5	0.0304363	-0.2533310	0.1999780	-0.0281792
5	6	0.0222994	-0.2134340	0.1149450	-0.0520004
6	7	0.0085053	-0.1257480	-0.0045386	-0.0687965
8	9	0.0420495	0.0171755	0.2203890	0.1254520
10	11	0.0800475	-0.2033950	0.3357040	0.0698825
10	11	0.0923729	-0.3277540	0.3594350	0.0167449
11	12	0.0859174	-0.3605080	0.3039310	-0.0298855
12	13	0.0630255	-0.3126540	0.1774950	-0.0713768
13	14	0.0242550	-0.1933110	-0.0103011	-0.1075210
15	16	0.0380441	0.0150788	0.2088310	0.1182440
16	17	0.0786709	-0.1914630	0.3253760	0.0707252
17	18	0.0938535	-0.3158800	0.3559690	0.0211823
18	19	0.0883131	-0.3556340	0.3060550	-0.0261918
19	20	0.0649252	-0.3159800	0.1817390	-0.0708862
20	21	0.0243956	-0.2031450	-0.0140357	-0.1146870
22	23	0.0353562	0.0149162	0.2035000	0.1153460
23	24	0.0768660	-0.1851150	0.3175240	0.0699279
24	25	0.0943673	-0.3075310	0.3510780	0.0229993
25	26	0.0899885	-0.3504860	0.3057230	-0.0236454
26	27	0.0660882	-0.3159020	0.1843470	-0.0695275
27	28	0.0236100	-0.2059420	-0.0130527	-0.1156460
29	30	0.0336027	0.0149610	0.2004960	0.1137840
30	31	0.0752205	-0.1813680	0.3120210	0.0690079
31	32	0.0938987	-0.3020350	0.3461240	0.0232877
32	33	0.0904386	-0.3458550	0.3035540	-0.0223508
33	34	0.0662527	-0.3137600	0.1845990	-0.0682429
34	35	0.0229770	-0.2052340	-0.0115943	-0.1145090
36	37	0.0327336	0.0154415	0.1985230	0.1129890
37	38	0.0739730	-0.1785310	0.3078600	0.0682994
38	39	0.0929429	-0.2977280	0.3417310	0.0232419
39	40	0.0899565	-0.3418090	0.3004900	-0.0218346
40	41	0.0658649	-0.3108110	0.1833780	-0.0673090
41	42	0.0225321	-0.2035920	-0.0109120	-0.1132820
43	44	0.0327171	0.0163739	0.1965770	0.1124470
44	45	0.0731628	-0.1757040	0.3040350	0.0677623
45	46	0.0917771	-0.2938220	0.3373970	0.0230101
46	47	0.0887854	-0.3378500	0.2971190	-0.0215152
47	48	0.0649113	-0.3077270	0.1815420	-0.0666318
48	49	0.0219491	-0.2018460	-0.0107465	-0.1122680
50	51	0.0335018	0.0177634	0.1939200	0.1117980
51	52	0.0727489	-0.1721090	0.2997300	0.0674066
52	53	0.0903752	-0.2893300	0.3327090	0.0229127

126

```
CUMNOR HILL
G BEAM
.................................................................
                        CALCULATIONS

SHEAR IN P S BEAMS TO BE2/73
SECTION CONSIDERED:SUPPORT

MAX SHEARS
  DL SHEAR                                                = 0.356
  HA SHEAR(NOT 112KN WHEELS)                              = 0
  HB OR 112KN WHEELS OR ACCIDENTAL LOAD SHEAR             = 0
  PARASITIC SHEAR                                         = 0
  MAX FACTORED ULTIMATE SHEAR  (1.5DL+2.5HA+P) Q MAX        MN= 0.534

ACTUAL SHEARS
  D.L. SHEAR                                              = 0.356
  HA SHEAR (NOT 112KN WHEELS)                             = 0
  HB OR 122KN WHEELS OR ACCIDENTAL LOAD SHEAR             = 0
  PARASITIC SHEAR                                         = 0
  ACTUAL FACTORED ULTIMATE SHEAR (1.5DL+2.5HA+P) Q          MN= 0.534

COEXISTANT MOMENTS
  D.L. MOMENT                                             = 0
  HA MOMENT(NOT 112KN WHEELS)                             = 0
  HB OR OTHER MOMENTS                                     = 0
  PARASITIC MOMENT                                        = 0
  COEXISTANT MOMENT (1.5DL+2.5HA+P) M                     MNM= 0

BEAM DIMENSIONS
  OVERALL DEPTH OF MEMBER                             D(M)= 1.03
  BREADTH OF MEMBER AT CENTROID                       B(M)= 0.26
  SECOND MOMENT OF AREA                            I(M↑4)= 0.068
  SECTION CENTROID TO EXTREME TENSILE FIBRE           Y(M)= 0.441

PRESTRESS
  EXTREME COMP FIBRE TO CENTROID OF TENDONS          D1(M)= 0.805
  EXTREME COMP FIBRE TO OUTER BARS OR TENDONS        D2(M)= 0.95
  STRESS AT CENTROID DUE SOLELY TO P S          FP(MN/M↑2)= 3.37
  MAX P S AT EXTREME FIBRE                     FEP(MN/M↑2)= 6.56
  VERT COMPONENT OF P S AFTER LOSSES                QP(MN)= 0

CONC AND REINFORCEMENT
  28 DAY CUBE STRENGTH                          UW(MN/M↑2)= 45
  DIAMETER OF STIRRUPS                             DIA(MM)= 16
  NUMBER OF LEGS PER SET                                  = 2
  ANGLE OF STIRRUP                                   ANGLE= 90
  CHARACTERISTIC STRENGTH OF STIRRUP           FYQ(MN/M↑2)= 425


MOMENT JUST SUFFICIENT TO CAUSE A FLEXUAL CRACK     (MN.M)= 1.477

SHEAR CAPACITY OF PLAIN SECTION UNCRACKED IN FLEXURE (MN)= 0.582

SHEAR CAPACITY OF PLAIN SECTION CRACKED IN FLEXURE   (MN)=
78871.142


  PROVIDE  16.000  MM LINKS AT 1838.144   MM CTRS
```

The detailed design of prestressed concrete sections usually involves frequent repetition of routine calculations, which can usefully be programmed in order to maintain consistent presentation of results and arithmetical reliability.

```
BURPHAM LANE BRIDGE
STRESS PICTURE        SUPPORT  3
.................................................................
                        CALCULATIONS

                 -----------------------------
                 !  VALUE   !   STRESSES     !  X-SECTION
                 -----------------------------
                 !          !  TOP  !  BTM   !  A = 7.663
                 -----------------------------  ZT= 1.563
                 !          !       !        !  ZB= 1.362
PRESTRESS        !   10.920 !  1.425!  1.425!
    TOP CABLE    !          !       !       !
FRICTION LOSS    !     8.1% ! -0.115! -0.115!
                 !          !       !       !
ECCENTRICITY     !    0.447 !  2.872! -3.296!
                 !          !-------!-------!
                 !          !  4.182! -1.986!
                 !          !       !       !
PRESTRESS        !   35.490 !  4.631!  4.631!
    BOTTOM CAB   !          !       !       !
FRICTION LOSS    !    10.7% ! -0.497! -0.497!
                 !          !       !       !
ECCENTRICITY     !    0.508 ! 10.291!-11.809!
                 !          !-------!-------!
                 !          ! 18.607! -9.661!
                 !          !       !       !
SELF WT.         !  -12.531 ! -8.017!  9.200!
    DECK SW      !          !-------!-------!
                 !          ! 10.590! -0.461!
                 !          !       !       !
LOSSES           !    13.5% ! -2.506!  1.301!
                 !          !-------!-------!
                 !          !  8.084!  0.840!
                 !          !       !       !
DEAD LOAD        !   -4.633 ! -2.964!  3.402!
    FINISHES     !          !-------!-------!
                 !          !  5.119!  4.242!
                 !          !       !       !
                 !          !       !       !         REVERSE BENDING
                 !          !       !       !!              !       !       !
LIVE LOAD        !    0.201 !  0.129! -0.148!!     -5.512   ! -3.527!  4.047!
    3 LANES HA   !          !-------!-------!!              !-------!-------!
                 !          !  5.248!  4.094!!              !  1.593!  8.289!
                 !          !       !       !!              !       !       !
```

Figure 21. Prestressing calculations.

```
·····················TENDER COMPARISON·····················
     1022      0.00      0.00   5564.48L              0.00   5564.48
```

```
     1023      0.00      0.00   2059.00L              0.00   2059.00
     1024      0.00      0.00   1420.00L              0.00   1420.00
     1025  25000.00H   8987.00L  17128.80             0.00  17128.80
     1026   2000.00L      0.00   6106.00H             0.00   4053.00
*WARNING*2* HIGH RATE  51% ABOVE AVERAGE - SUM DIFFERS BY   2053.00
     1027      0.00    720.00L   4686.00H             0.00   2703.00
*WARNING*2* HIGH RATE  73% ABOVE AVERAGE - SUM DIFFERS BY   1983.00
     1028      0.00      0.00   1541.24L              0.00   1541.24
     1029      0.00      0.00    582.20L              0.00    582.20
     1030      0.00      0.00    426.00L              0.00    426.00
     1031   4500.00L  10093.50  13629.80H             0.00  10093.50
*WARNING*2*  LOW RATE  55% BELOW AVERAGE - SUM DIFFERS BY   5593.50
     1032      0.00      0.00   1207.00L              0.00   1207.00
     1033      0.00    720.00L   3585.50H             0.00   2152.75
*WARNING*2* HIGH RATE  67% ABOVE AVERAGE - SUM DIFFERS BY   1432.75
     1034    250.00L   1220.00  11928.00H             0.00   1220.00
*WARNING*1* HIGH RATE GIVES A SUM  10708.00 ABOVE AVERAGE
     1035      1.00L      1.50      6.15H             0.00      1.50
*WARNING*2* HIGH RATE 310% ABOVE AVERAGE - SUM DIFFERS BY   1395.90
     1036      0.40L      0.60      1.42H             0.00      0.60

     BILL  1   SECTION  1   SUB-TOTALS
           56972.00  39007.50  193707.12             0.00


     BILL  1   TOTALS
           56972.00  39007.50  193707.12             0.00
```

Assessment of tenders is an operation involving extensive, repetitive arithmetic. A program offers consistent accuracy plus item by item comparison between tenders, identifying those items which show differences outside a prescribed range.

```
TORQUAY - PAIGNTON RING ROAD
BILL  8   EDGINSWELL RAIL BRIDGE
·····················TENDER COMPARISON·····················
             8103      4.00     228.39      913.55
             8104      6.00     232.13     1392.80
             8105    579.00      13.20     7642.80
             8106     17.00     616.64    10482.85
             8107     17.00     137.32     2334.41
             8108      1.00      99.00       99.00
                               TOTAL      63615.85
   SECTION 7
             8109   1071.00       1.86     1990.99
             8110     35.00      10.67      373.38
             8111      1.00     104.43      104.43
             8112      1.00    4271.28     4271.28
             8113    225.00      36.44     8197.88
             8114    225.00       4.13      929.25
             8115    923.00       0.98      901.77
             8116    923.00       0.95      872.24
             8117    190.00       8.51     1615.95
             8118    230.00       0.96      219.88
             8119    820.00       7.05     5781.82
             8120    150.00       1.00      150.15
                               TOTAL      25409.02

                          BILL TOTAL     240044.25
```

Figure 22. Tender comparison.

developing the design, adjustments may need to be made to the sectional properties, to the prestressing force and to its eccentricity – even assuming that the moments due to the applied loading were correctly calculated initially. There are other types of calculation where precise analysis can only be approached on a trial-and-error basis, such as evaluating the stresses in a column section that is subject to load which is eccentric about both axes.

Accepting that much design is a matter of trial and error, it is often possible to make the best use of programmed calculations by adopting the approach of analysing a section given by the engineer, rather than by trying to evolve design equations. In some cases it may be possible to prepare a program that incorporates automatic convergance on required output, but in many instances the intervention of the operator will be necessary to move toward the desired solution. Indeed the latter makes better use of the equipment because it means that the design process remains in the control of the engineer, who can then experiment with various solutions.

CHAPTER 10

Economic evaluation

Where the form of construction chosen for each component of a bridge is functional, well proportioned and appropriate for the conditions imposed by the layout and location of the structure, then it is likely that the overall solution is an economic one. The appropriateness of various forms of construction to differing situations and ranges of span is a judgement usually attributed to experience. Economics are a fundamental consideration, and involvement in the design and construction of varying types of structure is the best means of developing a keen sense of their suitability in differing situations. It is not often that a detailed assessment has to be made of the relative cost of alternatives, because most offices have a fund of knowledge from which conclusions can be drawn without the need to resort to specific calculations.

Optimization calculations, whether for material content or for cost, are more commonly a subject for debate in the academic sphere than among practical engineers. It is certainly a waste of effort to carry out lengthy calculations on optimization for component parts within a solution which is itself inappropriate. In most engineering design situations there are myriad practical constraints on the proportions and options open and, in any event, for the design of bridges of small to medium span there is only a limited choice of possible forms of construction.

There is, however, a place for a calculated assessment of the relationship between the cost of alternatives, whether such alternatives are differing constructional forms or for the optimum proportions within a given type of structure.

Some of the most commonly-quoted factors relating to economy can yield disappointing results. It is often stated that contractors prefer methods of construction which are speedy to erect. Once committed to a project the contractor's preferences are likely to be very much orientated in that direction, but this is not to say that he would give the best tender price for the solution which offers the most rapid construction.

Within a highway contract there may well be individual structures which are critical in terms of allowing access through a site, but differences in the overall cost on the project which might result from the delayed or early completion of such a structure are unlikely to be reflected in the costs attributed to it in the bills of quantities so that, even where rapid erection is an important economic factor, evidence to support this may be hard to find.

Great emphasis has been placed at times on the potential economies arising from precasting, but prices obtained against contracts where both precast and cast-in-situ designs have been prepared often suggest a different story from the general climate of opinion at the time.

There are no permanent rules about the comparative costs of differing solutions for construction, because changes take place in the relative cost and availability of labour and materials from one time to another, and developments in constructional techniques or new materials can also make a significant impact.

In the UK alternative designs are seldom produced at the tendering stage. Where this does happen the opportunity has often been created by the original design having been poorly conceived. It is therefore a mistake to base judgements on such incidents without a full knowledge of the circumstances.

There are inevitable difficulties in forecasting the cost of civil engineering works, and these are aggravated during times of economic uncertainty or rapid inflation. Quite apart from the general financial climate of the country, the rates adopted by contractors are obviously influenced by their current work-load, so that keen pricing cannot be expected during a period when the construction industry is heavily committed.

If there are difficulties about forecasting the overall cost of civil engineering works these problems are accentuated when it comes to identifying the cost of component parts within a contract. Costs in tenders submitted by several contractors frequently show marked disparities in the sums of money assigned to individual portions of the work, even where the total tender prices may be comparable. Bridge designers have always been sensitive to this problem because the cost of the bridges is commonly only part of the total cost of a highway project. There may therefore be wide discrepancies between the prices placed against bridgeworks by different competitors, within overall tender prices which may be close. There can also be widely differing rates against measured items on what appears to be comparable work within separate contracts.

A tenderer's policy may involve putting large sums of money against certain sections of the work because they will be completed early and the money thus recouped at an early stage in the contract, or because he anticipates other financial benefits, perhaps as a result of anticipated claims relating to that portion of the work. All such factors can distort data selected from tenders as a basis

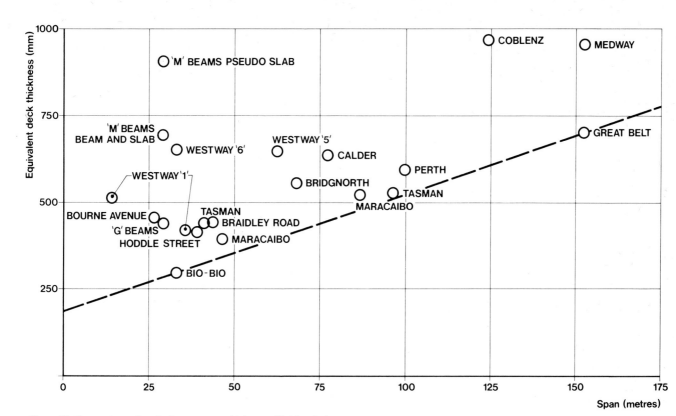

Figure 23. Comparison of equivalent concrete thickness of bridge decks.

for building records of cost information.

Whatever the difficulties may be, however, the problem still remains that the cost must be forecast and the designer has to make decisions about a choice of forms of construction with a view to achieving an economic design.

In order to make valid cost comparisons between alternative solutions there are two important factors to guide any evaluation. These are that comparisons should be made on a common basis, and that significantly varying items should be identified so that they can be examined more closely where necessary. For example, in making a comparison between the relative costs of box construction or of a voided slab, the soffit formwork will represent a substantial proportion of the total cost, but the difference in the cost of the formwork required whichever form of construction is adopted will be negligible. Errors in pricing the soffit formwork will therefore not invalidate

the comparison although they will misrepresent the total cost. On the other hand an error in selecting the correct rate for the reinforcement or the prestressing equipment could seriously distort the picture, and errors in the rate chosen for the concrete would also be significant.

Having identified the significant rates, the degree of sensitivity of the comparison to the sums of money put against them can be established, which usually leads to a sound judgement as to the validity of the comparison. Obviously, the greatest difficulty arises in making comparisons between work that is not similar. A comparison of the difference between deep spread footings in difficult ground and the use of piling, would be sensitive to certain rates which therefore require detailed examination to confirm their reliability.

One must also be alert to the fact that similar items may demand significantly different rates within alternative

---

Length of cable = 80m over anchorages.
Cable size = nineteen 15mm Dyform strand.

Cost of materials:
Strand: 19 × 82m = 1558m
 i.e. 1.715 tonnes @ £250 per tonne = £428.75
Sheath: 80m @ 80 p per m = £ 64.00
Sheath couplers: = £ 3.00
Anchorages: Two @ £60 each = £120.00
Reinforcement spiral (two) = £ 3.00

Cost of plant:
 Dumper transporting materials for 1 hour = £ 3.50

Cost of labour:
 Assemble and fix cable:
 12 hours @ £1.50 per hour = £ 18.00
 ―――――
 £640.25
 20% on-cost = £128.05
 ―――――
Total cost = £768.30

Note: The rates given in the figure are fictitious and are included for illustrative purposes only.

Figure 24. Specimen rate for providing and installing prestressing cable.

solutions. An obvious example is the formwork required to abutment wall construction if the options are between a plain surface for a cantilevered wall, and the shaping required to form counterforts. The rates for the formwork in such cases will be markedly different.

It is also important to identify an appropriate unit for making cost comparisons. It can be misleading to assume idealized conditions when making comparisons between alternatives. Most choices of this kind bring in their wake a number of peripheral issues, some of which may be significant in terms of cost.

It can be very satisfying to produce comparative estimates and to see figures purporting to demonstrate a particular conclusion, but with so many pitfalls involved in forecasting the cost of alternative forms of construction, perhaps the most important aspect of any economic assessment is a proper evaluation of the validity of such figures.

There can be other valuable guidelines to the economy of a form of construction, apart from direct calculations of cost. For example, the content of materials – concrete, reinforcement or prestressing steel – expressed per unit area of bridge deck and plotted against the span in the form of a graph is a useful guideline to economy; such a graph is illustrated in Figure 23.

Data Sheets 77 to 81 give general guidance concerning economic evaluation. Data Sheet 77 is devoted to economic trends when using voided-slab or box decks while the general relationships between span and cost for various types of construction are illustrated on Data Sheet 78. Data Sheet 79 discusses the determination of the economic depth of a voided-slab deck, Data Sheet 80 is devoted to the relative costs of different types of abutment construction, and Data Sheet 81 illustrates the economic trends relating to hollow-abutment construction.

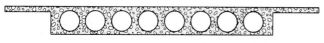

Voided slab

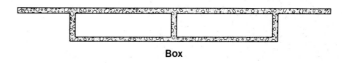

Box

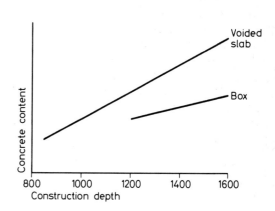

Practical considerations regarding access for striking formwork eliminate box decks of less than 1.2 m deep.

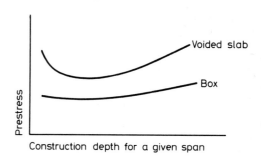

There is an optimum depth for a given span to minimise prestress. Very shallow decks require high prestress.

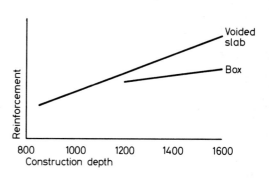

A box with thin walls may require heavy reinforcement to resist local bending, but there is little change with increases in depth.

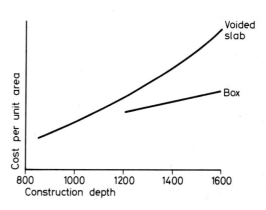

The cost comparison is sensitive to the slenderness of the deck in relation to the span. An actual comparison is therefore necessary for the span under consideration.

The choice of spans is often controlled by the practical constraints of the site. However, for long structures a choice may be possible regarding the number and lengths of individual spans.

The minimum dimensions for a pier are likely to be dictated by the height of the deck above ground level, as well as by the loadings imposed. Because of this the cost of a single pier is relatively insensitive to the span chosen for a high-level bridge deck.

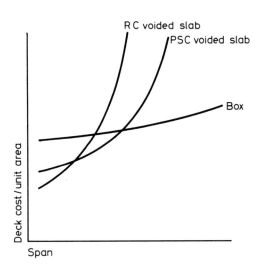

Whatever form of construction is adopted the unit cost per square metre of a bridge deck tends to increase with the span.

If the cost of an individual pier is fairly constant, it is apparent that the total cost of the piers in the substructure will reduce with increases in the span where the structure is sufficiently long to allow options on the number and lengths of spans.

The cost of bridge finishes will be constant, regardless of the span lengths adopted.

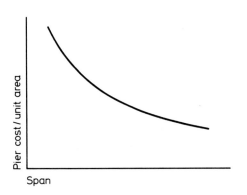

As the span increases, deck unit costs become greater, and pier unit costs become less. The economic choice of spans therefore involves striking a balance between these two factors. Since pier costs are primarily related to height, the economic span increases with the height of the deck above the ground. Where particular factors, such as the speed of construction, have a direct bearing on the cost, they may of themselves influence the economic choice.

For a given span the economic depth for a bridge deck results from balancing the contributive costs of major items.

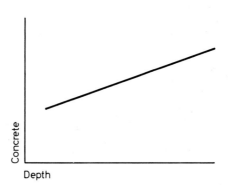

In addition to the direct cost of the concrete, the increased weight on the substructure has some influence on the cost—but this is usually marginal.

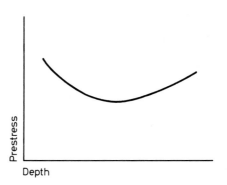

If a very slender deck is adopted, high stresses develop which demand a high prestress. The shallowest deck is not, therefore, the most economical.

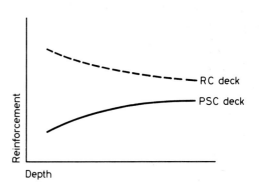

Some details, such as diaphragms, require less steel with greater depths. But the general trend is an increase of steel with depth for a prestressed deck.

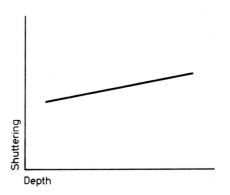

The major item of formwork is the soffit which is only marginally affected by increases in depth, because falsework loadings increase. However, side shutters and void forms obviously increase with increasing depth.

Abutments

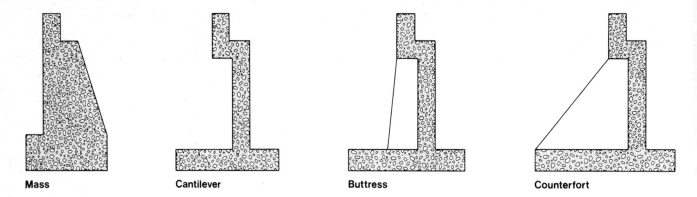

Mass   Cantilever   Buttress   Counterfort

The lower quality of concrete called for in mass concrete construction will attract lower rates.

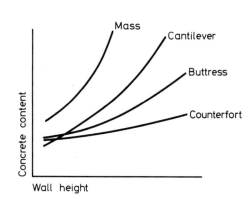

For high walls the reinforcement needed in cantilever construction can become very heavy. There will be differences in the rates between large and small diameter bars.

The more complex shapes needed in counterfort and buttress construction attract higher rates.

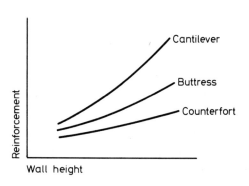

In addition to economic considerations the choice between wall types may be influenced by the speed of construction and practical considerations relating to the concreting of wall sections at a given height—particularly where the standard of finish is important.

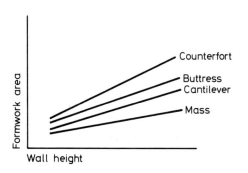

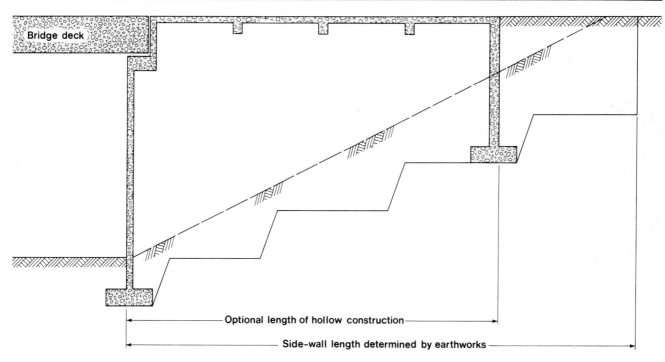

Optional length of hollow construction

Side-wall length determined by earthworks

Where the height of an abutment is great enough to make hollow construction economic, and the length of the side-walls is dictated by ground levels and earthworks shapes, there remains the option for locating the rear wall within the length of the side-walls.

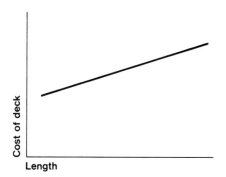

The cost of the deck slab on the abutment is obviously proportional to its area, except that any supports provided within the hollow abutment will be more expensive as their height increases.

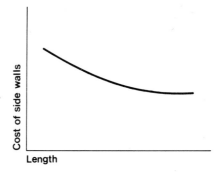

Within the hollow construction the side-walls are simple props, whereas behind the rear wall they act as retaining walls, becoming more expensive with increases in height.

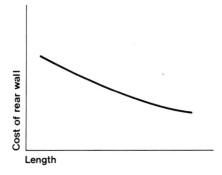

As the rear wall has to retain embankment fill its costs increase markedly with height.

In addition to the above factors earthworks costs also have some influence. The correct balance between these factors to produce an abutment of minimum cost depends on the controlling dimensions and the geometry of the site. There may be instances where the position of the front wall of the abutment is optional, so that the balance of costs between the abutment and the bridge deck construction needs to be included in an economic evaluation.

137

CHAPTER 11

Contract documents

Contract documents consist of drawings, a specification, conditions of contract and bills of quantities. It is also becoming general practice to issue bending schedules to tenderers, which has the effect of giving them the status of part of the contract documents since they then become information on which the contractor bases his tender.

Drawings are the primary vehicle for a designer to communicate his intentions to the people building a structure. It is important that the impression they give is clear, unambiguous and yields the required information without prolonged searches through a maze of apparently randomly assembled details.

The first requirement for a drawing is to define clearly the shape and relative positions of the various components forming a structure and it is often desirable, in the interests of clarity, to separate this from the more-detailed information concerning the reinforcement. Close conformity to the elementary principles of technical drawing in selecting the relative positions for plans, elevations and sections will also assist clear presentation.

The first operation on site is the setting out of the structure with a view to commencing work on the foundations, so that setting-out information is best indicated on the sub-structure layout drawing.

To achieve a clear set of drawings, thought has to be given as to the way in which information is presented, and to arranging the sequence of drawings in relation to the progress of the work. A natural mistake often made in preparing sets of drawings is that they develop by the process of recording the designer's thoughts, and therefore tend to be assembled in a design sequence. On site, the sequence in which information is required is related to the constructional procedure, and a set of drawings needs to be set out with this in mind.

Accepted scales for drawings of civil engineering works are 1:1, 1:2, 1:5, 1:10, 1:20, 1:50, 1:100, 1:200, 1:500, 1:1,250, 1:2,500 and 1:10,560 (i.e. six inches to one mile). Drawing sheet sizes are set out in BS 3429.

Titles for drawings should be helpful and informative. A number of overworked words are used in drawing titles which have probably lost much of their significance. Such words as "details" and "arrangements" have become no more informative than "whatsits" or "doodahs".

Information relating to contract documents is summarized on Data Sheet 82.

Specification

British bridges are built to the "Specification for road and bridgeworks" published by the Department of the Environment (DoE). Additional or modified clauses will be necessary to suit the particular requirements of individual contracts. These are written as revised and supplementary clauses.

For drafting specification clauses two distinctive approaches can be made. The method of working may be stipulated, or a description given of the required end product. Contractors prefer the latter "performance" type of specification because it leaves them freedom of choice in their way of working. A "method" specification does not of itself guarantee the quality of the end product, since it is quite possible to do a job the right way but badly. But in some circumstances an engineer may feel justified in employing method specification in the confidence that it describes one way in which the required end product can be successfully achieved. A performance specification is appropriate when the objective can be clearly defined. To specify the required density of fill after compaction is meaningful – in fact it better defines the end product than does the asking for a set number of passes with a certain-sized roller. The weakness of a performance specification occurs where it may be extremely difficult to describe a standard of quality – like that of a concrete surface. In practice there is then seldom any alternative to persuading a contractor to use methods of proven value to achieve results of the required standard.

Nominated subcontractors

Although it is possible to nominate specific sub-contractors for specialist work it is generally regarded as advisable to avoid doing this since it can cause complications in administering a contract, in the event of a nominated sub-contractor defaulting or causing delay in some other way. Nevertheless there are items where the engineer will wish to restrict the choices made by a main contractor. In these instances it is possible to include in a specification details of acceptable sources of specialist equipment. For example, if the engineer wishes to limit the choice of bridge bearings to be adopted he can send out enquiries to manufacturers before the main tenders are invited, make a selection of specific types of bearing from several suppliers, and include in the documents a schedule of bearings from these several suppliers which may be used. In this way the main contractor is given a choice, commercial competition is maintained, but the difficulty is avoided of having bearings offered by the main contractor from a source which is unknown or of a type which the engineer does not feel best fits the circumstances.

Conditions of contract

The Institution of Civil Engineers published in 1974 the fifth edition of the "General conditions of contract for civil engineering works". These form the usual basis for contract documents in the UK. Where third parties are involved in a contract it is often necessary to include additional conditions to meet their particular requirements. The most common of these parties are the statutory undertakers: electricity, gas, water and telephones. Other public bodies may also be involved, such as British Rail, the National Trust and local authorities.

Bills of quantities

The Department of the Environment has published a method of measuring quantities specifically related to highways contracts: the "Method of measurement for road and bridge works" (MMRB). The initial desire to produce a simplified bill with a small number of items is to be applauded. At the same time the writers strayed from the underlying principle of the "Standard method of measurement for civil engineering quantities", which is based on the initial premise that every item relates to completed work and includes all the materials, labour, plant and other costs involved. The MMRB gives a detailed item coverage for each item within the bill of quantities. If the writing of a particular bill requires the introduction of items not included in the MMRB, then new item coverage has to be written.

The weakness of this system is that it is too easy to overlook detailed factors contributing to the overall cost. In the light of the number of revisions that have already had to be made it is apparent that this has been the case.

A set of contract documents normally includes the following items:

Instructions for Tendering

Location and Brief Description of the Works

Collusive Tendering Certificates

Form of Tender

Forms of Agreement

Form of Bond

Conditions of Contract
    General Conditions of Contract
    Special Conditions of Contract
    Variation of Contract Price
    Noise Control
    Traffic Control
    Diversion of Public Utilities

Special Requirements in relation to:
    Central Electricity Board
    Area Electricity Boards
    British Rail
    National Coal Board
    Post Office
    Area Gas Board
    Area Water Authority
    National Trust
    Navigation Authorities

List of Drawings

Specification
    Reference to Standard Specification
    Additional and Revised Clauses

Bills of Quantities
    Preambles
    Bills
    General Summary

CHAPTER 12

Contract supervision

The brunt of the work involved in supervising the construction of bridgework falls on the Engineer's representative on the site, and it is important that he should have a clear understanding of what is expected in this rôle. The obvious need for previous experience in the practicalities of construction and an appreciation of the design of the structures to be built are not necessarily of themselves sufficient to equip an engineer to fulfill the rôle of Resident Engineer. Specific guidance should be given to the person about to take up the appointment, and a written brief setting out the main functions of the job can be a valuable aid. Obviously no document of this type can be comprehensive, but it may provide a valuable starting point for anyone commencing in such an unfamiliar rôle.

Specific details of the brief should be varied to suit the scope and nature of the work, and the experience of the person appointed. The following notes assume the work consists of a substantially-sized contract involving a resident engineer's staff of Section Engineers, Assistant Engineers and Inspectors.

Resident Engineer's duties

The objective of the Resident Engineer and his staff should be to ensure that the works are completed in accordance with the contract documents, and to keep the Engineer fully informed on all relevant matters. Their basic terms of reference are the specification, contract drawings, conditions of contract and bill of quantities. If these documents are contravened by the contractor or found to be in error, conflict or omission, the Engineer must be referred to for guidance.

The Resident Engineer should plan ahead and discuss future work with the contractor's agent to ensure that the phasing of the works is properly planned to suit the programme. This close collaboration between Resident Engineer and agent may also allow the consideration of design changes proposed by the contractor, and the submission of proposals to the Engineer for his approval.

The principal duties of the Resident Engineer are set out on Data Sheet 83. Many of his responsibilities will inevitably be delegated, wholly or in part, to members of his staff, and they must each be given a clear picture of what is expected of them. The job descriptions set out on Data Sheets 84, 85 and 86 could form the basis for a written brief to be given to each member of the Resident Engineer's staff. These briefs will require writing to suit the actual staffing arrangements on individual contracts.

Training

Resident Engineer's staff are often undertaking this work for a limited period, in order to gain experience of construction. This aspect of the job should not be lost sight of under the pressures of getting the job done. It is important for the individual, for his employers and for the profession as a whole that the experience gained should be of the greatest value. Engineering staff should therefore be given the maximum opportunities to understand, and to partake in, all aspects of administering the contract. Rigid job demarcation is an unnecessary evil in this respect. The functions outlined on Data Sheets 80 to 83 should be regarded as an ordered means of working as a team — not as a strait-jacket — within which a measure of flexibility can be accepted to advantage.

Safety

One area of potential confusion on civil engineering sites is the question of responsibilities regarding safety. Under the civil engineering contract between the contractor and the employer, responsibility for the safety of all operations on the site rests with the contractor. However, this does NOT mean that the Engineer (and hence all the Resident Engineer's staff) have no interest or responsibility in matters of safety. Under the professional contract between the Engineer and the employer, the Engineer has a responsibility to the employer to ensure the safe and expeditious completion of the work. In turn, however, this does NOT mean that the contractor can hand over his responsibility regarding safety to the Engineer.

The adequacy of temporary works, both as regards design and construction, and the adoption of safe methods of working on the contract are of paramount importance.

For the Resident Engineer's staff the implication is that the Resident Engineer must be informed of any case of suspected unsafe working or temporary works. Where prompt action is needed, the guideline should be that work must not be permitted to proceed in a manner considered to constitute a threat to the safety of persons. The Resident Engineer is empowered to stop the job at any time, by issuing the necessary site instruction.

Figure 25. Falsework for bridge deck.

Checking temporary works

The checking of temporary works is done primarily to check the safety of the permanent structures, but the Engineer cannot escape his responsibility for care. He must therefore satisfy himself that the contractor has a well-worked-out scheme, even if he does not actually check the calculations for falsework.

Where detailed checking of complex proposals is necessary, this should be done by the Engineer off the site. Other pressures may be too great for the Resident Engineer's staff to undertake long and careful checking of calculations, to give the approval urgently required by the contractor.

Resident Engineer's reports

The following extract is taken from "Civil engineering procedure".

> Progress reports
> The Engineer will maintain a check on progress through reports submitted to him by the Resident Engineer. These reports must be in a form that will give the Engineer a clear and concise picture of the progress made and the extent to which this is ahead of or behind the contractor's programme; they should be accompanied by such progress charts or diagrams as may be necessary for this purpose. If progress is behind programme on any items of work the report should state the reasons for the delay and the steps which the contractor is taking to remedy matters.

Good handling and minutes of the site meeting will relieve the need for a good deal of verbiage in reports.

In addition to progress, reports should call for any information needed from head office for the contract, and give brief details of any problems, physical, technical or contractual, arising on the job. It should also note visitors to site and any other points of interest to the Engineer.

A written report must be submitted regularly to the Engineer, together with copies of all correspondence with the contractor, of routine test results obtained on site, and of all site instructions issued.

Site meeting

The Resident Engineer should call and take minutes of site meetings at monthly intervals. The general purpose of such site meetings is to provide a regular opportunity for the contractor and the Engineer to monitor jointly the progress of the contract, and to record items of contractual importance or interest. Such meetings are not the occasion for raising or discussing points of detail, and the contractor should be dissuaded from any tendency to do this.

The first site meeting should be used to establish the intended pattern, and to advise everyone of the contribution required of them. The following basic points should be clarified and minuted.

> The contractor's staff structure.
> The levels of communication to be employed (i.e. the acceptance of instructions).
> The contractor's safety officer.
> Agreement as to site levels.
> Written notification for inspections.
> Dayworks. (The Resident Engineer's staff may sign for hours for record purposes, but only the Resident Engineer can sign for payment.)
> Standing orders for material testing.
> Signing of contracts.
> Access to land.

A typical agenda for a site meeting is set out on Data Sheet 87.

Site instructions

All instructions given to the contractor should be confirmed in writing, whether or not they have financial implications. The instructions should be concise and unambiguous. Careless wording can be exploited by a contractor, apart from the possibilities of misunderstanding.

All the relevant references (the drawing number, the specification clauses, the bill item number, and a clear statement of the part of the works affected) should be noted on the instruction. This can save frustrating searching at a later date, when one's memory is blurred.

When the instruction involves extra work not covered by the drawings, the basis for payment should be stated on the instruction: i.e. as dayworks, at existing bill rates, or at rates to be negotiated.

Variation orders

There are significant differences between the practices adopted on building and civil engineering contracts in respect of variation orders.

For civil engineering contracts it is only necessary to issue a variation order for a significant departure from the works as shown on tender drawings, such as the omission or addition of items of work, or for substantial amendments to the quantity of measured work. Such alterations will, in the first instance, be covered by site instructions. The variation order follows as a definition of the financial implications. It should state the measurement and rates applicable for any additional work, arriving at a sum to be included in the final account. It follows, therefore, that the variation order will come after negotiations have taken place on rates for the additional work. Also, new items added to the bill of quantities should be covered by such variation orders.

The Resident Engineer should draft variation orders where they are needed and pass them to the Engineer who issues them.

Methods of working

There are a number of operations during the construction of a bridge where the method of working that is adopted may be critical, not only in terms of ensuring the smooth progress of the work, but also because the soundness of the end product may be prejudiced if a wrong approach is taken. It is normally because of this latter possibility that the Engineer takes a particular interest in the question of the methods of working adopted, since a contractor will himself have progress very much in mind when making his own decisions, and should be at least as well informed as the Engineer on the issue. For example, during excavation there is the possibility of disturbance to the adjoining ground. In particular, when ground-water problems exist either in the form of artesian pressure or a high standing-water table, the Engineer will want to be satisfied that the contractor will deal with this effectively, bearing in mind the fact that the formation could be prejudiced unless appropriate measures are taken.

The methods employed to place the concrete should not only ensure that an appropriate rate of delivery can be achieved but also that the placing and compaction can be controlled. Where high lifts are being carried out within forms, trunking may be necessary to ensure that good access to the point at which the concrete is to be placed

can be maintained. The Engineer should also have played his part by detailing the reinforcement in such a way that such access is possible. A choice also has to be made between the use of immersion or external vibrators.

Prestressing operations may be sensitive to the exact procedure adopted, in terms of making the result compatable with the design calculations, so that the Engineer will be very much concerned with how these operations are carried out. The grouting of prestressing cables is an operation of critical importance to the serviceability of the structure. A subsequent inspection of the results is often impossible and in any event, if defects are found, the problem of suitable remedial action still remains. Close control of the procedure is therefore the only way to ensure a satisfactory result.

Confirmation of the quality of materials fabricated or manufactured off the site is usually undertaken by independent testing houses. This applies to reinforcement, prestressing strand and specialist equipment such as bearing, stressing anchorages and the like.

Approvals

During the currency of a contract, the Engineer must evaluate a number of proposals concerning the contractor's method of dealing with the work, and the materials he intends to use. On commencing the works the contractor is required to produce a programme setting out the sequence in which he intends to tackle the work and giving sufficient details to enable the Engineer to make a reasonable assessment of whether it is in fact an appropriate sequence of operations compatable with constructional requirements and that can reasonably be achieved within the contract period. It may be necessary to ask the contractor to supply additional information about the plant and labour he intends using on those parts of the work where there may be doubt as to the practicability of completing the items within the time assigned within the programme. At this early stage of the contract it is not reasonable to assume that such a programme can be an exact instrument. Physical circumstances may change and the contractor is constantly having to balance available resources of labour, plant and materials against his intended progress, so that it frequently becomes necessary to recast a programme as work proceeds.

The responsibility of the Engineer in examining this initial programme is therefore limited to checking that the contractor's intended sequence in no way conflicts with the requirements of the design, or any restrictions on the contract such as the availability of land, the maintenance of traffic routes through the site, and the phasing of associated work being carried out by, for example, public utilities which may not be under the direct control of the main contractor.

It may be necessary to make clear to the contractor the limited nature of the Engineer's assessment of the programme at this stage. In the event of difficulties arising in the course of the contract, which lead to the disruption of the contractor's working arrangements, negotiations on such questions as an extension of time or compensatory payment may focus on this initial programme. In giving his consent the Engineer may therefore find it prudent to point out to the contractor that this does not bestow on his initial programme the status of a mathematical instrument which might be used to re-evaluate the contract period by the adjustment of variables within the equation.

At the time of submitting his programme, the contractor will usually give some indication of the intended methods of construction he will employ relating to bridges. Whether at this stage or later in the contract, detailed proposals for the falsework and formwork should be submitted for the Engineer's approval. A sensible appraisal of these proposals is of prime importance if the Engineer wishes to retain control over the quality of the finished work. Although in theory, it may be possible to allow a contractor to proceed with the construction of elements of the work and then to make judgements about their finished quality, either accepting or condemning them, it is rarely possible to justify the condemning of a significant item of work and to have it pulled down simply because one is disappointed with the quality. To justify such measures the work usually has to be defective rather than merely disappointing. To ensure the quality of the end product it is necessary to keep abreast of all the contractor's intended ways of working to achieve it, either as regards the temporary works and materials to be incorporated, or the methods of working to be adopted.

The prime requirement for falsework is obviously that it should be stable under the loads which will be imposed on it during construction. Its deformation under load is also important so that the works can be completed to line and level within acceptable tolerances. The basic principles involved in falsework construction are much the same as the structural principles involved elsewhere, but added problems arise from the temporary nature of the structure. Many of the joints are less positive than would be the case in a permanent structure. The alignment of beams seated on scaffolding poles cannot, by the nature of the structure, comply with the same tolerances expected from a connection between beam and column in permanent works. Unhappily it is often the case that where these tolerances are likely to arise the structure is particularly sensitive to variations, but this is not often appreciated by the operatives on site, and is even overlooked quite frequently by falsework designers and engineers.

A high proportion of the failures of falsework are due to oversights in relation to the susceptability of temporary structures to problems of this type. It should be a salutary thought that almost all the failures of bridge structures take place during the period of construction, and that a high proportion of these failures result directly from failures of the falsework.

In examining falsework failures a number of recurring themes arise. The sensitivity of rolled steel I-sections to the buckling of the web under direct load is frequently overlooked. It is often assumed that if a beam of this type is capable of sustaining a certain bending moment and shearing force it is therefore adequate to support the associated loads – a false conclusion. This situation is aggravated by any tendency for the support conditions to produce an eccentricity of load in relation to the axis of the web, a condition quite common in falsework. The remedy is to provide adequate bracing of the member or to introduce web stiffeners at the points of concentrated load or reaction, or both.

The temporary nature of falsework structures means that they are normally supported on improvised foundations. These are liable to settle in most instances, this settlement not necessarily being uniform. For certain types of structure this behaviour may be significant in the way that the loads are distributed within the temporary structure, and local overloading can lead to distortion and even to failure. Fork-heads at the tops of scaffold poles can easily be loaded in an eccentric manner and become susceptible to failure by bending or buckling.

Such details of seatings and connections within falsework are a fruitful field for finding deficiencies to which attention must be paid.

Formwork

In studying proposals for formwork which is intended to provide a high standard of finish, attention needs to be concentrated particularly on the joints, whether they are the joints between adjacent plywood panels, between abutted shutter panels, at corners, or between the forms and the work previously cast. If the resulting concrete is to be sound, without "boney" patches or discoloration, then the formwork must prevent any loss of grout or moisture from the mix during placing. All the joints must therefore be grout-tight and remain so under the vibration that results during the placing and compacting of the concrete. Positive and preloaded connections are necessary to achieve this and the spacing adopted must be such that the panel is stiff enough to resist any deformation between the points at which it is held. If props are used, these must extend back to something which is rigid.

If all these jointing details are given proper attention then the major source of defects will have been taken care of. Provided that the shutter surface is in a reasonable condition, modern release agents are such that difficulties from bad striking are relatively rare nowadays.

Where some form of profiled relief is provided in the surface by planting timber or plywood block-outs on the face of the form, the interface between the making-out pieces and the surface of the form must be sealed to prevent the grout gaining access between the two surfaces. If this is not done, spalling of the concrete edge and a progressive movement of the block-out away from the original face of the form will occur.

The remaining point to consider in order to achieve a satisfactory finish is to make proper arrangements for terminating the height of concrete placed at one time. The inclusion of a grout-check provides a means by which the concrete can be finished off to a clean line. Where the top surface of the concrete being placed is to be a finished surface a grout-check can only be provided as a temporary measure while the concrete is being placed, and must be removed at the end of the operation so that the top surface can be finished with a float. To achieve a good line on this upper surface it is either necessary to use forms made to the true height or, after removing the grout-check, to employ a string line as a guide to which the finisher can work in producing the finished top edge.

Disputes

During the progress of the contract, issues inevitably arise over which the contractor and the Engineer have differing points of view. Such difficulties may take the form of circumstances which the contractor regards as disruptive and not necessarily foreseeable, or requirements for additional work, or delays due to operations outside of the direct control of the contractor, or disputes over the standard of work being produced.

Those responsible for supervision have to decide whether or not a contractor's requests for additional payment or for an extended time for completion are reasonable within the terms of the contract.

The rôle of the Resident Engineer in this respect should be to seek to minimize any areas of disagreement. This task involves clearly identifying those issues over which differences can arise, giving prompt instructions where these are necessary to resolve a difficulty and, where differences still remain, keeping a record of work in progress, instructions issued and discussions between the parties involved.

If the contractor's and the Resident Engineer's staffs are prepared to discuss difficulties as they arise and to seek agreement on the course of action to be taken, then disputes can be minimized. It is usually possible to agree on the course of action needed to resolve a difficulty, even if the question of the responsibility for costs cannot be agreed at the time. But if this spirit of co-operation can be fostered it usually has the effect of paving the way for the easier settlement of claims as well as achieving agreement for physical action on the site.

Where both parties are prepared to agree that it is desirable to minimize areas of dispute, then such interests are usually best served by arranging the maximum personal contact and discussion of issues, prior to the establishment of a written record in the form of correspondence or minutes of discussions. Correspondence without prior discussion generally has the effect of widening any areas of dispute.

An open and constructive approach toward the settlement of differences requires that both parties should be experienced engineers, confident of what they are doing and enjoying the confidence of their superiors. An excessive reliance on correspondence in disputes generally indicates that the parties are more interested in establishing their own positions than in seeking agreement. At worst, this degenerates into an endless debate on the significance of the conditions of contract, leading to the distressing spectacle of those who should be engineers acting out the rôle of amateur lawyers.

The principal routine duties of the Resident Engineer aided, where appropriate, by his staff are as follows.

1. To organise and phase the duties of his staff to suit the construction programme.

2. To supervise the permanent work to ensure that it is executed to the correct line and level, and that the materials and workmanship comply with the specification.

3. To execute or supervise tests carried out at the site, and to inspect materials and manufacture at source other than that which may be carried out by the Engineer's head office staff.

4. To issue instructions and drawings to the Contractor's Agent.

5. To agree departures from the contract documents, in consultation with the Engineer.

6. To draft variation orders and pass them to the Engineer.

7. To keep a diary constituting a detailed history of the work of construction and of significant happenings at the site, and submit regular periodic progress reports to the Engineer.

8. To keep records of inspections, variations, testing, and points of contention.

9. Where the Contractor claims payment for additional work, to agree with the Contractor and record all relevant circumstances, including the cost of labour and materials, seeking agreement on matters of fact before any question of principle has to be decided by the Engineer or an arbitrator.

10. To record and check the progress of the work against the programme.

11. To measure, in agreement with the Contractor's staff, the quantities of work executed, and to check daywork and other accounts for interim and final payments due to the Contractor so that they may be certified by the Engineer.

12. To examine methods proposed by the Contractor for executing the work, and temporary works, to ensure the safe and satisfactory execution of the permanent work.

13. To redesign work to the extent that this may be delegated by the Engineer.

14. To record on drawings prepared for the purpose, the actual level and nature of all foundations, the strata encountered in excavation, and full details of any deviations from the working drawings which have been made during the execution of the work.

15. To observe the behaviour of the finished works, recording movements, settlements, etc.

16. To keep all the Resident Engineer's staff fully informed on matters which may affect their work, including copies of the relevant site instructions and correspondence.

1. To supervise and co-ordinate the activities of the Assistant Resident Engineers, Inspectors and Clerks of Works, to organise them to provide most effective supervision of the contract within agreed policy, and to ensure that their work is of an acceptable standard.

2. To supplement the existing supervision policy in consultation with the staff and the Resident Engineer.

3. To monitor the Contractor's programme for his section, advising the Contractor and the Resident Engineer of potential bottlenecks.

4. To draft site instructions for any required variations from, or in addition to, the contract documents, and to pass them to the Resident Engineer.

5. To agree, for record purposes only, the hours and quantities involved in any part of the works for which the Contractor claims additional payment, and to make recommendations to the Resident Engineer as to whether such payment is due.

6. To draft correspondence and pass to the Resident Engineer.

7. To make a weekly written report to the Resident Engineer.

8. To keep a daily diary of dealings with the Contractor and other items of interest.

9. To inspect and approve foundations before the blinding concrete is placed.

1. To check the correctness of the basic setting-out drawing for the contract relative to existing ground features.

2. To check, by independent calculation and measurement, the setting-out of all parts of the works, to record discrepancies observed and to inform the Section Resident Engineer.

3. To check the level and alignment of the formwork, to record discrepancies and to inform the Section Resident Engineer and the Contractor where these are outside the specified tolerances. When concreting is in progress on piers and walls, to observe the formwork to check for movement.

4. To prepare, in conjunction with an Inspector, a list of any points requiring attention where the Contractor has called for inspection. A copy of this list should be passed to the Section Resident Engineer.

5. To keep records of the setting-out calculations and methods adopted.

6. To mark up prints of the contract drawings with variations made during construction and to pass these to the Resident Engineer.

7. To observe progress, methods, workmanship and materials, and to inform the Section Resident Engineer.

8. To supervise routine testing and to record results.

9. To keep a daily diary of the weather, the setting-out he has checked, any points of contention with the Contractor, and other items of major interest, plus details of his own hours of attendance on the site.

10. To keep other Resident Engineer's staff informed on matters which may influence their work.

11. To report daily, in person, to the Section Resident Engineer.

12. To undertake any other work requested by the Section Resident Engineer.

1. To check the workmanship and materials for conformity with the drawings, specification and site instructions, and to inform the Section Resident Engineer and the Contractor where this is not achieved.

2. To note site instructions and any other relevant directives onto the drawings used in inspection, to ensure that they are taken into account during an inspection.

3. To check the reinforcement against the drawings and to inform the Section Resident Engineer and the Contractor of any discrepancies. This inspection must be carried out prior to the erection of any formwork which would impede access to the steel.

4. To prepare a written list of any points which may require attention, in conjunction with an engineer, where the Contractor has asked for an inspection. To pass the list to the Contractor's foreman. To check that these points have been rectified or agreed before this part of the works is covered (by concreting, erecting formwork, or earthworks as the case may be), unless the Section Resident Engineer advises him that relaxation of requirements has been agreed. A copy of this list should be passed to the Section Resident Engineer.

5. To attend during concreting, to ensure that the workmanship is satisfactory and to observe the formwork. To check the workability of the concrete.

6. To inspect the concrete when the forms are struck, to note any defects and to inform the Section Resident Engineer.

7. To attend operations where full records are required: *e.g.* piling, prestressing, grouting, etc.

8. To check the levels of the foundations after placing the blinding concrete (or earlier if extra digging is involved) and to inform the Section Resident Engineer of any significant discrepancies. To agree levels with the Contractor's Quantity Surveyor where extra digging is involved.

9. To keep a daily diary recording the weather, the work in progress, inspections carried out, concrete placed, movements of key plant, points of special difficulty or contention, other items of special interest, and his own hours of attendance on the site.

10. To note the hours worked on any item designated as daywork, or any other work which may involve extra cost, and to inform the Section Resident Engineer.

11. To note minor variations which may affect payment and to notify the Section Resident Engineer.

12. To record the ground conditions in foundations on the layout drawings.

13. To notify the Section Resident Engineer of any accidents on site, and record these in his diary.

14. To keep record drawings marked with the dates when concreting takes place.

15. To keep a record of the Contractor's staff and the sub-contractors on site.

16. To ensure that general disciplines such as the curing and protection of fresh concrete, the provision for traffic through the site, and safe working conditions are maintained. These can best be kept under control by requiring items in this category to be put in order before inspecting for concreting.

17. To keep other Resident Engineer's staff informed on matters which may affect their work.

18. To report daily, in person, to the Section Resident Engineer.

19. To undertake any other work requested by the Section Resident Engineer.

20. To supervise routine tests where requested.

The agenda for a typical site meeting should be on the following lines:

1.1 Minutes of the previous meeting

These provide an opportunity for anyone to raise points of detail regarding the record of the preceding site meeting, which will have been circulated, and to agree the record.

1.2 Matters arising

To further the progress of any items unresolved previously.

1.3 Agents report

The Contractor should report on the progress achieved since the last meeting, giving reasons for an unexpectedly poor or good performance, and drawing attention to any items which may affect future performance relative to the programme. His report should also give details of:

1. The labour and principal plant on the site, together with the changes planned for the coming month.

2. Any changes in site staff (from Section Foreman and Section Engineers upward).

3. The names of sub-contractors to be employed on any part of the works, together with a description of the work they are to undertake.

4. Any claims for additional payment not accepted by the Resident Engineer. The grounds for the claim should be stated briefly.

Salient points of the Agent's report should be submitted in writing to the site meeting for inclusion in the record.

Questions concerning the Agent's report present an opportunity to plug any gaps in his submission.

1.4 Construction programme

A discussion of the past and the future, assessing performance against programme and airing any remedial action to be taken, if necessary.

1.5 Contractor's proposals

The proposals under consideration should be itemised. A request should be made for specific proposals needed in the forthcoming month, as foreseen by the Engineer.

1.6 Information required

The itemisation of information awaited by various parties to the contract.

1.7 Interim certificate

To record the present situation in terms of the amounts certified, paid and claimed.

1.8 Claims

The site meeting is not the place for facilitating the progress of or for settling claims, but points of principle may be aired to advantage. A catalogue of outstanding claims may be presented and progress towards agreement or non-agreement entered in the minutes.

1.9 Date of next site meeting

This should be recorded in the minutes.

1.10 Any other business.

The system of numbering illustrated above embodies the site meeting number as the prefix and can be adopted to advantage in the minutes.

INSTITUTION OF CIVIL ENGINEERS. *Civil engineering procedures*. London. First published 1963, Reprinted with Amendments, 1976. London. pp. 62.

INSTITUTION OF CIVIL ENGINEERS. *Conditions of contract and forms of tender, agreement and bond for use in connection with works of civil engineering construction*. Fifth edition. London, 1973. pp. 37.

DEPARTMENT OF ENVIRONMENT. *Model contract documents for highway works contracts*. London, D.o.E., 1972. pp. 98.

DEPARTMENT OF TRANSPORT. *Specification for road and bridge works*. London, H.M. Stationery Office, 1976. pp. 195.

DEPARTMENT OF ENVIRONMENT. *Notes for guidance on specification and method of measurement*. London, D.o.E., 1972. pp. 98.

H.M. STATIONERY OFFICE. *Method of measurement for road and bridge works*. London, 1969. pp. 94.

FEDERATION OF CIVIL ENGINEERING CONTRACTORS. *Schedule of dayworks*. London. First published September 1975. Amended, August 1976. pp. 40.

JOINT COMMITTEE REPORT. *Falsework*. Report of the Joint Committee of the Concrete Society and The Institution of Structural Engineers. London, The Concrete Society, 1971. pp. 52. Publication No. 52.020.

RICHARDSON, J. G. *Formwork notebook*. London, Cement and Concrete Association, 1972. pp. 94. Publication No. 12.047.

KINNEAR, R. G. et al. *The pressure of concrete on formwork*. London, Construction Industry Research and Information Association. April 1965. Research Report No. 1. pp. 44.

BLAKE, L. S. *Recommendations for the production of high quality concrete surfaces*. London, Cement and Concrete Association, 1967. pp. 40. Publication No. 47.019.

TILLER, R. M. and WARD, F. W. *Concrete finishes for highway structures*. London, Cement and Concrete Association, 1972. pp. 25. Publication No. 46.001.

APPENDIX A

Notation

A_c	Area of concrete	f_y	Characteristic strength of reinforcement
A_{cf}	Area of effective concrete flange	G	Shear modulus
A_{ps}	Area of prestressing tendons	h	Overall depth of section in plane of bending
A_s	Area of reinforcement	h_f	Thickness of flange
A_0	Area enclosed by median wall line	I	Second moment of area
a	Deflection	i	Radius of gyration
a'	Distance from compression face to point at which crack width is being calculated	K	A constant (with appropriate subscripts)
a_b	Distance between bars	k	A constant (with appropriate subscripts)
a_{cent}	Distance from centroid of concrete flange to centroid of composite section	M	Bending moment
		M_0	Moment recessary to produce zero stress
a_{cr}	Distance from point (crack) considered to surface of nearest longitudinal bar	M_u	Ultimate resistance moment
a_s	Distance from centroid of steel to centroid of net concrete section	P_o	Prestressing force in tendon at jacking end (or at tangent point near jacking end)
a_t	Distance from neutral axis to tension face	P_x	Prestressing force at distance x from jack
b	Width of section	Q	Design constant for reinforced concrete
b_e	Width of contact surface (between cast-in-situ and precast components)	r	Internal radius of bend
		r_{ps}	Radius of curvature (of prestressing tendon)
b_w	Breadth of web or rib of member	S_c	First moment of area of concrete to one side of contact surface about neutral axis of transformed composite section
C	Torsional constant		
d	Effective depth of tension reinforcement	s_b	Spacing of bars
E_c	Modulus of elasticity of concrete	s_v	Spacing of links along member
E_s	Modulus of elasticity of steel	T	Torsional moment
e	Eccentricity	$T°$	Temperature in degrees
F	Ultimate load	u	Perimeter
F_b	Anchorage value of reinforcement	V	Shearing force
F_{bst}	Tensile bursting force	V_c	Ultimate shearing resistance of concrete
F_{bt}	Tensile force due to ultimate loads in bar or group of bars	V_{co}	Ultimate shearing resistance of section uncracked in flexure
F_h	Horizontal component of load	V_{cr}	Ultimate shearing resistance of section cracked in flexure
F_k	Characteristic load	V_d	Total vertical shear due to design service load
f_{bs}	Bond stress	V_p	Shear due to prestress
f_{co}	Stress in concrete at level of tendon due to initial prestress and dead load	v	Shearing stress
		v_c	Ultimate shearing stress in concrete
f_{cp}	Compressive stress at centroidal axis due to prestress	v_h	Horizontal shearing stress per unit area of contact surface
f_{cu}	Characteristic concrete cube strength	v_t	Torsional shearing stress
f_{pb}	Tensile stress in tendons at (beam) failure	v_{tu}	Ultimate torsional shearing stress
f_{pe}	Effective prestress (in tendon)	x	Depth to neutral axis
f_{pt}	Stress due to prestress	y	Distance from neutral axis to extreme fibre
f_{pu}	Characteristic strength of prestressing tendons	z	Lever arm
f_{s2}	Stress in reinforcement	α_e	Modular ratio
f_t	Maximum principal tensile stress		

APPENDIX B

Metric units

Subject	Imperial Unit	S.I. Unit	Symbol	Conversion factor
length	mile	kilometre	km	1 mile = 1.609 km
	yard	metre	m	1 yd = 0.914 m
	foot	metre or millimetre	m or mm	1 ft = 0.305 m = 304.8 mm
	inch	millimetre	mm	1 in = 25.400 mm
area	square mile	square kilometre	km²	1 mile² = 2.590 km²
	acre	square kilometre or hectare	km² or ha	1 acre = 0.004 km² = 0.405 ha
	square yard	square metre	m²	1 yd² = 0.836 m²
	square foot	square metre	m²	1 ft² = 0.093 m²
	square inch	square millimetre	mm²	1 in² = 645.16 mm²
volume	cubic yard	cubic metre	m³	1 yd³ = 0.765 m³
	cubic foot	cubic metre	m³	1 ft³ = 0.0283 m³
	cubic inch	cubic millimetre	mm³	1 in³ = 16 387.1 mm³
capacity	gallon	litre	litre	1 gal = 4.546 litre
mass of materials	ton	tonne	tonne	1 ton = 1.016 tonne
	hundredweight	kilogramme	kg	1 cwt = 50.802 kg
	pound	kilogramme	kg	1 lb = 0.454 kg
	ounce	gramme	g	1 oz = 28.350 g
density	pound per cubic foot	kilogramme per cubic metre	kg/m³	1 lb/ft³ = 16.019 kg/m³
	pound per cubic yard			1 lb/yd³ = 0.593 kg/m³
force	pound force	newton	N	1 lbf = 4.448 N
	ton force	kilonewton	kN	1 tonf = 9.964 kN
	pound force per foot	newton per metre	N/m	1 lb/ft = 14.591 N/m
	ton force per foot	kilonewton per metre	kN/m	1 ton/ft = 32.690 kN/m

Subject	Imperial Unit	S.I. Unit	Symbol	Conversion factor
pressure	pound force per square foot	newton per square metre	N/m^2	$1\ lbf/ft^2 = 47.880\ N/m^2$
	pound force per square inch	newton per square millimetre	N/mm^2	$1\ lbf/in^2 = 0.006\ 89\ N/mm^2$
	ton force per square foot	kilonewton per square metre	kN/m^2	$1\ ton/ft^2 = 107.250\ kN/m^2$
	ton force per square inch	kilonewton per square millimetre	kN/mm^2	$1\ tonf/in^2 = 0.0154\ kN/mm^2$
stress	pound force per square inch	newton per square millimetre	N/mm^2	$1\ lbf/in^2 = 0.006\ 89\ N/mm^2$
	ton force per square inch	newton per square millimetre	N/mm^2	$1\ tonf/in^2 = 15.444\ N/mm^2$
	ton force per square foot	kilonewton per square metre	kN/m^2	$1\ tonf/ft^2 = 107.250\ kN/m^2$
modulus of elasticity	pound force per square inch	newton per square millimetre	N/mm^2	$1\ lbf/in^2 = 0.006\ 89\ N/mm^2$
bending	pound force inch	newton millimetre or newton metre	N mm or N m	$1\ lbf\ in = 112.985\ N\ mm$ $= 0.113\ N\ m$
	pound force foot	newton metre	N m	$1\ lbf\ ft = 1.356\ N\ m$
	ton force foot	kilonewton metre	kN m	$1\ tonf\ ft = 3\,037\ kN\ m$
section modulus	in^3	mm^3	mm^3	$1\ in^3 = 16\,386\ mm^3$
second moment of area	in^4	mm^4	mm^4	$1\ in^4 = 416\,210\ mm^4$

APPENDIX C

Department of Transport Technical Memoranda

NUMBER	TITLE	DATE
	PRE-1975 MEMORANDA TEMPORARILY RETAINED	
H2/69	Metrication. Orders and land acquisition procedures	2/5/69
H11/70	Site investigation procedure	19/10/70
H6/71	Trunk roads and motorways. Alternative tenders for flexible, composite and concrete pavement construction	30/4/71
H9/71	Cross-section design of road verges and central reservations on or under bridges	30/7/71
	1972 MEMORANDA	
H1/72	Manual of standard highway designs: rural motorways: typical cross-sections: verge and central reserve treatment	March 72
H5/72	Notes on the treatment of old filled mine shafts and disused shallow coal workings	30/6/72
	1973 MEMORANDA	
H1/73	Criteria for traffic light signals at junctions	16/1/73
H5/73	The COBA method for the economic appraisal of inter-urban road schemes, economic highway notes	27/3/73
H8/73	Traffic noise prediction and L10 measurement	20/8/73
H9/73	Safety fences Corrigendum: 8/3/74 Amendment 1; 1/9/75 (incorporating correction to Amendment 1) Specification clauses only are superseded by 1976 Specification (HMSO)	18/10/73
H10/73	Computerised forecasting of item rates	24/8/73
	1974 MEMORANDA	
H2/74	Suite of road design and analysis programs Program HECB/R/12 (FREEWAY)	11/3/74
H5/74	Suite of road design and analysis programs Program system (HOPS)	15/5/74
H6/74	Design flows for motorways and rural all-purpose roads (Corrigendum: 1/4/75)	12/8/74
H9/74	System of drainage and analysis programs Program HECB/R/7(DAPHNE) and HECB/R/11 (SAFRON)	3/9/74
	1975 MEMORANDA	
H1/75	Interim criteria for the provision of crawler lanes on rural roads (Corrigendum; 6/3/75)	3/1/75

NUMBER	TITLE	DATE
H2/75	Roundabout design (Corrigendum; 18/2/75)	3/2/75
H4/75	Police observation platforms on motorways	26/2/75
H6/75	Design of rural motorway-to-motorway interchanges. General guidelines	25/4/75
H9/75	Grass cutting and hedgerow treatment on trunk roads and motorways	11/7/75
H10/75	Clearance to bridges on dual two-lane roads	25/7/75
H13/75	Highways optimisation program system (HOPS). Hops user guide	11/9/75
H15/75	Suite of road design and analysis programs. Program HECB R/18 (SETTLE)	30/9/75
H17/75	Design of rural motorway-to-motorway interchanges. Single-lane links	1/12/75
H18/75	Design of rural motorway-to-motorway interchanges. Merging and diverging lanes	1/12/75

1976 MEMORANDA

NUMBER	TITLE	DATE
H3/76	Model contract document for site investigation	Feb 1976
H6/76	Bus priorities—implementation of	
H7/76	Standardisation in format and preparation of drawings	4/6/76
H9/76	Design flow for urban roads	23/7/76
H10/76	Deflection measurement and their application to structural maintenance and overlay. Design for flexible pavements	6/8/76
H11/76	Design of major/minor priority junctions	29/8/76
H12/76	Design of weaving areas for motorways and all-purpose roads	12/11/76
H14/76	Noise barriers. Standards and materials	30/11/76
H15/76	Introduction to specification for road and bridge works 1976 and notes for guidance on specification	17/12/76
H16/76	Specification requirements for aggregate properties and texture depth for bituminous surfacings to new roads	29/12/76

1977 MEMORANDA

NUMBER	TITLE	DATE
H1/77	Superseded by Supplement No. 1 to the Specification for road and bridge works 1976 (HMSO).	
H2/77	Bus priority at traffic signals using selective detection. Corrigendum 25/10/77	31/3/77
H3/77	Suite of highway maintenance analysis programs. Program suite HECB/R/16 (CHART)	15/6/77
H4/77	Standard terms of appointment for testing firms employed on roadworks	21/6/77
H5/77	Method of measurement for road and bridge works 1977 and notes for guidance and library of standard item descriptions	29/6/77
H6/77	Suite of slope stability programs Program HECB/R/22 (CIRCA 1.0).	9/12/77

1978 MEMORANDA

NUMBER	TITLE	DATE
H1/78	Specification for road and bridge works amendment to specification for sub-bases and road-bases — frost susceptibility	10/1/78
H2/78	Highway cost model system program HECB/R/20 (COSMOS)	11/1/78
H3/78	Notes for guidance and library of standard item descriptions for use with the method of measurement for road and bridge works 1977 Corrigendum 1/3/78.	12/1/78
H5/78	Model contract document for topographical surveys	Feb 1978
H6/78	Road pavement design	13/4/78
H8/78	Technical publications arrangements	1/5/78

NUMBER	TITLE	DATE

PRE-1975 MEMORANDA TEMPORARILY RETAINED

NUMBER	TITLE	DATE
IM 4	Pulverised fuel ash. Backfilling to structures	19/12/69
IM 5	Formation of continuity joints in bridge decks	21/1/70
IM 7	Use of stainless steel in bridge works	27/7/70
IM 9	Line and level on long-span structures	14/8/70
IM 11	PTFE in bridge bearings	23/10/70
IM 12	New proprietary products	30/4/71
BE 5	The design of highway bridge parapets (Third revision; 16/11/73)	30/9/70
BE 11	Lightweight aggregate concrete for use in highway structures	20/4/69
BE 13	Fatigue risk in Bailey bridges	8/4/68
BE 14	Headroom standards (Addendum 1; 29/1/71)	11/12/68
BE 16	Provisional fatigue requirements for steel bridges	Jan/69
BE 18	Suite of bridge design and analysis programs	10/7/69
BE 23	Shear key decks	27/11/70
BE 27	Waterproofing and surfacing of bridge decks	17/6/70
BE 28	Unauthorised access to motorway bridges	11/6/71
BE 29	MOT/C&CA standard bridge beams	2/7/71

1972 MEMORANDA

NUMBER	TITLE	DATE
BE1/72	Department of the Environment suite of bridge design and analysis programs	28/3/72
BE3/72	Expansion joints for use in highway bridge decks	31/10/72
BE4/72	Street lighting columns of steel construction	30/3/72
BE7/72	Appointment of testing firms employed on bridgeworks	15/8/72

1973 MEMORANDA

NUMBER	TITLE	DATE
BE1/73	Reinforced concrete for highway structures (1st Revision; 9/8/73)	30/1/73
BE2/73	Prestressed concrete for highway structures	30/1/73
BE3/73	The assessment of highway bridges for construction and use vehicles	28/2/73
BE6/73	Application of the Merrison Committee's interim design and workmanship rules for steel box-girder bridges	9/10/73
BE7/73	Rules for the design and construction of preflexed beams in highway bridges	9/10/73
BE8/73	Approval in principle and calibration of computer programs for use in DoE highway structures on trunk roads and motorways	12/11/73

1974 MEMORANDA

NUMBER	TITLE	DATE
BE1/74	The independent checking of erection proposals and temporary work details for major highway structures on trunk roads and motorways	28/2/74
BE2/74	Suite of bridge design and analysis programs Program HECB/B/12 (COLDES)	1/5/74
BE3/74	Suite of bridge design and analysis programs Program HECB/B/11 (MUPDI)	21/8/74
BE4/74	Suite of bridge design and analysis programs Program HECB/B/13 (STRAND)	21/8/74
BE5/74	High-alumina cement concrete	16/8/74
BE6/74	Suite of bridge design and analysis programs Program HECB/B/15 (ORTHOP) and design charts HECB/B1/5	15/10/74
BE7/74	Lateral loading on piled foundations	17/12/74

NUMBER	TITLE	DATE

1975 MEMORANDA

BE1/75	List of computer programs examined by the Highway Engineering Computer Branch Corrigendum; 7/2/75)	21/1/75
BE3/75	Suite of bridge design and analysis programs Program HECB/B/14 (QUEST)	19/2/75
BE4/75	Suite of bridge design and analysis programs Program HECB/B/16 (CASKET)	20/2/75
BE5/75	Rules for the design and use of Freyssinet concrete hinges in highway structures	7/3/75
BE8/75	Painting of concrete highway structures	24/10/75

1976 MEMORANDA

BE1/76	Design requirements for elstomeric bridge bearings	13/2/76
BE2/76	List of computer programs examined by the Highway Engineering Computer Branch (Department of the Environment)	5/3/76
BE3/76	Interim rules for design and construction of plate girders and rolled section beams in bridges	31/3/76
BE4/76	Suite of bridge design and analysis programs Program HECB/B/13 (STRAND 2)	25/3/76
BE5/76	Evaluation of highway structures	20/8/76
BE6/76	Suite of bridge design and analysis programs Program HECB/B/20 (PREBEM)	5/11/76
BE7/76	Suite of bridge design and analysis programs Program HECB/B/8 (RETWAL)	20/12/76

1977 MEMORANDA

BE1/77	Standard highway loadings	
BE2/77	List of computer programs examined by the Highways Engineering Computer Branch, DTp	18/2/77
BE3/77	Suite of bridge design and analysis programs Program HECB/B/9 (GRIDS)	22/3/77
BE4/77	The inspection of highway structures	1/4/77
BE5/77	Suite of bridge design and analysis programs Program HECB/B/7 (PGROUP)	1/4/77
BE6/77	Amendments to the 5th edition "Specification for Road & Bridgeworks"	18/4/77
BE7/77	Departmental standard (Interim) motorway sign/signal gantries	25/4/77
BE8/77	Use of Department of Transport bridge paint manual	31/5/77
BE9/77	Suite of bridge design and analysis programs Program HECB/B/17 (MINIPONT)	16/11/77

1978 MEMORANDA

BE1/78	Design criteria for footbridges and sign/signal gantries	17/2/78
BE2/78	List of computer programs examined by the highway engineering computer branch DTp	29/3/78
BE3/78	Reinforced earth retaining walls and bridge abutments for embankments	27/4/78

Subject index

Page numbers in italics indicate Data sheets

Author index

14

WITHDRAWN